AF251038

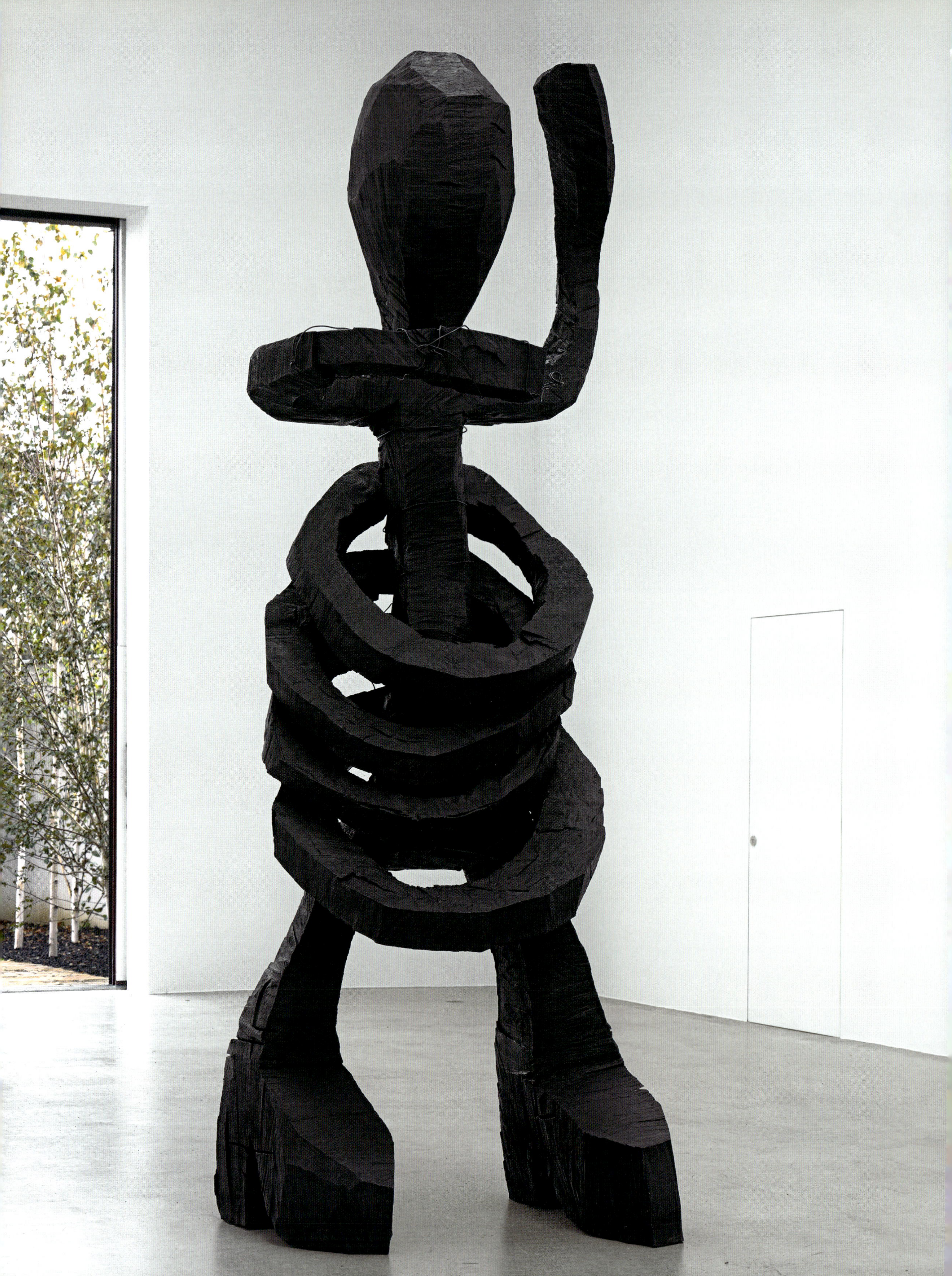

H A U S D E R K U N S T

PRESTEL Munich · London · New York

Edited by Ulrich Wilmes

With essays by
**Georg Baselitz, Eric Darragon, Okwui Enwezor,
Michael Semff, Katy Siegel, and Ulrich Wilmes**

GEORG BASELITZ
BACK THEN, IN BETWEEN, AND TODAY

CONTENTS

For several years the Haus der Kunst has engaged with a very particular kind of exhibition thesis, namely one that investigates a specific aspect within an artist's oeuvre that may have been overlooked, underexposed or not yet fully explored in a comprehensive way. Key examples are: Robert Rauschenberg's show *Traveling '70–'76* (2008), which examined rarely seen work groups employing predominantly cardboard and fabric that developed from Rauschenberg's personal travel experiences in the nineteen-seventies; Gerhard Richter's *Large Abstracts* (2009) that focused entirely on Richter's abstract paintings since the mid-nineteen-seventies onwards that testify to the artist's continued examination of the conditions of painting; and Ellsworth Kelly's *Black & White* (2011–12), which focused solely on his black-and-white works.

This survey exhibition of Georg Baselitz curated by Dr. Ulrich Wilmes, the chief curator of Haus der Kunst, is conceived along thematic strands and clusters of figures, motifs, and iconography in Baselitz's painting practice. It offers an illuminating examination of works that span fifty years. With the exhibition, Haus der Kunst offers a study of stalwart continuity in themes, as well as refreshed analysis of the figurative tradition that has been at the core of the work of one of the most rigorous painters of our time.

The renewal and critical reflection of his own work has always been a defining feature in the art of Georg Baselitz. In the past decade, the new interpretation of programmatic works—set against a new temporal background—has assumed a more dominant role. In the *Remix* series, the artist thus revisits earlier paintings, such as *The Great Friends* or *The Big Night Down the Drain*, in a dynamic process. Here Baselitz appropriates the motifs using a very different

Okwui Enwezor

FOREWORD

formal approach that virtually contradicts the original versions' significant features. The previous effect of the powerful ductus of the saturated opaque paint opposes the lucid transparency of the paint drippings, which seem to liquefy the motifs and graphically dissolve them. The ease of this approach liberates the representation of content and meaning, which transposes the artist's thinking and work into a contemporary key. In this sense, the *Black Paintings*, produced since late 2012, appear as a logical consequence in which the pendulum of the analytical penetration of one's own actions swings into the opposing remote realm of one's own being. In its symbolically charged gravity, the eagle motif—firmly embedded in the work of Georg Baselitz since the early nineteen-seventies—seems, like no other motif, to be predestined to trace this mysterious process.

The exhibition at Haus der Kunst presents this new series of works alongside the monumental bronze sculptures that were created during the same period. The formal and contextual renewal to which Baselitz repeatedly subjects his own work, is demonstrated retrospectively using related and complementary examples from 1965 to today. Haus der Kunst is honored to be hosting this exhibition in close collaboration with Georg Baselitz. Our deep and warmest gratitude goes to the artist himself, for the enthusiasm and the dedication with which he has engaged in our joint conversation and for the generosity that underpins his close relation to our institution. We would like to include in this gratitude Elke Baselitz for her emotional support throughout the whole project.

In the artist's studio, Detlev Gretenkort and Julia Westner have been a steady font of knowledge and irreplaceable members of the project team. They have also provided much appreciated help with the conceptual planning and installation of the exhibition. Our great thanks of course also belong to all institutional and private lenders of the exhibition without whose willingness to temporarily separate from their works no exhibition could be realized. We further would like to thank the authors Katy Siegel, Eric Darrgon, and Michael Semff for their extremely thoughtful and enlightening contributions which make this project an important piece of research on the oeuvre of Georg Baselitz.

We are deeply thankful to the Gallery Thaddaeus Ropac, Gagosian Gallery, and White Cube who are representing Georg Baselitz's work worldwide and who gave not only substantial financial support, but also helped us to gain all information necessary for the succesful completion of the exhibition. We would namely like to thank Thaddaeus Ropac, Arne Ehmann, Stefan von Ratibor, Andrea Schlieker, and Jay Jopling for their patience in giving answers to our endless flow of questions.

We further owe thanks to Prof. Roland Berger and Bangke Chen, Council Member Chinese People's Institute of Foreign Affairs, who helped us to establish the cooperation with the Powerstation of Art in Shanghai and its director Ms. Gong Yan. We very much appreciate that one of most distinguished Chinese institutions of contemporary art will host the exhibiton.

Members of our staff in Haus der Kunst, across all departments deserve special acknowledgment for their tireless engagement in all the phases of the realization of this exhibition.

Many thanks to Prestel Publishers, namely to Katharina Haderer, Gabriele Ebbecke, Cilly Klotz, Florian Frohnholzer, Sophie Reinhardt, and Leina González for their extremely professional and sympathetic collaboration on the creation of this eminent publication.

Last but not least we would like to thank Freistaat Bayern, the Schörghuber Group, and the Gesellschaft der Freunde Haus der Kunst for their yearlong engagement in supporting the work done by Haus der Kunst.

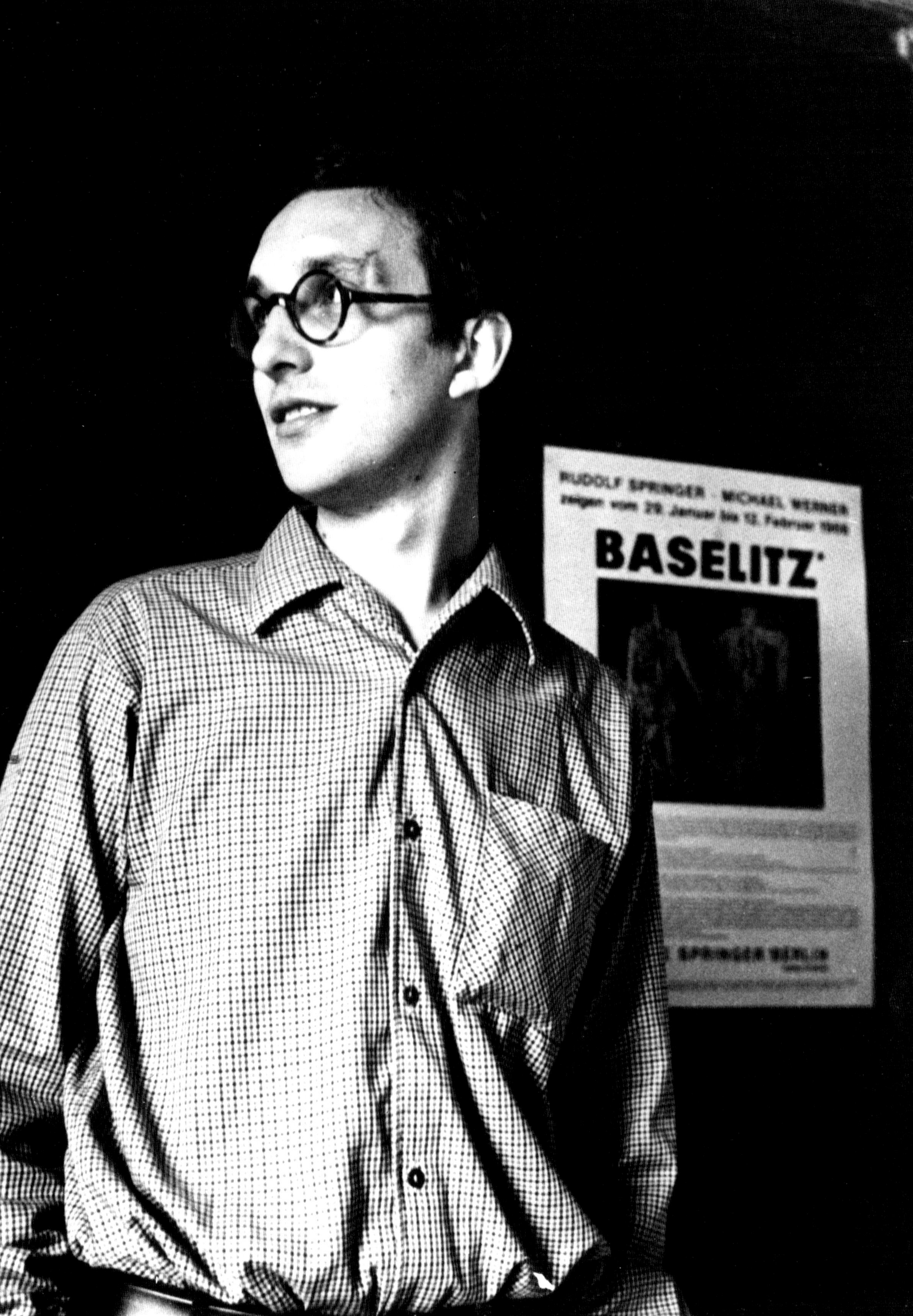
RUDOLF SPRINGER · MICHAEL WERNER
zeigen vom 29. Januar bis 12. Februar 1966
BASELITZ
SPRINGER BERLIN

ENWEZOR Though, I believe all the questions I am going to pose to you have been covered extensively in the large amount of literature your work and practice as a painter have generated, I want to begin with the most recent projects and exhibitions. You've just had—this past winter—an incredible season: Georg Baselitz in London. There were three major exhibitions, all related to your work or to your interests as a collector. There was *Germany Divided: Baselitz and His Generation* an exhibition of drawings of postwar German artists at the British Museum. The second show at the Royal Academy focused on your collection of mannerist prints in tandem with similar material drawn from the collection of the Albertina Museum in Vienna; and finally, *Farewell Bill*, a show of new paintings that was your hommage to Willem de Kooning on view at Gagosian Gallery. These different shows received enormous critical coverage, a kind of robust acknowledgment of your stature as a key artist of your generation. Then this autumn there will be a big survey of your paintings, along with recent monumental sculptures at Haus der Kunst that traces your career back fifty years with many recent paintings and sculptures included in the exhibition. So it seems you're incredibly busy. Right now you seem unstoppable. What makes Georg Baselitz tick?

BASELITZ It's a culmination. I am increasingly preoccupied with my past; there are so many exhibitions where I have to realize that my paintings are already more than fifty years old. To some extent, that's terrifying, but at the same time, very maddening, since quite a lot has happened in all those years. In England, I'm not very well known, or so I thought. And now it turns

GEORG BASELITZ IN CONVERSATION WITH OKWUI ENWEZOR

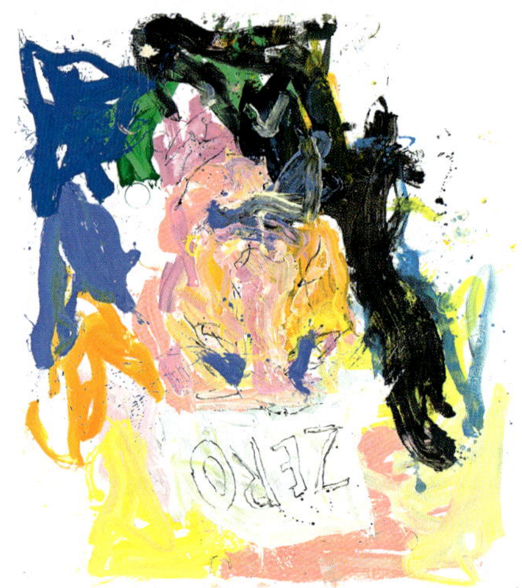

Georg Baselitz, *Baf ell we rill*, 2013

out that I am well known there. My first gallery exhibition was in London in 1982 and my first museum exhibition, in the Whitechapel Gallery, was in 1981 already. Since then more and more followed with continuity, and then I lost track of things. When it comes to the early Old Master prints, you could say that I have been a professional collector since 1965, without any regard for the fact that I'm active as an artist myself. I'm someone, then, who wants to own things. This desire is shared by all collectors. Of interest in the case of London is the fact that there were no claire-obscure woodcuts in England during the Renaissance. But that's an aside. What worries me or drives me (to return to your question) is that I continue to be dissatisfied with what I've done until now, so I think to myself: That can't have been all. Because I began as a student at a time when it was being said that painting was at an end, that panel painting was at an end. I didn't believe it, but in subsequent years, I didn't see any paintings. Now, there are many pictures by a much younger generation, and I'm always curious whether I make an appearance in these pictures, just as de Kooning can see that he appears in mine. Which he can no longer see, because he's dead, of course. And this curiosity, or this game, is very interesting to me because I have always assumed that I'm making something that doesn't yet exist. Which is to say, there is no group, no style, no generation to which I belong—or at least I flatter myself that it's so. It's really true. And today, I'm constantly asking whether my start, my attempts to promote painting, to paint the best political pictures, whether that was really a good idea. Because meanwhile, I've noticed more and more that this general "forwards" simply doesn't exist, there is no general validity, that subjectivity doesn't exist, and

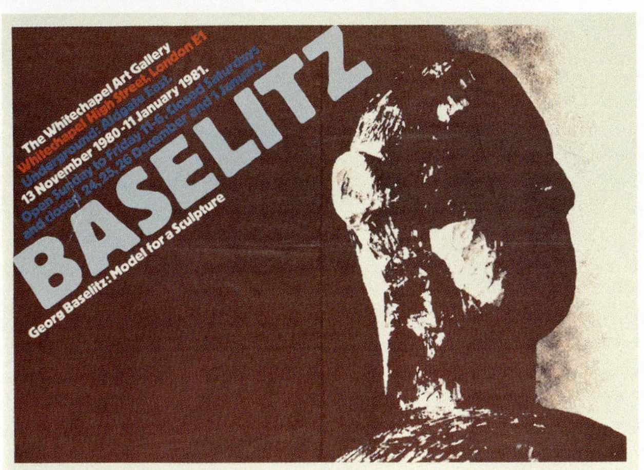

Exhibition poster, *Georg Baselitz: Model for a Sculpture*, The Whitechapel Art Gallery, London, 1980–81

so forth and so on. And I noticed that this or that exists, and myself as well.

ENWEZOR You seem to have covered quite a lot of ground. In the sense that you have offered both a summation and an introduction to your beginning and to your evident dissatisfaction with the world of representation, with painting, and with the process of your own work, which seems to be deeply marked by the continuous search for the meaning of form in your paintings. But I want to return to very early in your career, especially since you have recently spoken about your relationship to contemporary art today, because you are a contemporary artist. But you did establish a position as a contemporary artist at the very beginning of your career, what I would consider the point of formal disobedience from the prevailing orthodoxy of abstraction that then ruled the international art world in the late nineteen-fifties and sixties. Though one can say that artists like Jasper Johns or Robert Rauschenberg at this particular time were also very much genuinely, questioning abstraction in this sense. But looking back at that period, do you still believe that such a binary position between abstraction and figuration is valid today, particularly given the complete liquidation of any notion of a singular artistic style that dominates contemporary art today?

BASELITZ My point of departure was what I came across, what existed before me. And what I came across as a student was the enormous dominance first of French art, and then immediately after that of American abstract painting. This dominance of American painting was so persuasive, and so consistent with my

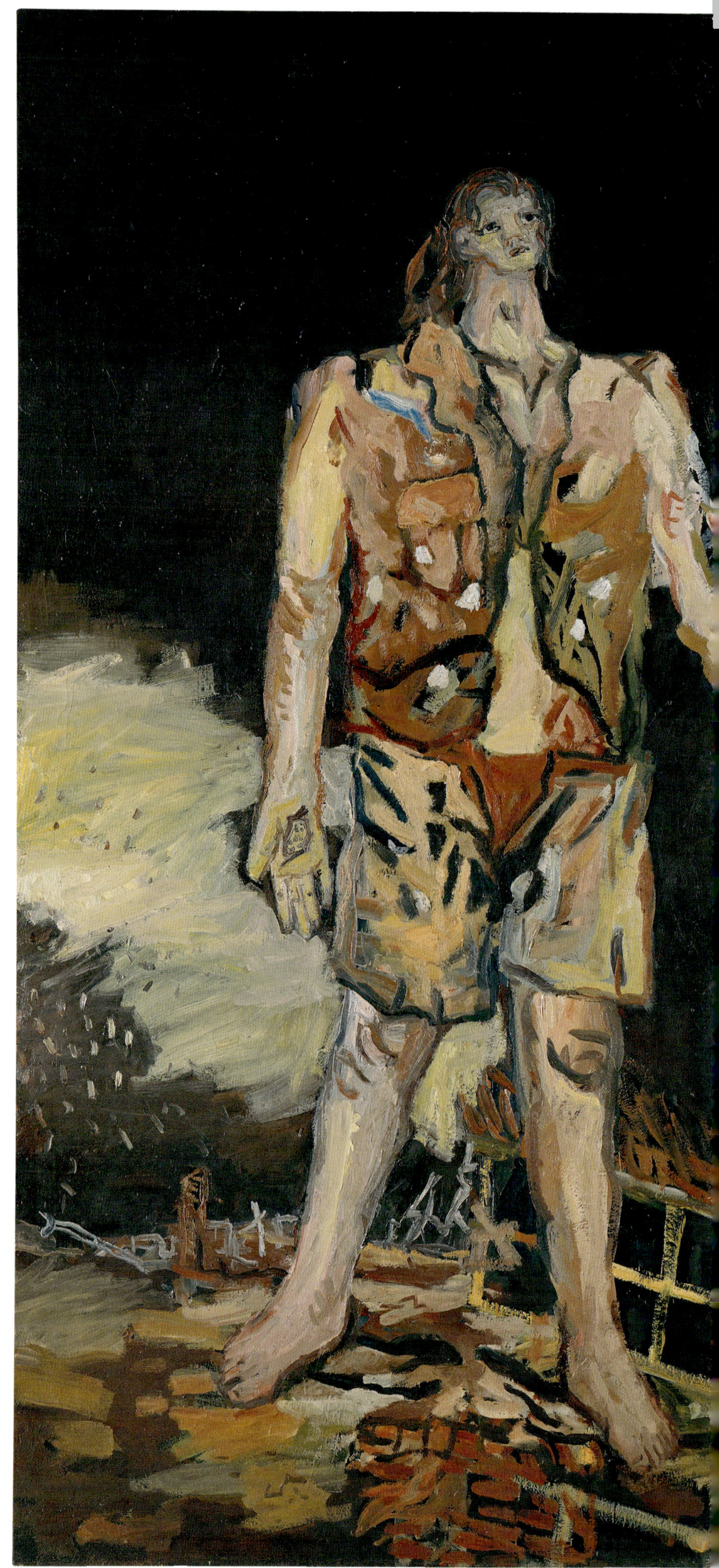

The Great Friends, 1965

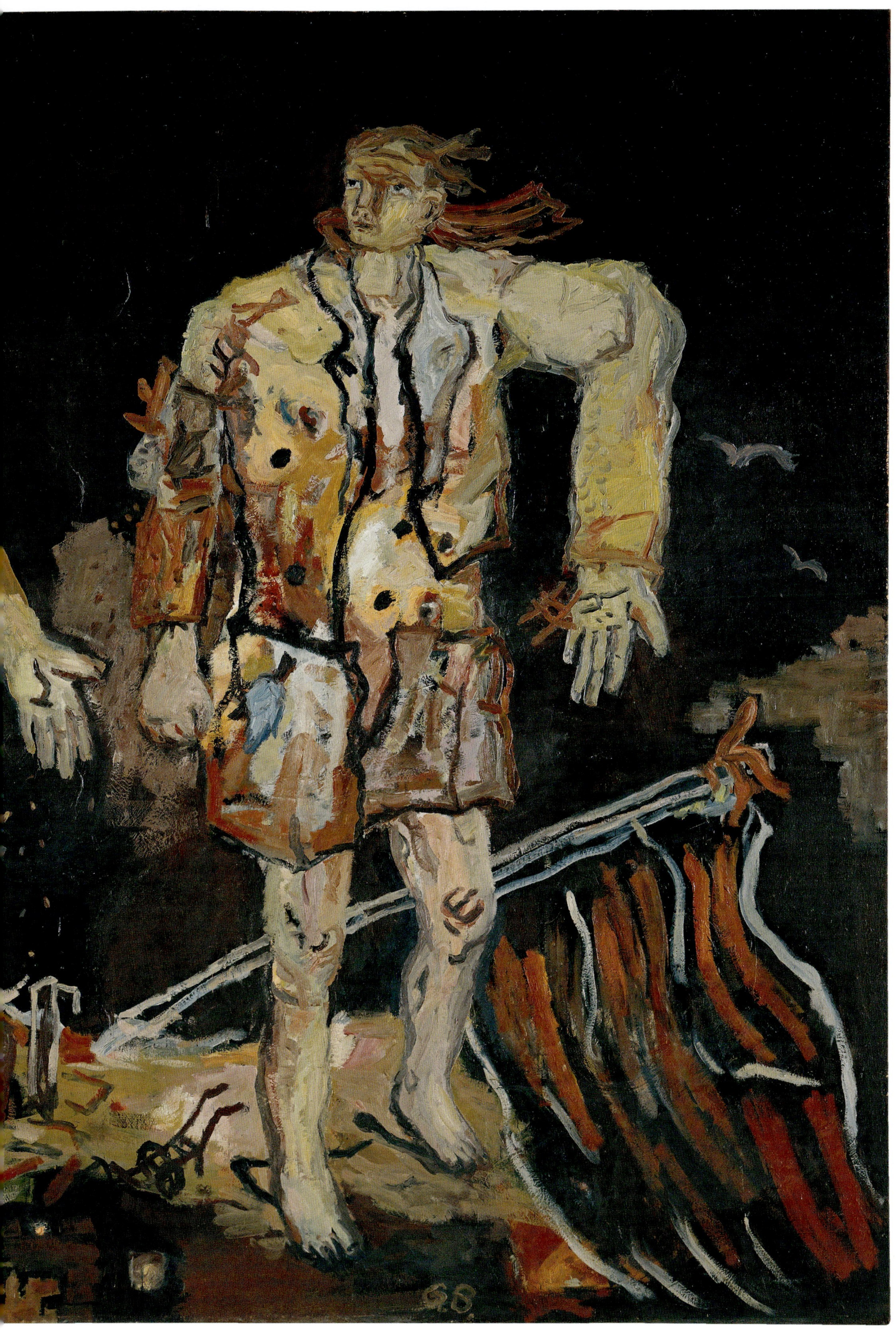

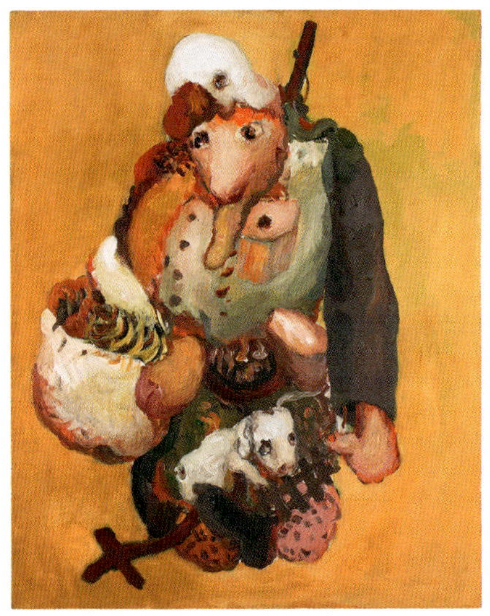

Georg Baselitz, *The Soldier*, 1965

convictions, that I had to say: Not only did you win the war, you've also completely trounced us when it comes to culture. If I'd been a good boy, I would've gone to school, would've become a good student. Mainly because I didn't contradict what I saw; I thought all of what I saw was fantastic, and I was totally uncritical. Today, when I see a picture by Baziotes, or Frankenthaler, or Gottlieb, or de Kooning, or Sam Francis, or Pollock, etc. etc., I say bravo, bravo, that was my time. Only, I wasn't a good boy, I had to do something else. Which is why I came up with a perhaps stupid, an anyway by no means intelligent answer, and did something that made my teachers say: That's anachronistic, stop doing that, that's unacceptable! But I did it anyway, and I'm still doing it. And today, I sometimes say, there are references and citations, and I recognize everything I've seen, by citing it. But my thing has become so manifest, I don't have to sell it anymore.

ENWEZOR   It's very interesting that you point to the critique of your teacher in relation to the anachronism that he found in your paintings, particularly when it was your strategy to depart from the domination, of what Clement Greenberg called the "American-type painting," that was so prevalent across many international networks in the fifties and at least in the early sixties. But in his essay "Figures of Authority, Ciphers of Regression: Notes on the Return of Representation in European Painting" the German art historian and critic Benjamin H. D. Buchloh launched a denunciation of the return to figuration in European painting, especially in the seventies and early eighties. He saw this return to figuration as symptomatic of a return to a certain kind of conservativism. You have made the opposite case for the doctrinaire conformism of abstraction, which

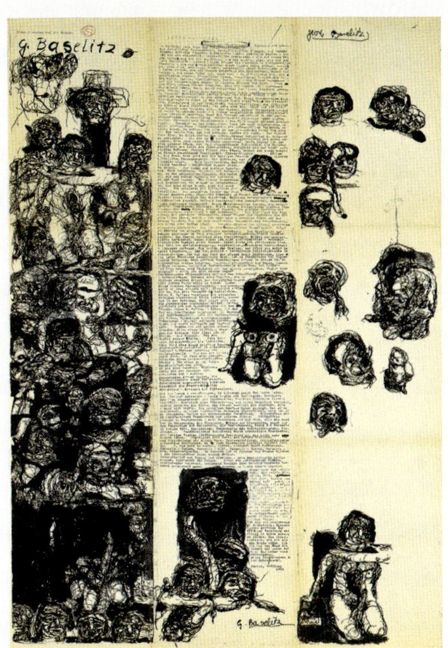

Georg Baselitz, *Pandemonic Manifesto II*, 1962

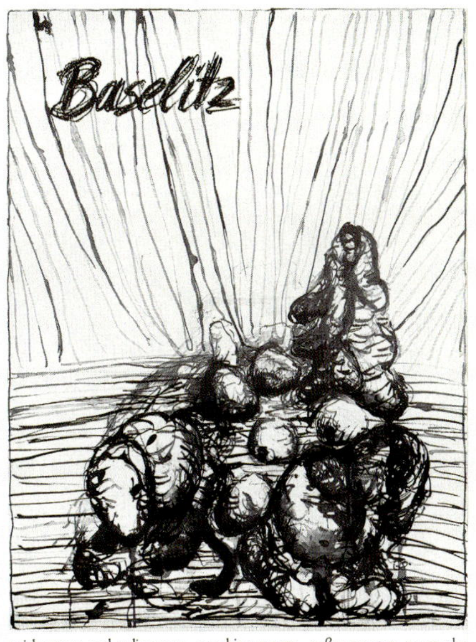

Exhibition poster, *Baselitz: Drawings and Etchings*, Staatliche Graphische Sammlung München, 1972

you attributed to American power, and to the global domination of American culture. The question I have is: Is it possible to find a more nuanced position of the uses of abstraction and figuration in painting today as it was then? Or when the partition between those two tendencies—figuration and abstraction—divided opinions? And why in your view was it necessary to so vociferously try to negate abstraction, especially with the kind of polemical stands you adopted in your first solo exhibition, with the pivotal painting *The Big Night Down the Drain* (1962–63) and of course the Second *Pandemonic Manifesto*?

BASELITZ   I believe that's a misunderstanding. The kind of painting I pursued was completely independent of what you saw back then. I never arrived at the idea of using a model, no matter what kind, whether human or landscape or still life, instead, I invented everything I did. Up until the inversion of 1969, I painted trees and animals, but they were all monsters, and only after the inversion were they recognizably realistic. Then there was this break, and this break—I think it took place around 1910 with Dadaism—this break that Sedlmayr, the professor from Munich, characterizes with the phrase "loss of the center." And this "loss of the center" meant that the world had been lost. That the world had been lost meant that its moral and aesthetic core has been lost. The antiwar paintings of Dix and other German artists, for example, they were all painted before the discussion began about whether one should paint abstractly or realistically. When I studied in Berlin, the discussion was about abstraction and representation, about Karl Hofer and Will Grohmann. It was a matter of saying that when you paint abstractly, you're immoral, and when you paint realistically, you're moral. Fortunately, the entire representational part was amputated in the West, while

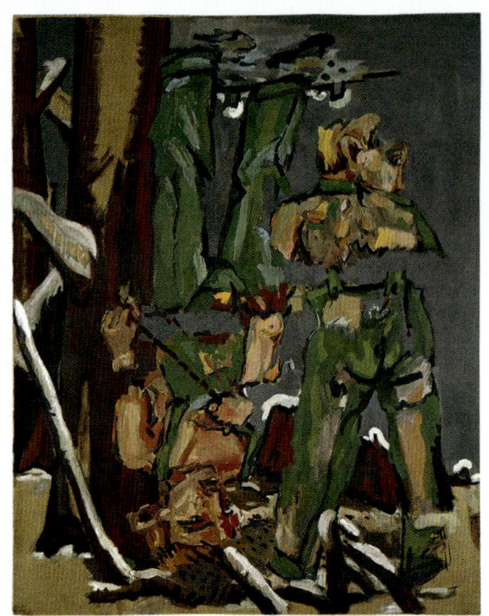

Georg Baselitz, *Woodsmen*, 1968

the East painted in a representational social realist way. And I came from there. For me, therefore, there was no question at all of this kind of schism. I became immersed in the underground, so to speak, and was preoccupied with the fantastical, the monstrous, with dreams, with crazy things, with the art of the mentally ill, with outsider art. That wasn't necessarily pleasant, but it kept me well isolated, always with regard to the fact that, manifestly, I regarded Pollock as the greatest.

ENWEZOR I still want to return back to Buchloh's denunciation, the fact that he ascribed the return to figuration in the seventies and eighties to a certain kind of return to conservativism. And I want to address this from the point of view of your radical break with abstraction, your formal disobedience with this formal conformity that was very prevalent in the postwar period, especially in the fifties and sixties in Germany. And I want to do that in relation to the fact that there this tradition of the avant-garde, in which the manifesto and thoughts of disobedience are seen to be how the artist breaks with a certain reality that combines the relationship to culture with a search for new forms. It seems that you were then searching for new possibilities in your paintings. But at the same time, while your paintings were radical to you at this particular time, it could not have been considered avant-garde in the sixties. Did you see any contradiction there, that figuration could not be avant-garde? And you may have ended up looking more like a reactionary painter than an artist willing to challenge the authority figures of aesthetic conformity. Were these thoughts part of the mental and cultural landscape that informed your own specific relationship to contemporary art in general in the sixties, when you were inventing these new forms?

Portrait of Elke I, 1969

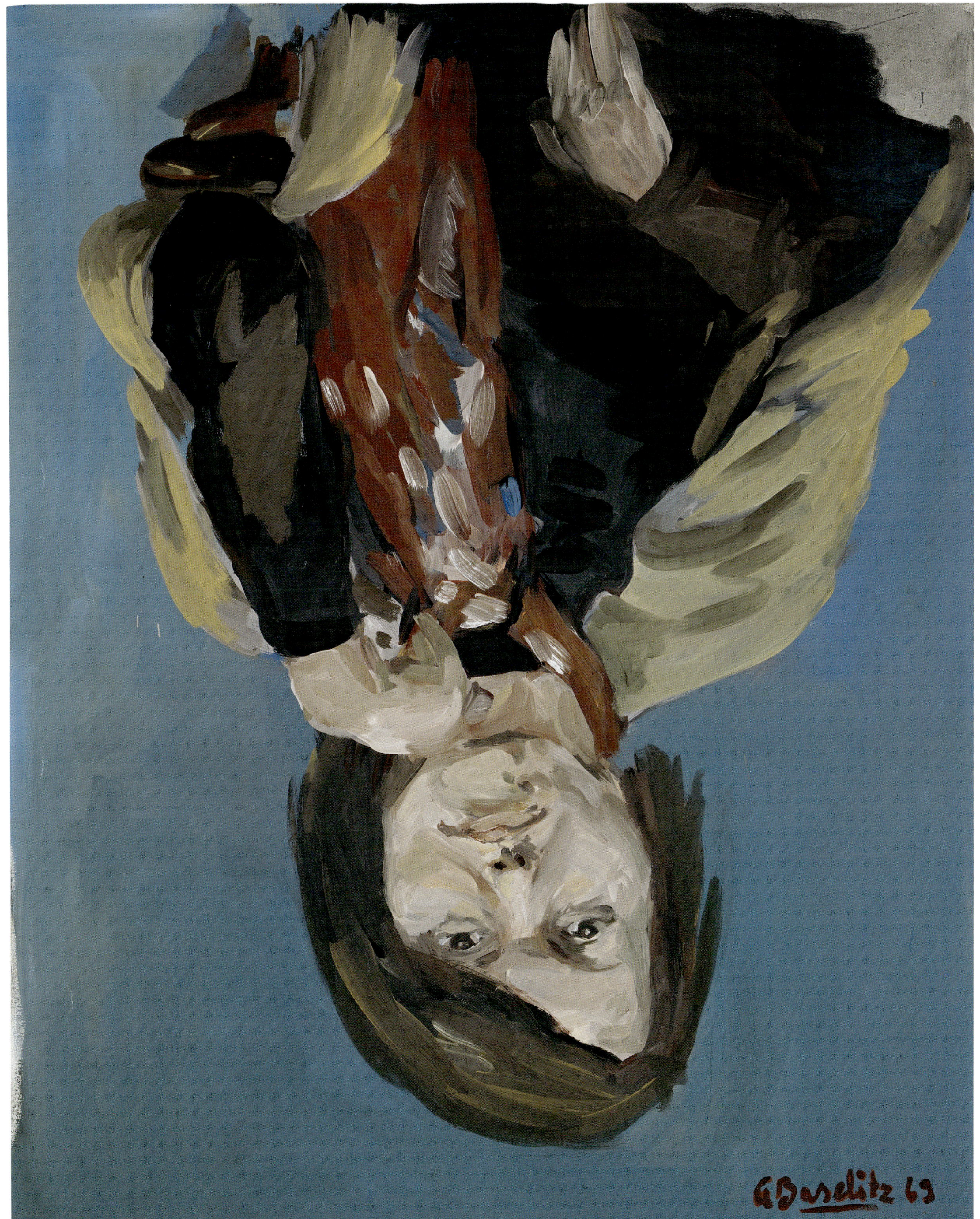

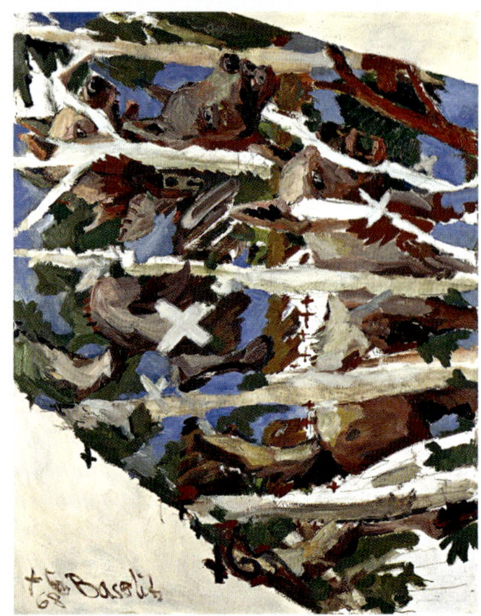

Georg Baselitz, _Three Dogs Upward_, 1968

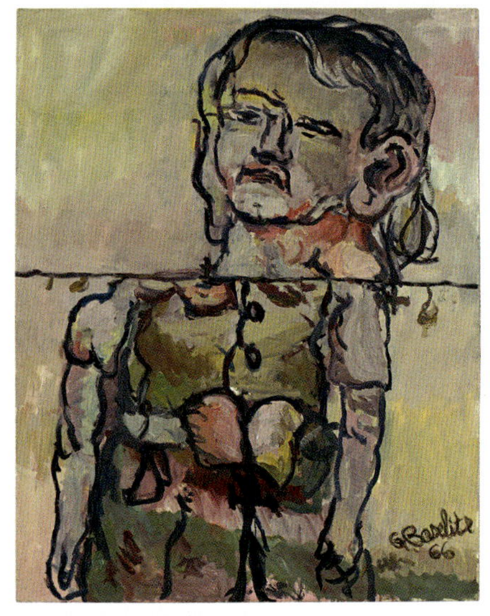

Georg Baselitz, _Divided Hero, 1966_

BASELITZ I believe that the art, the attitude, isn't clean. I believe that what goes on in the heads of artists is to begin with rather dirty, unclean, that analyses doesn't take place there at all. You react to what you see. And what I saw, the main current, was the École de Paris, abstract expressionism from America. And there, not only were the canvases clean, what you found on them was marvelously clean, without being decorative. And the aim of this art was the demonstration of a better life without philosophy. The philosophy only referred to what an artist is capable of. My exemplars, my heroes, were of a completely different kind. If we accept that Schoenberg was the most avant-garde musician of the nineteen-twenties, then actually, you have to accept that he was also the most avant-garde painter of the nineteen-twenties, but no one does, only I do. There are many examples of this kind that I could mention, in order to present this contradiction simply.

ENWEZOR Very interesting, because I think that with the mention of the heroes, we go back to what could be the formative aspects of your career. Your first exhibition in London could have been a museum exhibition. It was at the Anthony d'Offay Gallery in 1982. It was the paintings from 1966 until 1969, featuring all this imagery that you had introduced into your painting: figures, landscapes, animals, and so on. But you had also introduced a mode of painting—the so-called _Fracture Paintings_ that in fact revealed that it was still possible to be radical within the space of very traditional mediums, such as painting. Did you feel that almost unquestionably embracing abstraction that the artists of your generation were seeking to protect themselves from exploring the kind of topics that you were exploring, because you went back looking at almost to the

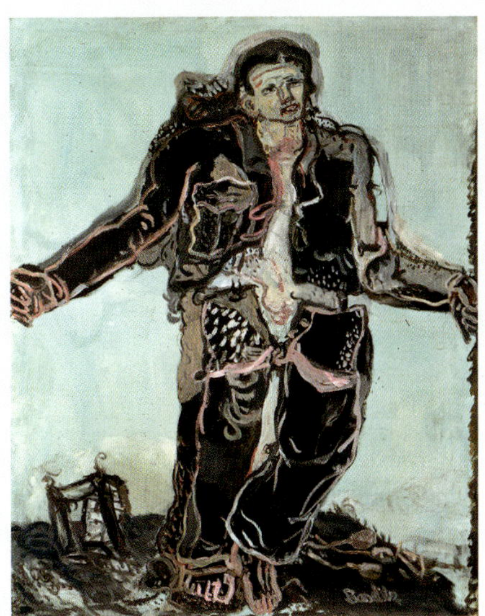

Georg Baselitz, *The New Type*, 1965

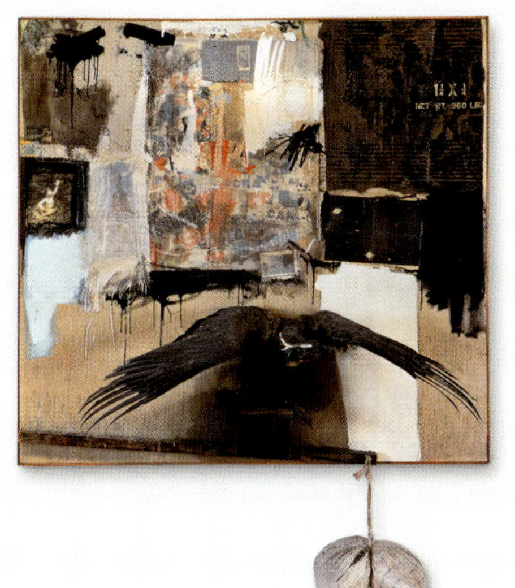

Robert Rauschenberg, *Canyon*, 1959

painters that seemed to be right out of German romanticism? In the *Heroes* and *The New Type* paintings, were you trying to touch the wound that abstraction was trying to cover up, in a sense, after the war by referring back to a certain kind of German archetypal figure?

BASELITZ The catalogue you mention, from the London exhibition, is really a wonderful example. To begin with, you can see I have absolutely no sense of humor. And when you look more closely, you can see that the contents of these pictures is, in formal terms, the "London School." By London School, I mean Bacon, Freud, Auerbach, Kossoff. And until now, no one has noticed that a correspondence exists between myself and these people. First and foremost, the artists themselves haven't noticed it. I made an offer, I wrote a letter, so to speak, but received no reply. And now, I've repeated the whole thing again this year with my exhibition at Gagosian. Now, there is some very, very positive criticism, astonishingly, but there is nothing further … aside from greetings from afar, Frank Auerbach, for example, doesn't say: My boy, you're right! How can he say it? Because I always say that this London School is Berlin's past. That is something that needs to be analyzed. How was it that after the war, Berlin painting was perpetuated in London by young people who had emigrated from Germany as children? That really is, for instance, a genuine historical irruption in the stringency of art history. Now perhaps people say that the English are very conservative by nature anyway, but these artists, they're not English. If they're anything, they're German. Now I suppose someone will whack me on the head for saying that, but that's how I see it. These artists didn't participate in the avant-garde race, they almost hid, stubbornly creating their remarkable pictures. I would

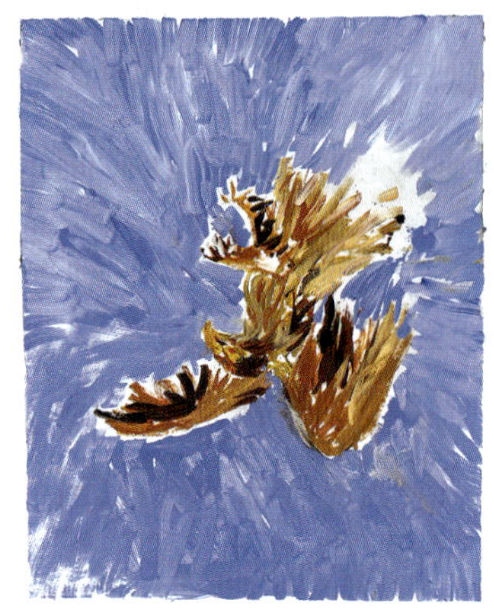

Georg Baselitz, *The Eagle (Remix)*, 2005

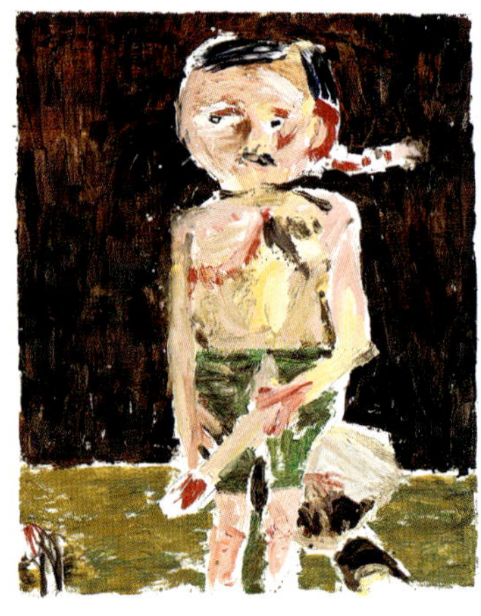

Georg Baselitz, *The Big Night Down the Drain (Remix)*, 2005

never dare to say, in normal speech, I mean in the literal sense, that they're conservative, instead, I've always thought they were avant-garde. It's a different kind of avant-garde. When I saw my first Rauschenbergs, I admittedly saw them through the filter of all the Schwitters I'd seen, but I would never have thought of comparing them, would never have said that he had plagiarized, that he copied, that he had raided Schwitters's stores. I find these schisms, which one perceives in retrospect, have become increasingly important, because they mean a greater wealth—and many other things.

ENWEZOR Do you then think that your *Remix Paintings* could be analogous to Rauschenberg's *Combine* paintings?

BASELITZ I saw the exhibition in New York at the Guggenheim, and found it magnificent. To begin with, I asked about prices. Unaffordable for my wallet. Really. I never thought that this isn't modern art, it has something to do with Dadaism, for example. I only looked: unfortunately, it wasn't possible for me to do it like that. Actually, I could've done it, but it had already been done. There was even an eagle.

ENWEZOR It's very interesting that you began by saying that you are in the process of looking back and that you have seen such distance that you have covered in your work. And the *Remix Paintings* sort of describe a kind of flashes of memory in the process of dissolution being recaptured in a very fluid, but also in a transitory way. When did you go back, return back to your own oeuvre, to excavate, to perform an archaeology of your own works in the *Remix Paintings*?

BASELITZ If you take the term remix from music (and I mean something similar), it means you rescue something in a new time, or, for example, you bring

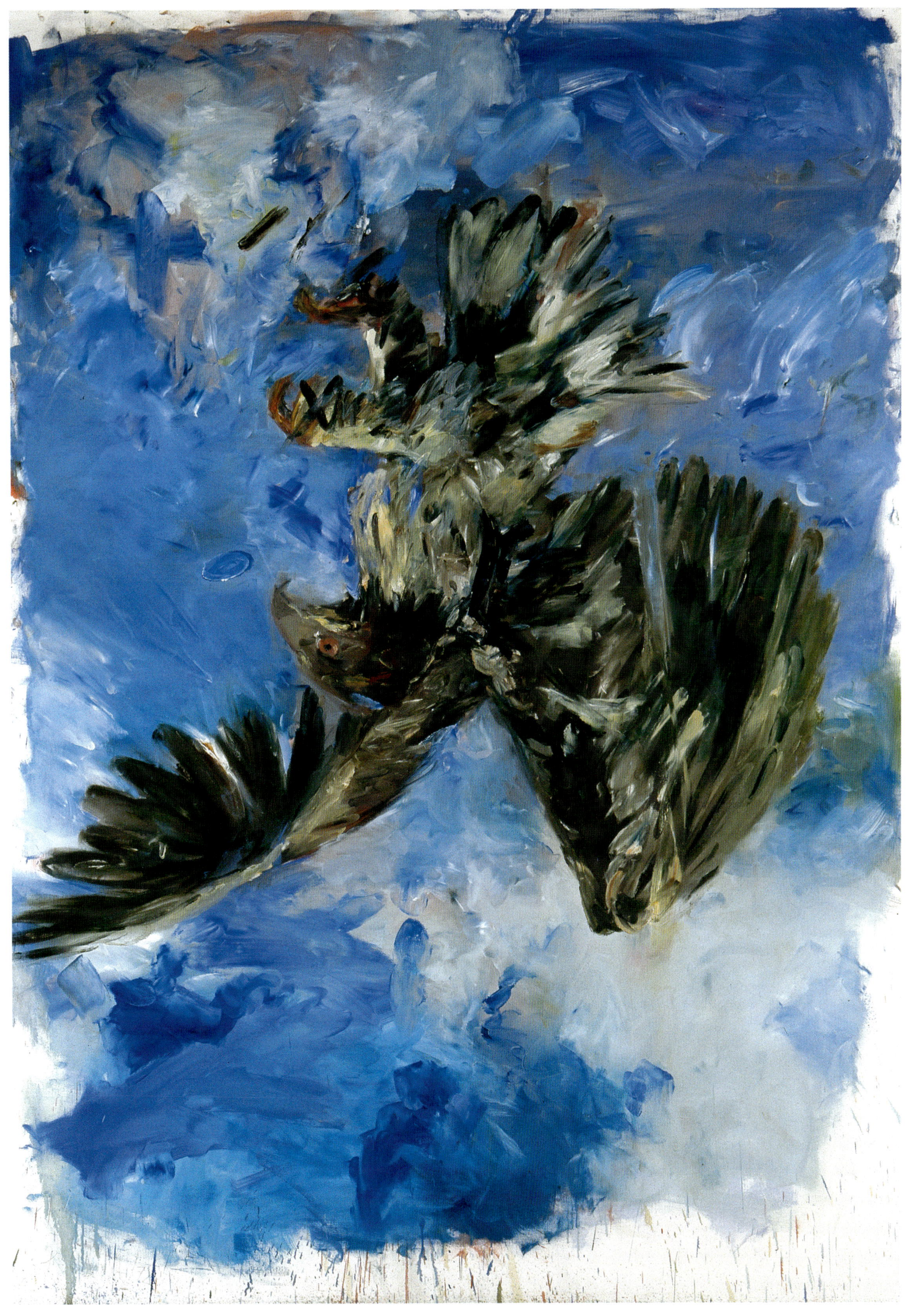

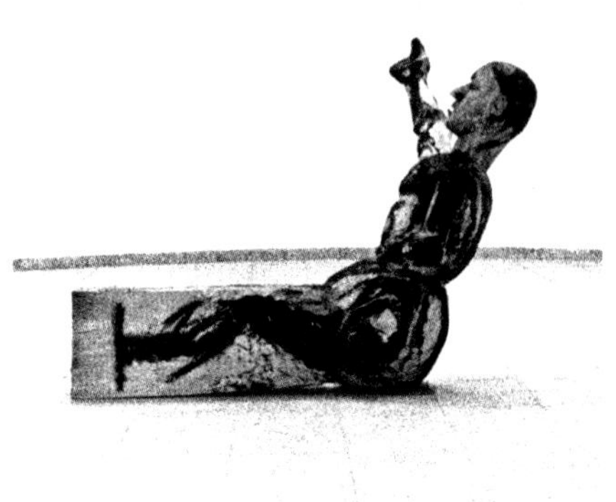

Model for a Sculpture, German
Pavilion, Venice Biennale, 1980

it into the new time. That doesn't mean you rehash it, but instead that you use quite specific essences, basic themes, in order to reformulate it. That means: larger, faster, wider, and so forth. When you grow older, you notice that everyone streaks passed you. They don't notice you anymore. They try to shove you into a ditch. And then I always say, that you have to plant your flag in the snowpile, in order to say: You're still there. I can't do it by calling out, instead, I have to do it with pictures. It's not a question of making the pictures I've already done better, since my pictures from the past are actually okay, instead, it's an entirely hermetic preoccupation with myself, with results that have an impact toward the outside, and that should impact the outside.

ENWEZOR It seems to me that this question of historical returns is present in your recent work. And I want to discuss your very first sculpture, which you presented in the German Pavilion at the Venice Biennale in 1980. In that exhibition you showed *Model for a Sculpture*, a piece whose rigid gesture of an outstretched arm and hand kind of suggested an oblique reference to the Nazi salute. This connotation, for a German artist, is a really very strong gesture. And recently you have made these new sculptures, *BDM Group*, which would seem to suggest that you constantly return to the subject matter that on the one hand might seem ambiguous, but on the other hand also is explicit in the references that it's trying to evoke. Do you see a connection between *Model for a Sculpture* and *BDM Group*? And if so, are you trying to continue this exploration of both your beginnings and the traumas that many German artists of the postwar generation had to confront in the fifties and sixties?

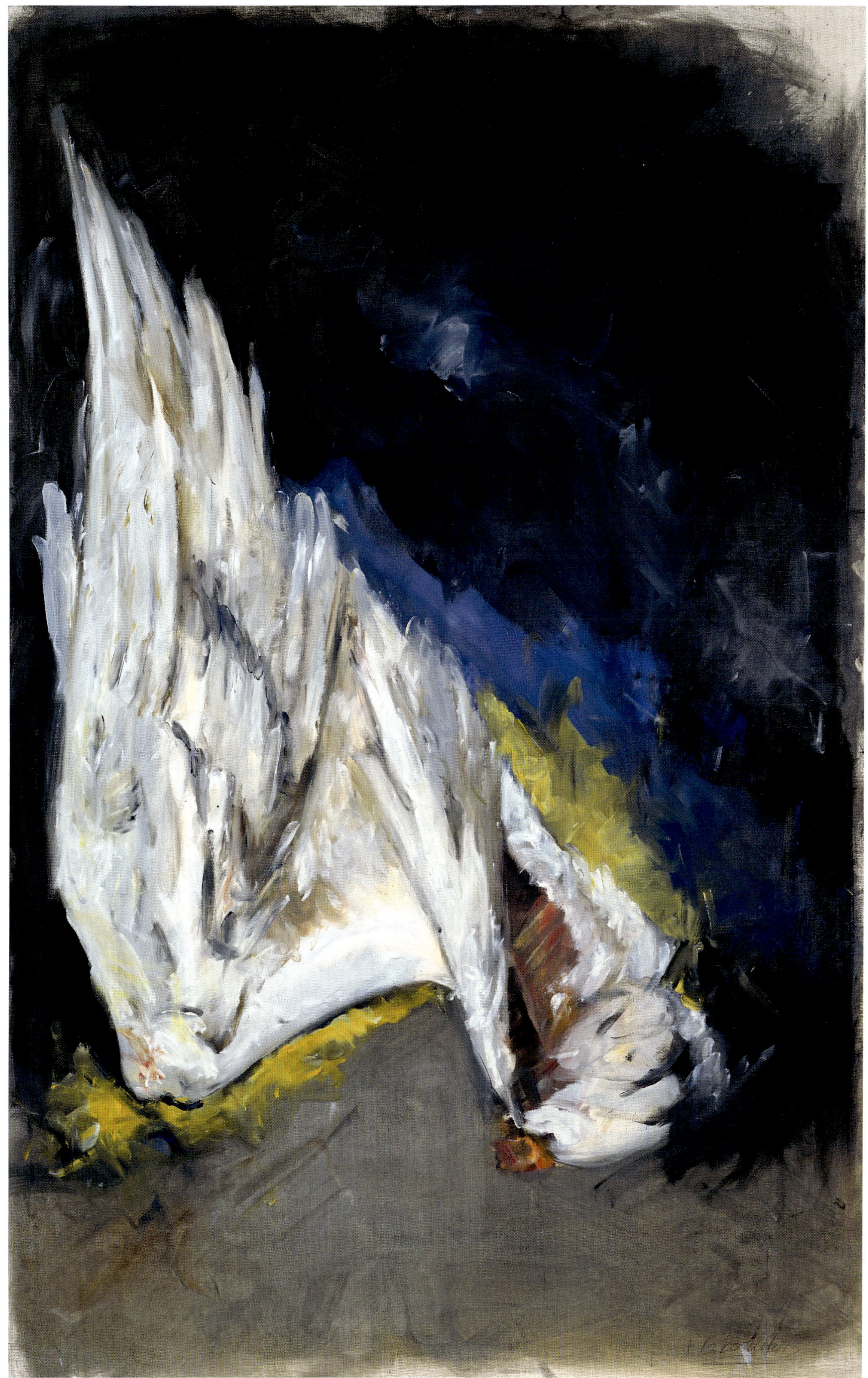

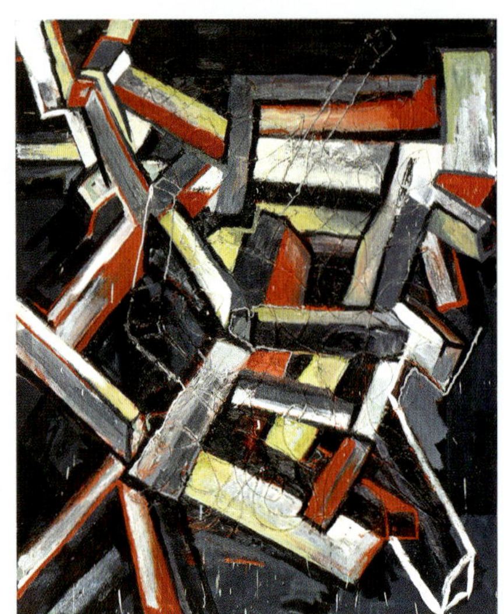

Martin Kippenberger, *With the Best Will in the World I Can't See a Swastika, 1984*

BASELITZ To begin with, it's the case that many people from my generation (and my generation in particular has the say, as a consequence of biology), if you consider their biographies, they aren't politically correct. In order to have a presence, you have to deny your past. Or you have to play hide and seek in a very intelligent way, like the way Kippenberger, for example, painted a picture: *With the Best Will in the World, I Can't See a Swastika*. To get mixed up in this kind of game always nauseates me. The discussion, for example, about whether a sculpture can be titled *BDM Group* or not. That would simply mean that I would have to discard a large portion of my past. Which I don't want to do. Independently of that, when I made my first sculpture (the one for Venice), I didn't know what I was doing, since I had no model. Which is why I called the sculpture *Model*, but I had no vis-à-vis, I didn't even have the idea of a vis-à-vis. I had a jumble, a mixed up head full of ethnological sculpture and archaeology, and I really assumed that you take a piece of wood, begin to hack into it, and it becomes something. Sort of like: I'm making something out of you. Something like that. The spirit inside of you … and so on. And gradually, through the years, I became sensible, so to speak, and now I simply have a model, I simply have a vision or a notion, my sister in BDM uniform or her friends in BDM uniform, and I make a sculpture. Or my wife and me with linked arms. Or a dancing woman, that became *Louise Fuller*. Therefore the chasm is the bridge that I have found a vis-à-vis in the sculpture.

ENWEZOR Why did you find it necessary, seventy years after the fact, to make the *BDM Group* sculpture, to refer to this history? Why was it important for you today?

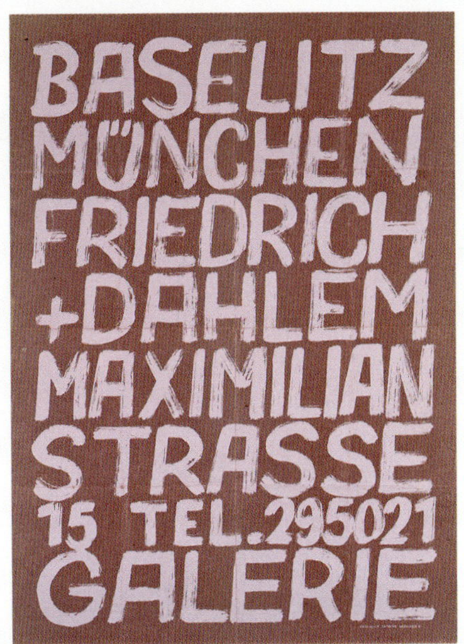

Exhibition poster, *Baselitz*, Galerie Friedrich & Dahlem, Munich, 1965

BASELITZ I live half in the night and half in daytime, and curiously enough, I've become used to incorporating into my work everything that happens in my dreams. And the images from my childhood, from the village square, simply are exactly like this sculpture.

ENWEZOR One of the important things in your sculpture and the search for a model is what one could describe as a deliberate primitivist turn in the fabrication and making of the sculptures. The sculptures seem less products of carving, as much as they are products of mark making. Even the current sculptures, while they are very skillfully crafted and carved, still very much involve, the visible essence of those sculptures is how your own gestures act upon the work itself. In that sense you see the sculptures as a continuation of your painting, are they gesturally different? What is the connection between the sculptures, the printmaking, and the drawings? Because each of them has a certain physicality to them.

BASELITZ Initially, there was the end of sculpture. There was Flavin, there was Judd, there was Sandback, all of them represented by my gallery, Friedrich and Dahlem in Munich. This meant the end of sculpture. I didn't want that. I didn't want to let it end like that. I thought to myself, you have to do something, you have to take a piece of wood, the way all the others have done, and make a different figuration … You must turn back. I don't believe in an international sculpture. I don't believe that there exists a single clean idea for a final sculpture. Instead I really believe that there is a German, a Saxon, an Upper Lusatian sculpture, just as there exists an Indian sculpture, a Nigerian sculpture, and so forth. I really do believe in this traditional origin. I don't believe the archetype exists, instead I believe that each makes a very special sculpture on the basis of his background, whether he participates in the contemporary competition or not. That's the first thing. Secondly, it is of course the case that my avant-gardism in painting is no different from my avant-gardism in sculpture. It's the same person, the same head that make both. Only a sculpture always presents itself differently. What I love most in sculpture is Calder. But I can't make a Calder. Unfortunately.

ENWEZOR So what we have identified in the artists you mentioned—Judd, Flavin, Sandback—is a certain removal of the artist's gesture from the sculpture, a turn towards a more industrially fabricated object that defines a completely different terrain of sculpture. And here we are dealing with a different notion of abstraction from the one that you dealt with in painting, because the abstraction you were dealing with was a response to gestural abstraction, whereas the work of Judd, Flavin, and Sandback reached a different point of understanding of abstraction, which is a complete removal of subjectivity in the production of the work. Do you think that the lack of subjectivity for a certain kind of pure objectivity of the medium, of the material is antithetical to sculpture that you understand?

BASELITZ I don't believe so. I think there are many [types of abstraction] and that both this one and mine are possible. The whole thing is not a religion, it's not a question of the ultimate best, or all of these clean moral backgrounds. Warhol's *Brillo Box*, defined as sculpture, I say: Bravo, fantastic. Jeff Koons: Fantastic. Piles of earth by Walter de Maria: Fantastic. Boreholes: Fantastic. I've experienced all these things. I don't work in terms of a statement against them, not at all, instead I'm doing something completely different. I don't want to say, they aren't artists

Bedroom, 1975

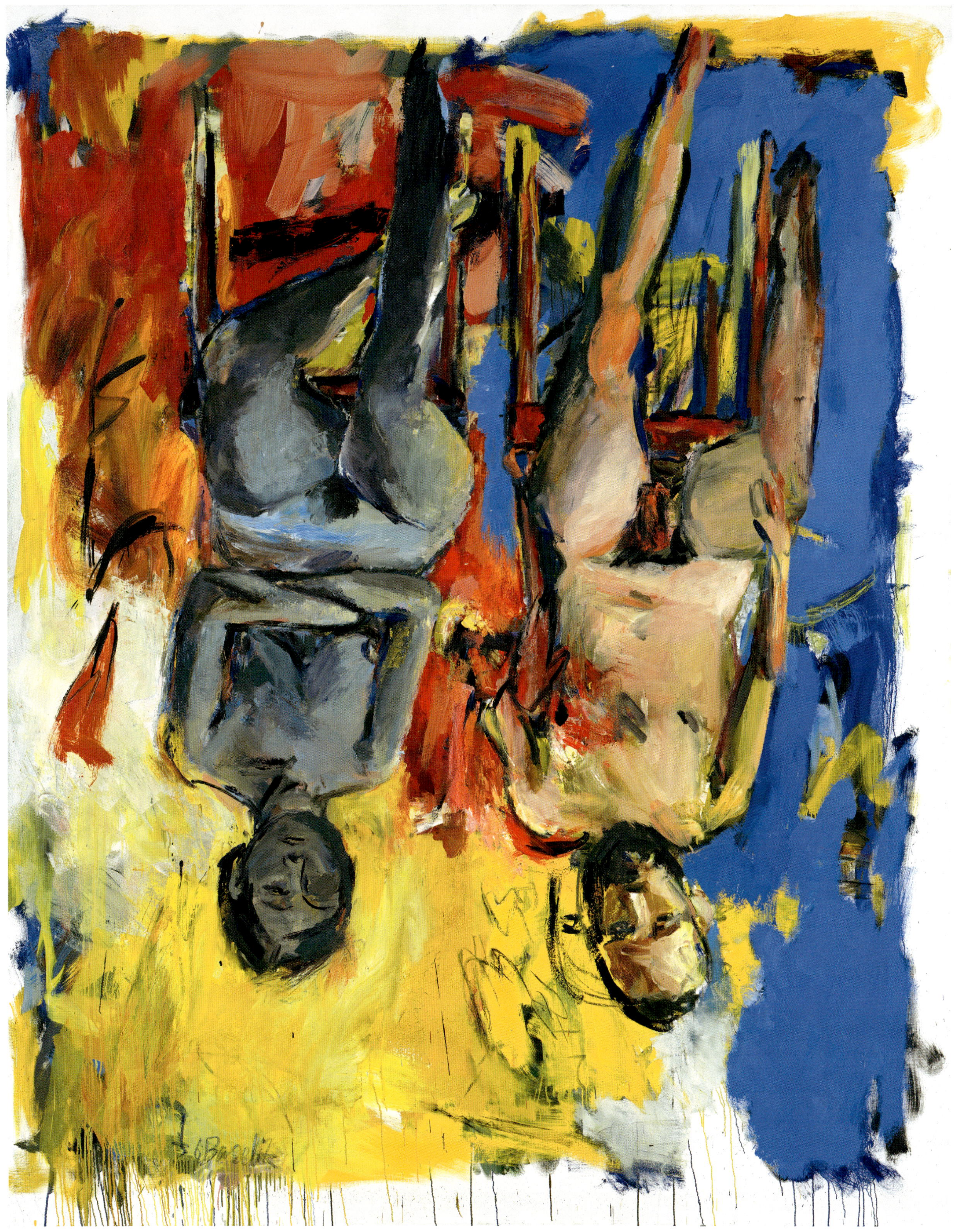

at all, but instead only engineers. No, no, I wouldn't say that. Perhaps I'm an engineer—privately, not as an artist.

ENWEZOR I would like to return to the paintings in our exhibition. Since *Finger-Painting—Eagle* (1972), the figure of the eagle has served as a sort of emblematic role in many paintings of yours. Lately, you've began a much more insistent examination of the motif of the eagle in the so-called *Black Paintings*, that will form the centerpiece of the exhibition in Haus der Kunst. Why are you invested in this subject matter?

BASELITZ At some point, I began with the inversion, and then I began painting eagles, because Franz Dahlem said: If you go to America, you have to paint eagles. I was able to go to America. That was in 1975. But there, I only painted flowers. With my eagles, I wasn't successful. Nevertheless, since 1970, the eagle has been one of my exam themes, and whenever I want to do something new and complicated, I imagine an eagle less as an emblem, or not at all, but instead as something out of my natural history book. And the recent pictures, the *Black Paintings*, that's really an experiment: How can I, finally, make the object almost disappear? How far can you go, how far can you shift the boundaries, and still make a picture that doesn't end up a total disaster? And this attempt, it's very simple. Every painter knows, there are pots of paint, bright colors and black and white, and if you want the greatest efficiency, then you use the strongest contrast between bright and dark, with the color scale as well, and then there are the contours. And if you intentionally disregard everything, it becomes difficult, but appealing. Which is why I mixed simple colored paints, can by can, with black, so that only a tiny nuance of color remained. And then I painted my eagle model,

almost blindly. The result was these pictures. And it worked. But it didn't function, if you began to introduce psychology, if you were would to think, these are
the last pictures, this is the end, and so forth, that has absolutely nothing to do
with it; instead it's an experiment, to shift the boundaries. You could do it just as
well with white.

ENWEZOR I want to return back to your first exhibition in England. When
I found this catalogue, I found it really quite fascinating, that what ostensibly
could have been really your first monographic museum exhibition in London
was in a commercial gallery, covering the period from 1966 to 1969. It is astonishing to me that more than a decade after you made these paintings that they
were still available. What does that say about the reception of your early work,
that these magnificent, very important paintings were still available to be shown
in a commercial gallery? Were they available or were they for sale? Because it
seems to contradict the view of the radicality of the paintings, the provocation
they produced. So people must have been repelled by that, people must have
been afraid of these particular paintings.

BASELITZ Of course, it really was so … I did something, always with an eye
toward being very avant-garde, progressive, revolutionary, subversive, and
I don't know what, but the other side, the reception, was arranged very differently. These paintings were unexpected, they didn't fit into what I would call
the mainstream. I understand that, too. Today, things are different. Back then,
you had to assert all of these biographies, not only mine, against great resistance. I would say, not only in Germany, but in all of Europe. In America, the
expectation of renewal was far greater, more accepted. But my things, or our

things, are accompanied by quite a lot of ballast. Often, they are not pleasant. I was told, for example, when I had my first exhibition in New York: Please keep your mouth shut, don't say anything! I asked: Why? I want to discuss things with Rauschenberg and so on. No! Keep your mouth shut! Americans won't like it if you open your fly. And I had a hard time going along with it, although I did try.

ENWEZOR How were the paintings received?

BASELITZ Not at all.

ENWEZOR Not at all. Silence?

BASELITZ Silence.

ENWEZOR How did you feel about that? Because now, in 2014, Georg Baselitz is a hero in London.

BASELITZ Thank you.

ENWEZOR What didn't they see in 1982? What did they miss?

BASELITZ I've always believed I'd receive a Nobel Prize for my texts, but never for the pictures, I've never believed that. No kidding. I said earlier that I totally lack humor, which can be seen in my pictures. And I think you need that. And when you know that my great model is Picabia, then you no longer understand anything at all, for I saw the first Picabia exhibition in Paris in 1964, and from that point onward, I never wanted to paint like Picabia, not like Polke, but instead like Baselitz, but in the spirit of Picabia.

ENWEZOR You made a statement that right now your generation of artists is dominant, and I take it to mean the fact that there is so much attention focused on your careers, on Gerhard Richter, Sigmar Polke, on yourself, and this seems to be where the separation happens. The other artists are not quite in the same

Elke Nude, 1976–77

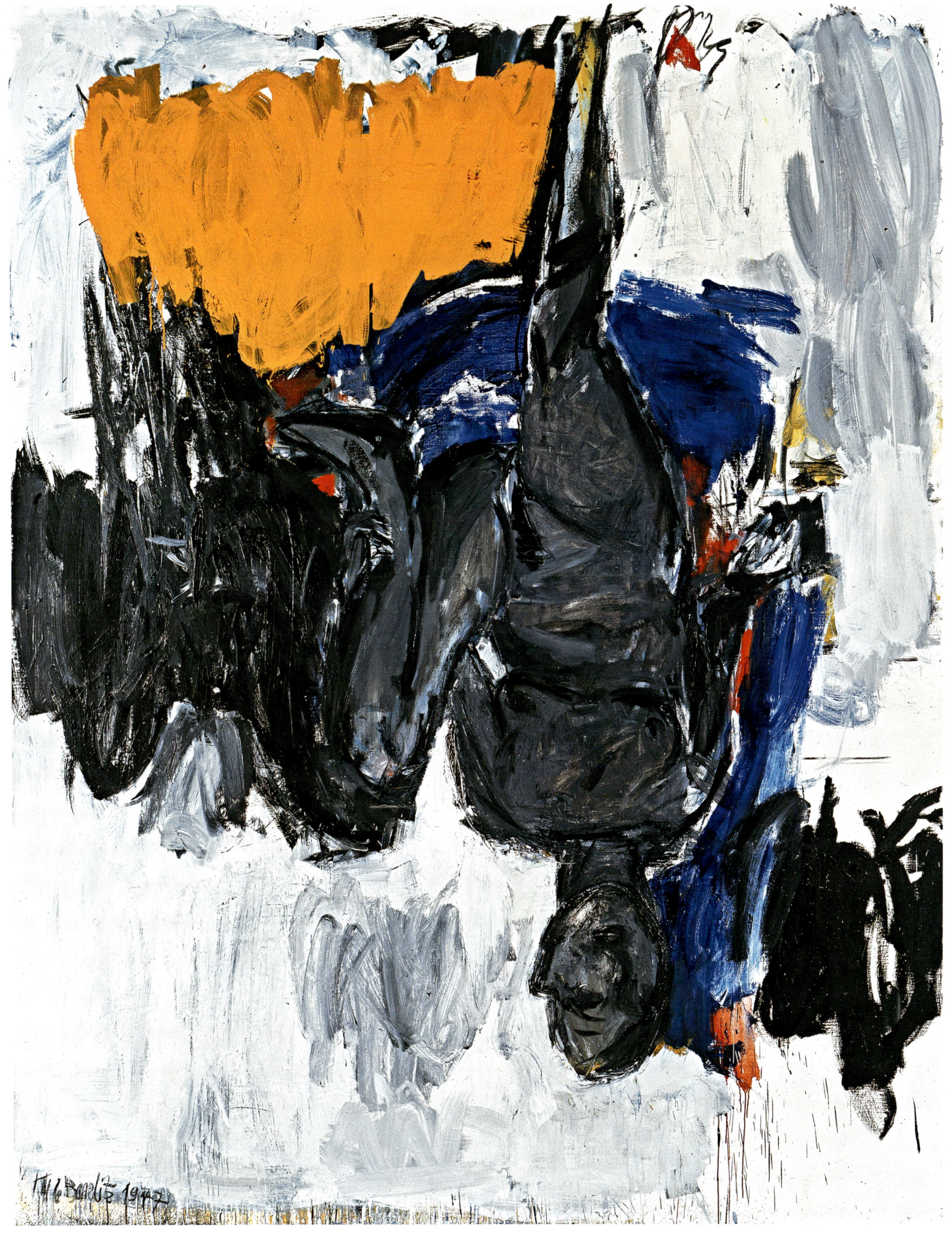

category as the three painters, who emerged strongly in the postwar period. Why do you think that this triangle between yourself, Polke, and Richter remains so prevalent and strong?

BASELITZ To begin with, there are biographical reasons, I think. Then you can't forget the performance with these types, the level of work performance. There was no expectation, no inheritance, no chance for a market, everyone really had to seriously work. You couldn't do anything frivolously. But these are the standard sayings I'm now offering. Then there is the culmination of various cultures, this mixture. What about American pop art, for example, isn't it European in origin? Of course, Richter took up something that belonged to him. It was developed somewhere else. It's like a Toyota that looks like a Mercedes. From the very beginning, I had a really, really strong skepticism, and I said, let them do that, let them look across the ocean, let them make socially critical, consumer critical things, even though in Germany, we have nothing to eat. I see all that, but I'm doing something different. Because I was deeply convinced that there was something in me, something different than the social aspect, this general aspect. I was preoccupied with very obscure things, in music, in literature, in art. And I never had the notion of doing the whole thing academically or pedantically. When I recall that all of my teachers—grammar school, gymnasium, art school—said to me: Not like that, please not like that! It's so. That's how it goes. No, no, not that way, that's how it goes. That was simply my problem.

ENWEZOR The last time I visited you at your studio we talked about younger artists you've been looking at, and you mentioned Jonathan Meese as one contemporary artist you believe is serious. Are there others? If you look between

Head—Elke in Profile, 1977

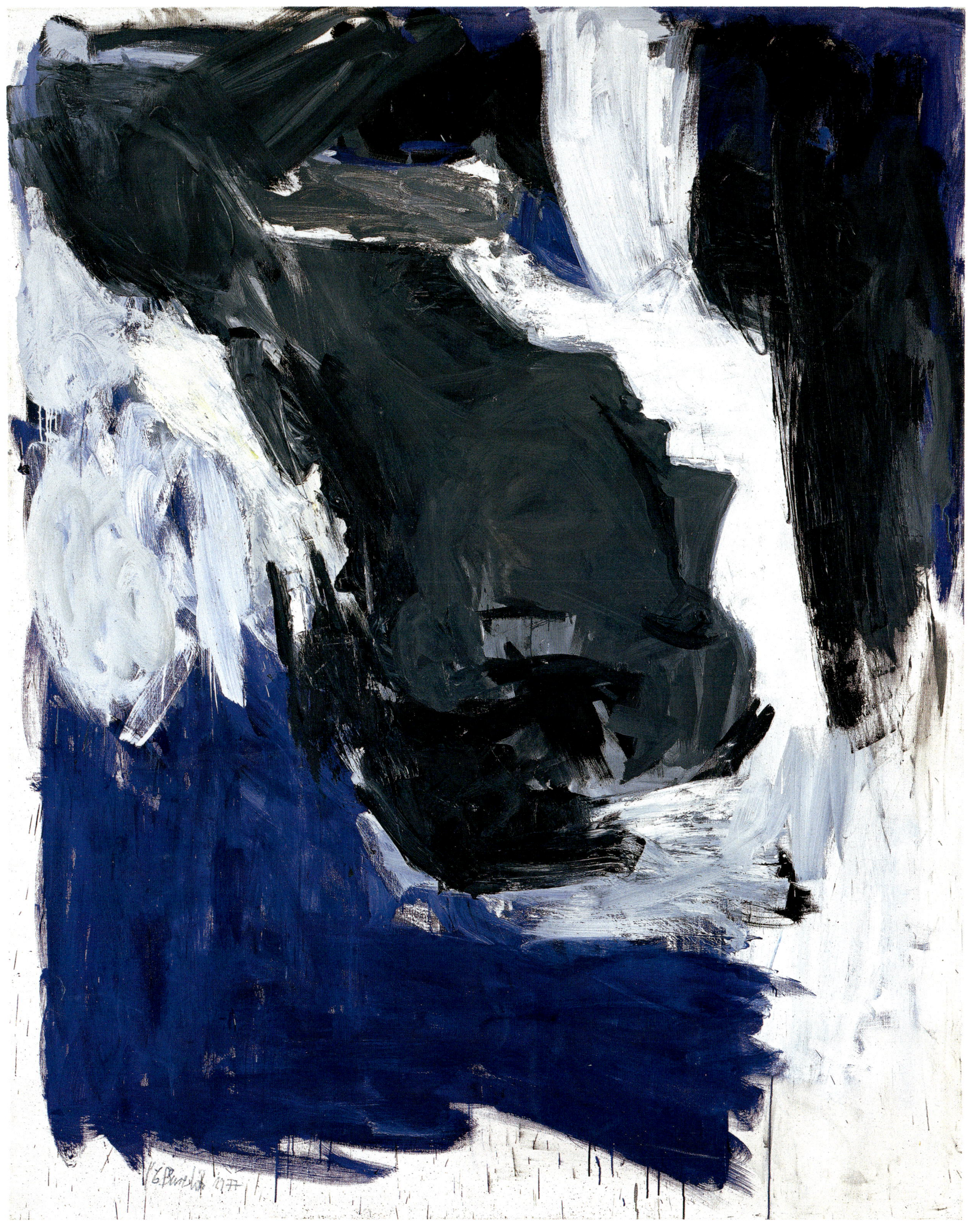

your generation and now, what are the other artists that you've been looking at, who, do you think, have absorbed a legacy of your struggle to form a unique voice within the landscape of international artistic practice?

BASELITZ We haven't talked at all about my immediate neighbor A.R. Penk. I find Penk to be an enormously important artist. Though, at the moment, his position is not contemporary. Another very important artist—and I experience him as coming a generation after me, but that's not true—is Anselm Kiefer. Actually, I find Anselm Kiefer to be the most distinctive artist, not just in Europe, but anywhere. It's quite strange what he does, and I admire it very much. And then, I have to say, I've seen so many artists in exhibitions in recent years, with great curiosity, where I have to say, the goals that were prescribed to us apparently no longer exist. Our prescribed goal was not only the socialization, it was always a question of a better life—always underlain with philosophy behind it—and of the greatest originality. There was never the trade union accommodation that we should be artists. And today, I have to say (and I experience it as pleasant), one uses all of these peculiar things from the past, appropriates them and declares them new. When I was still spying on de Kooning furtively through the keyhole, Richard Prince had long since painted a de Kooning. And when I saw it at the Guggenheim, I thought, this can't be. What has happened? And meanwhile, I see such things. And there are thick auction catalogues with high prices that treat this theme especially. I say "in my time," that is to say, in my past, this principle was valid only in socialism, because socialism had an explicit goal, which

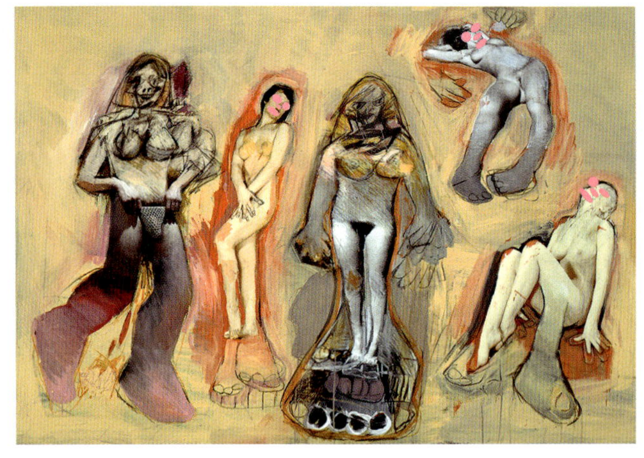

Richard Prince, *Untitled (de Kooning),* **2008**

applied to everyone, but that contradicted individualism very strongly. And I can't really deal with that. That's how I see it.

ENWEZOR I should like to end by reading you a quote from Norman Rosenthal, one of your great admirers and interpreters. He wrote in an article in *The Guardian* in 2007 during the great exhibition you had at the Royal Academy in London. And it says: "As I look back over the many years I have known Baselitz and his art, I think there is a striking comparison to be made with Picasso. In their early years, both artists painted works that came from an inner necessity, the intensity of which frightened each of them. Both borrow from others, ruthlessly adopting ideas for their own purposes. Picasso used, among others, Raphael, Ingres, Delacroix, and Cézanne. As well as taking from Cranach, Pontormo, Goltzius, Munch, Kirchner and indeed Picasso himself, Baselitz, too, has found affinities in the rough, anti-traditional, anarchic painting of the young Cézanne." How are you anti-traditional?

BASELITZ Who said that? Norman said that? I'm very much in that tradition. Only some biographical paraphernalia is missing. When the Second World War came to an end, I was seven. And Picasso had lived through several wars. Simply missing from my biography are these world upheavals. I have to make my own war. All of these controversial things are things from my head, outside of social contexts. Can you imagine that during the war, I became the director of the Nationalgalerie in Berlin, like Picasso was of the Prado? I can't imagine it, I really can't.

ENWEZOR Why?

BASELITZ I think the skepticism people have in relation to my work is, fortunately, very great. I'm mistrusted. I have the certain feeling they don't trust me an inch. Time and again, I realize that I'm not taken seriously—around here, in this country; after all … that's how it is. Just read one of the critics in our great daily newspaper, the *Frankfurter Allgemeine Zeitung*, written not long ago, you can read it there.

ENWEZOR Well, I certainly hope that the Haus der Kunst exhibition will continue to prove them wrong. Thank you, Mr. Baselitz.

Eagle, 1977

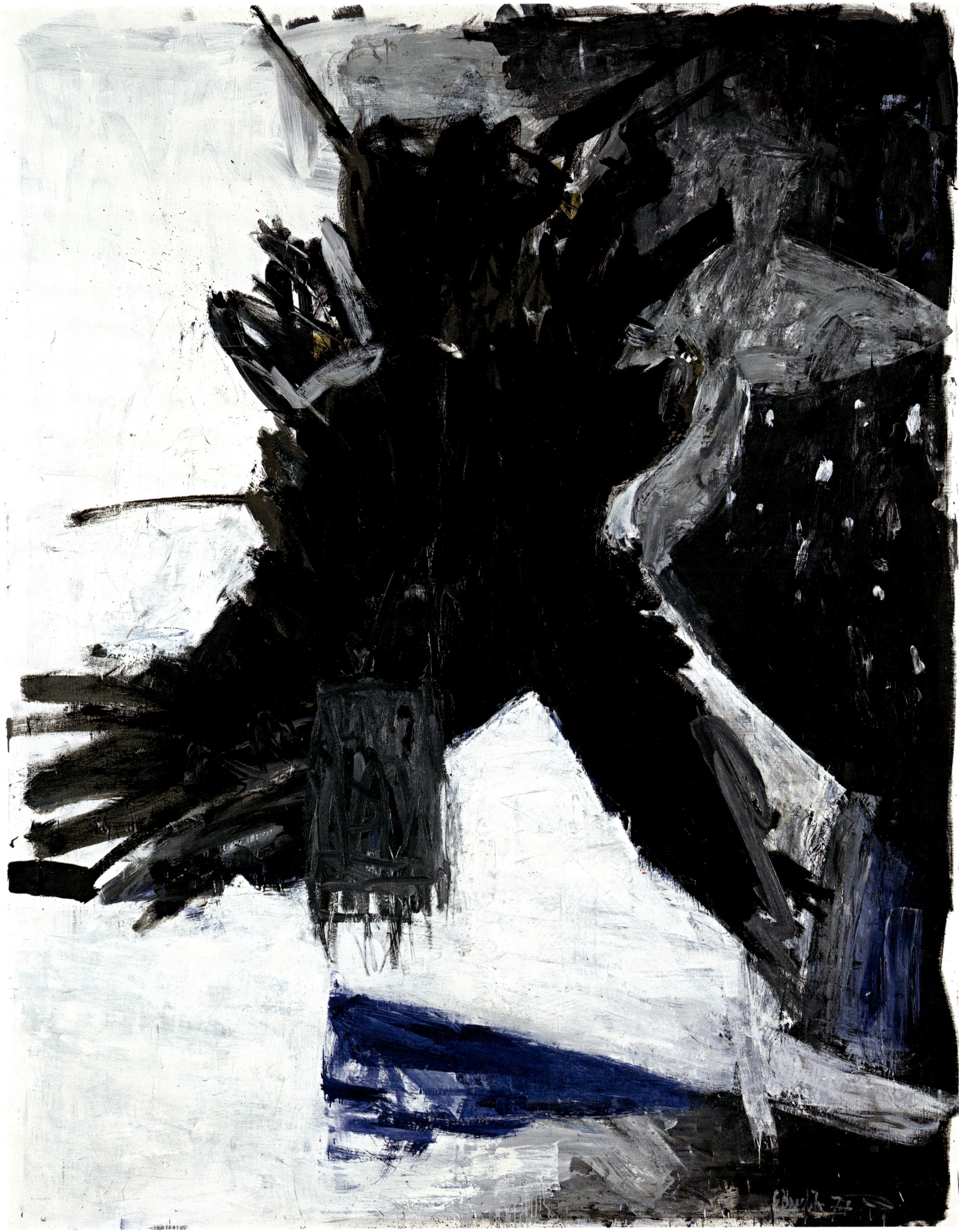

Eagle, 1977–78

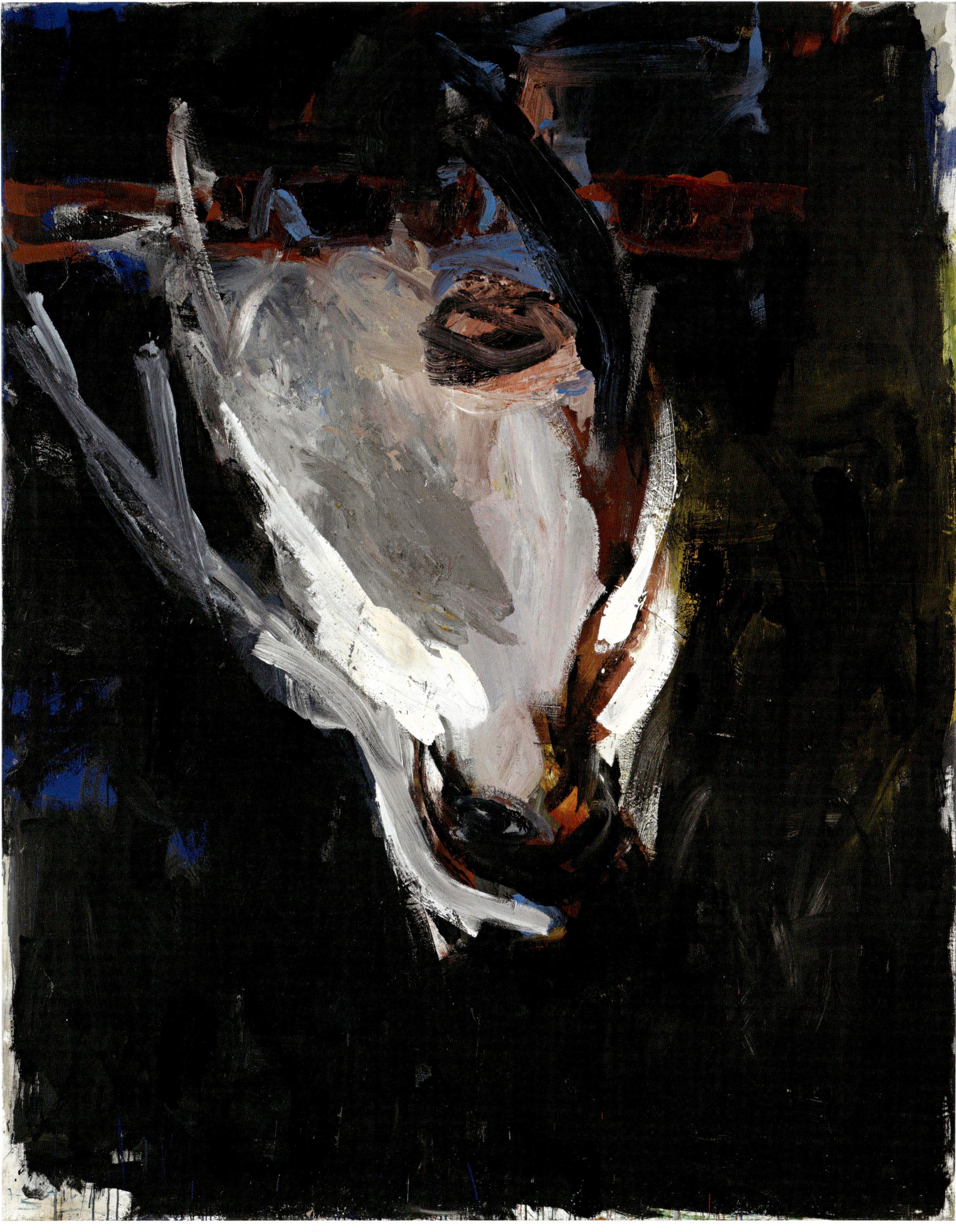

Eagle, 1978

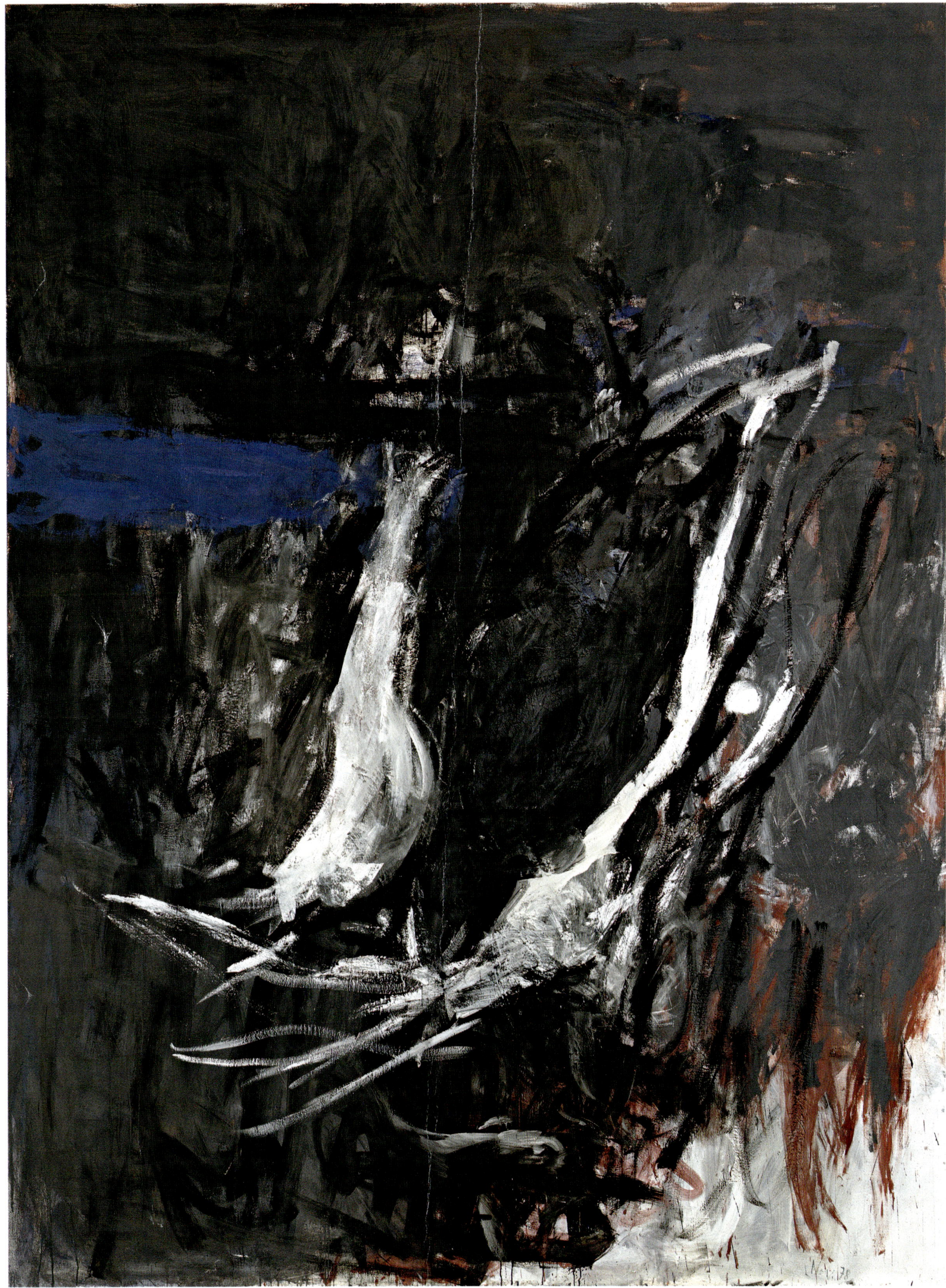

Eagle, 1978

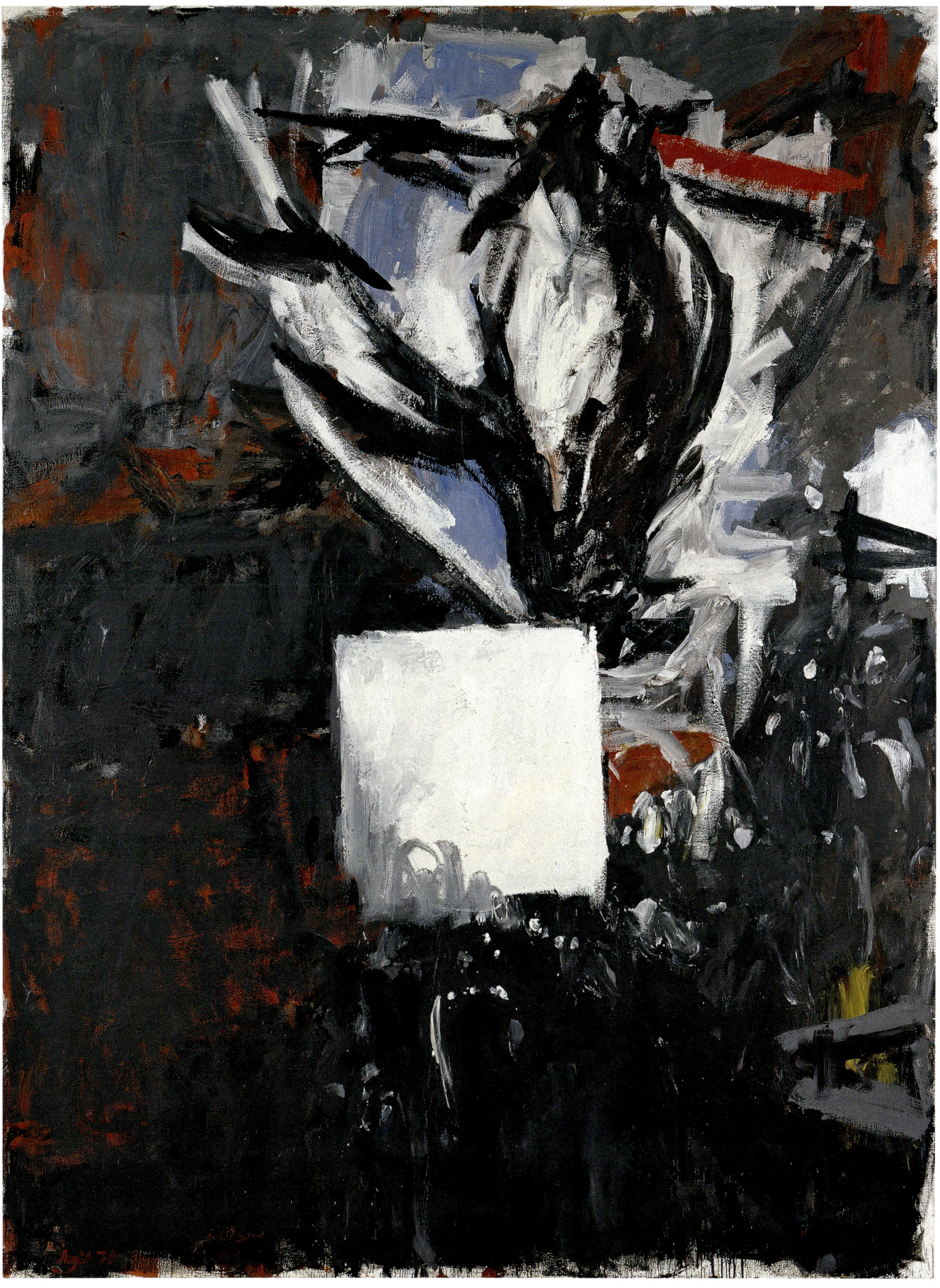

Still Life, 1977

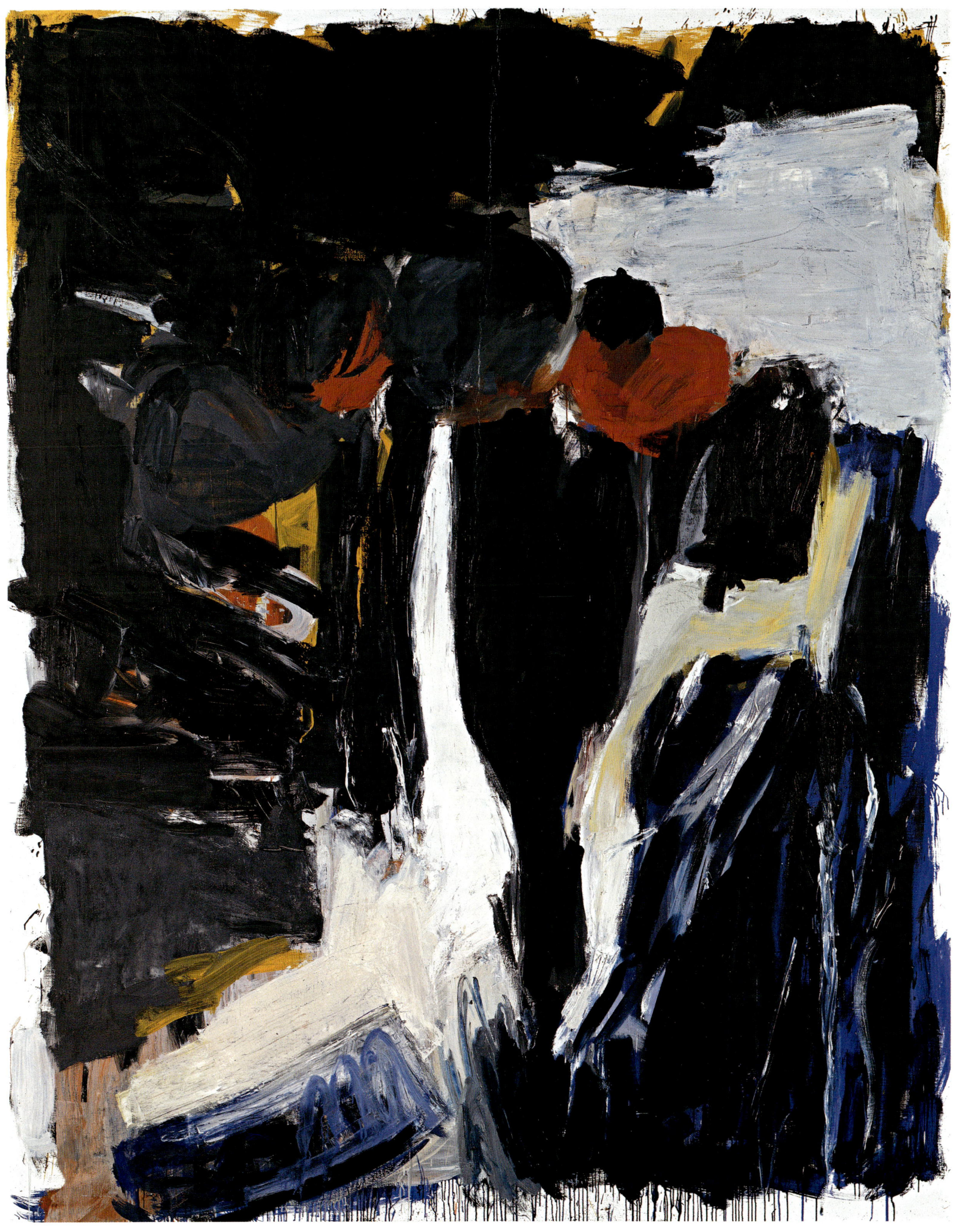

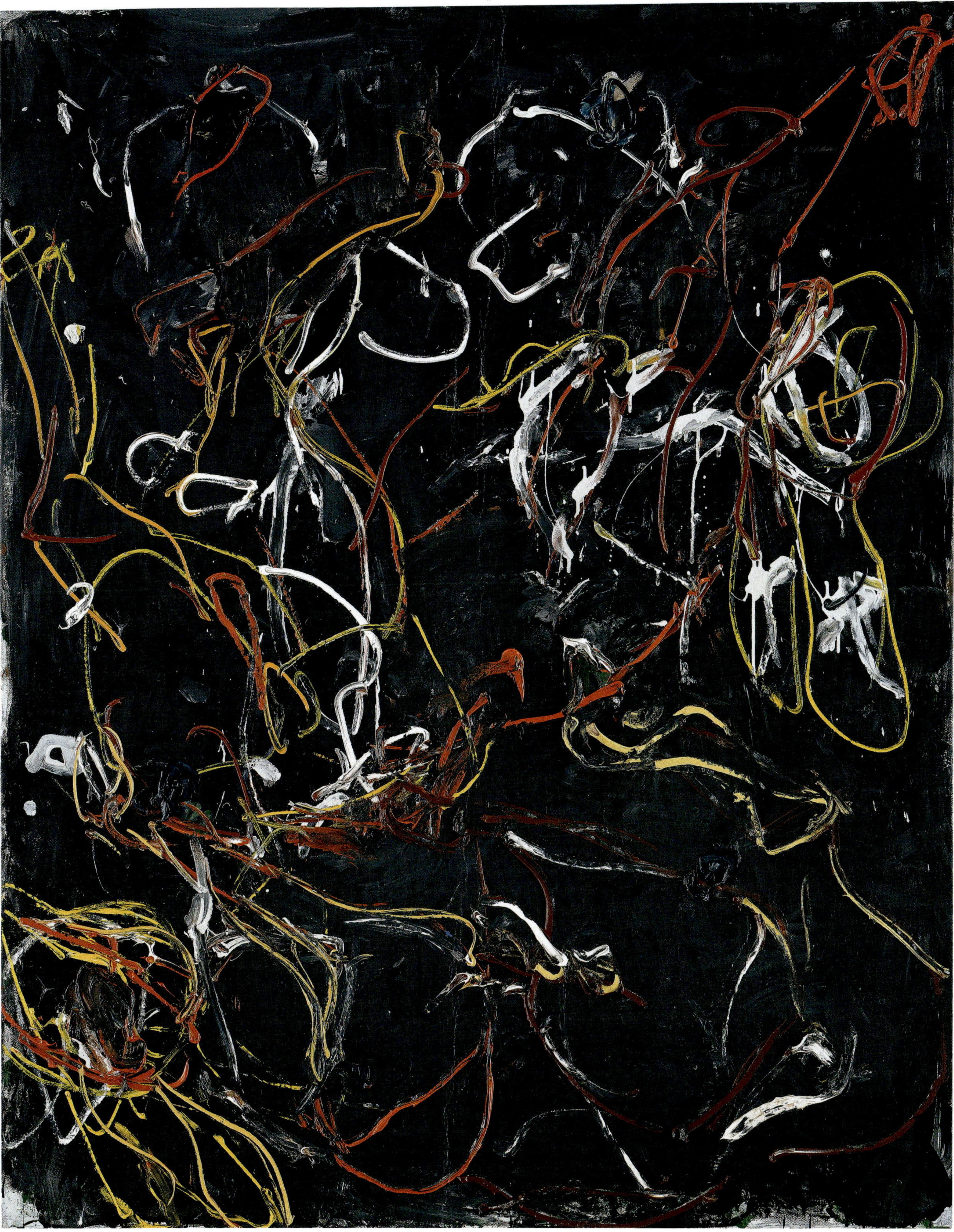

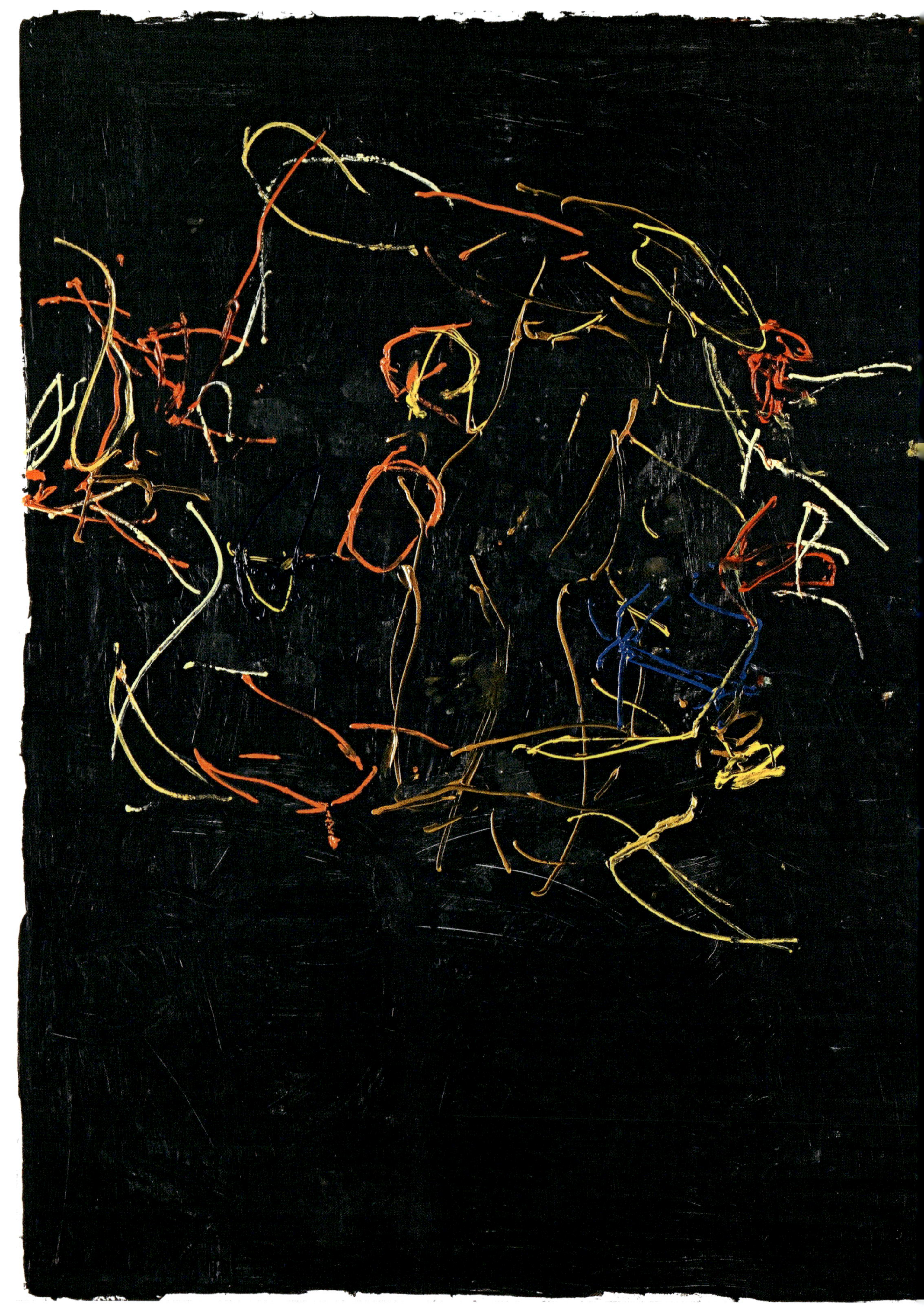

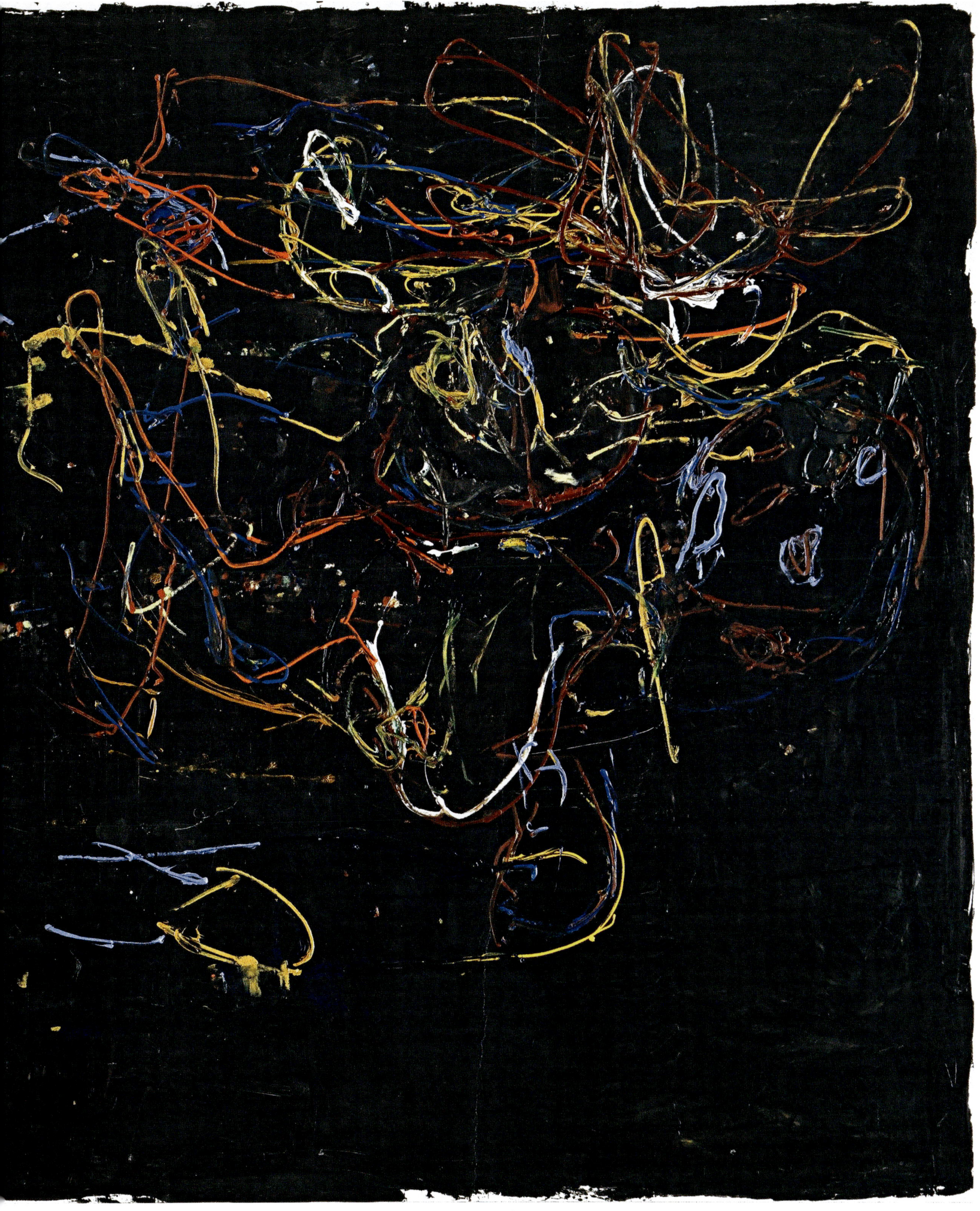

Picture Sixteen, 1993

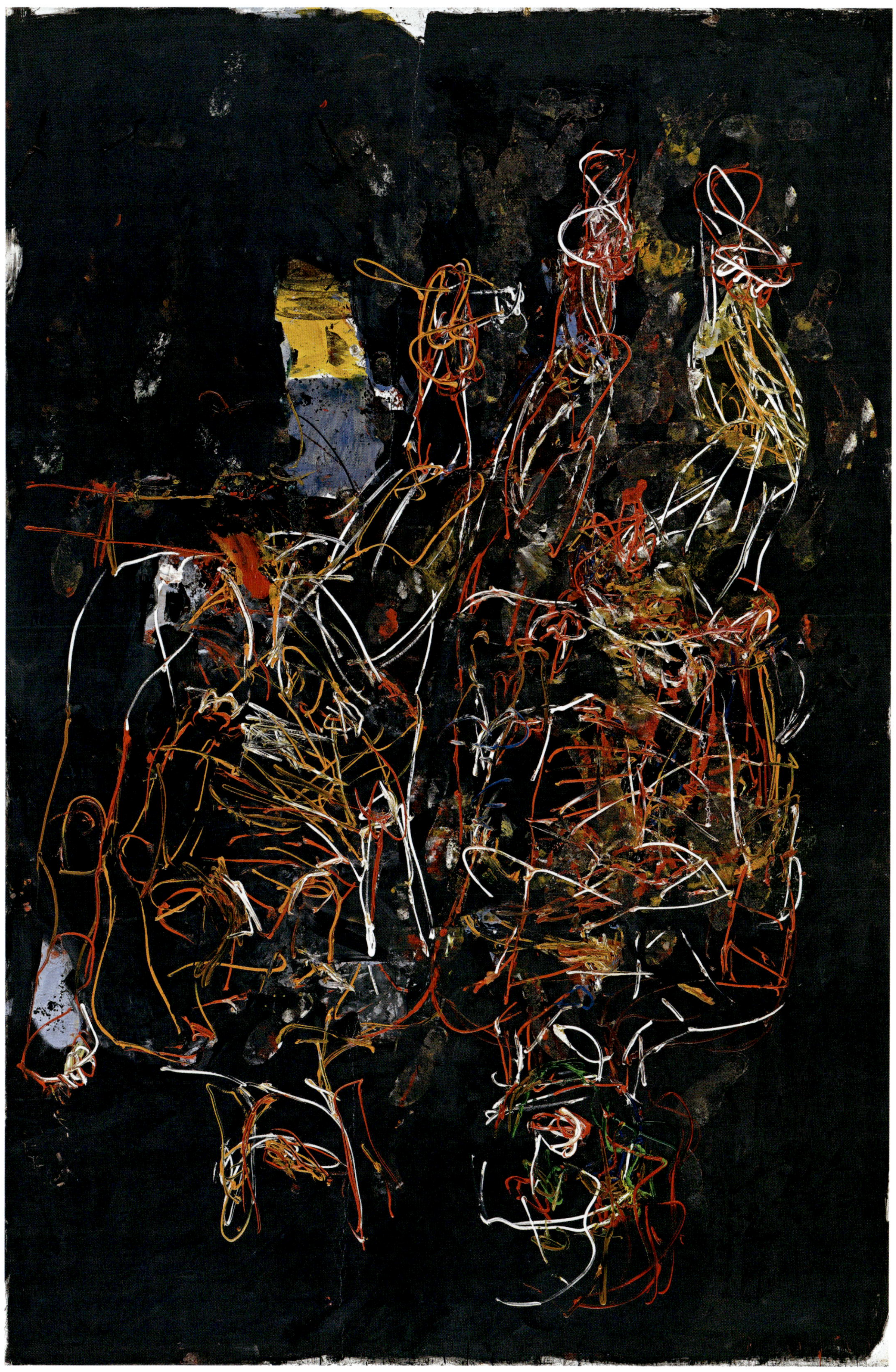

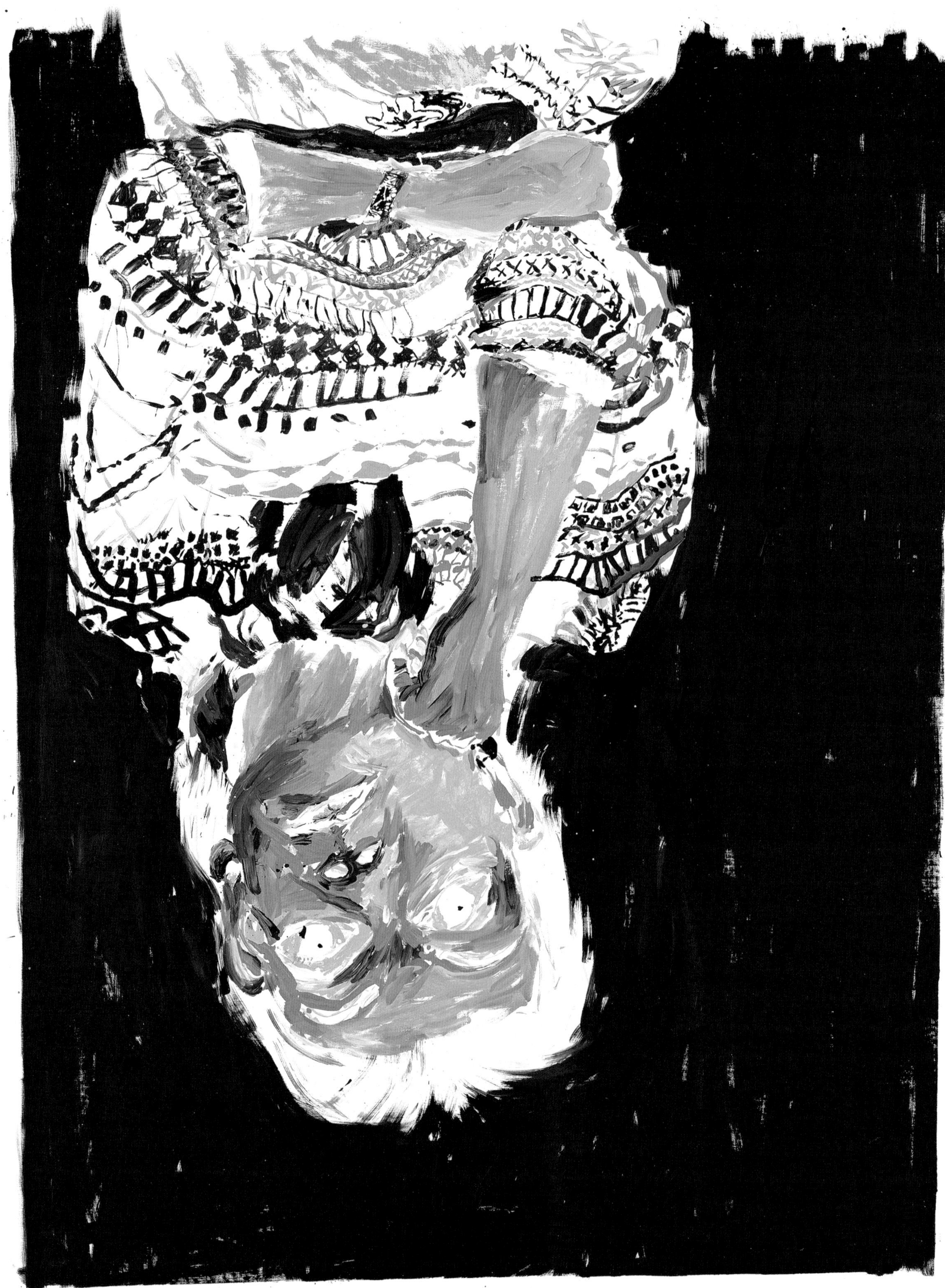

One of the defining traits of Georg Baselitz's development as an artist is—historically speaking—his historical reflexivity, which seems to expand exponentially. This opens up to him the expanded possibilities of self-reference in many ways, and concerns both his pronounced awareness of the historical contexts that permeate his biography, and which have therefore influenced him in a sustained way, as well as his artistic practice, which propels his contemporaneity through an interrogation of his own history, exposing him to the risk of reinterpretation.

His conception of the function and significance of the image involves both his art-historical as well as his contemporary circumstances, which he grasps in a progressive, irreversible process of continuous regeneration and renewal, one whose results he consequently never regards as being complete.

Figuratively speaking, Baselitz has always regarded himself as an immigrant, one who perceives himself as having been involuntarily driven from his biographical and artistic homeland. After his rejection from the Akademie der Künste in East Berlin, he entered an unknown land with his decision to attend the Hochschule für Bildenden Künste in West Berlin in 1957. He searched for a third path that diverged from the narrative orientation of socialist realism on the one hand and from nonobjective Tachist painting on the other, which together represented the antithetical poles of mainstream art for this young, recalcitrant, and rebellious artist. With his uniquely irreverent self-confidence, he strived for a form of artistic expression that would challenge the stereotypes of formal categorizations. From this spirit of contradiction, he developed a provocative stance that reacted against the conformist controls of the art world.

Ulrich Wilmes

DEEP, DARK TIME

In his artistic practice, Baselitz assumes the perspective of a "neutral narrator" who exits the work in order to shape an experiential situation from the outside. The revival of motifs that were shaped and elaborated years and even decades earlier subsequently detaches them from their historical backgrounds, thus allowing the relevance of a given theme to enter into a new and unforeseeable perspective, one that this painter regards as indispensable. He is aware of the risks to which he exposes his works, and even provokes the risk that such redeployments will limit the work's historical significance—in the sense that the current reading of the object will inundate the interpretation of the original presentation. In this respect, the question of the object is proscribed, as if it would have imposed itself now. The question of the narrative perspective of the painter, who exposes his own work to a revision, appears significant here as well with regard to the selection of the motif (whether a figure, eagle, portrait, group-portrait, or nude), and as concerns art-historical references. Baselitz has always situated the motivation that prompted him to adopt a specific theme in the realm of the personal. His method is to close off objects from any narrative interpretation by the beholder, and to confine them to their function in the image. The ambiguity of this undertaking is therefore entirely intentional, because it presupposes and regards as self-evident, the divergent perspectives of painter and beholder in relation to the image.

"I want personal content, but it should come through the painting. I wanted to use typical subjects, like landscapes, nudes and portraits, because they are a standard subject. You have to paint something, but the point is not to begin with something personal. You must have the will to deny content in order to begin to make a painting that will exist for itself … I begin with an idea, but as I work the picture takes over. Then there is the struggle between the idea that I preconceived in advance and the picture that fights for its own life."[1]

This revolt against conformism has manifested itself repeatedly at historic turning points when decisive political or social upheavals formed the backdrop for equally radical transformations in the aesthetic constitution of art. Serving as crucial guideposts for the present consideration of Georg Baselitz's artistic achievement and continuing development is his attitude during periods of transition from modern to contemporary art. Addressed here, as a consequence is his relationship to mannerism, which served—not at all accidentally—as a consistent stimulus to his artistic convictions and pronouncements. The historical arc that can be traced from the sixteenth to the twentieth centuries is based on the concept of modernity, one derivable historically and indisputably, from a variety of perspectives, not unlike the concept of mannerism, which has been developed in contradictory ways throughout the course of art-historical debates. The intellectual and philosophical departure of modernity that emerged as a break with tradition in all spheres of life during the turn from the fifteenth to sixteenth centuries was based on the humanism of the Renaissance and the Reformation, while the aesthetic and artistic manifestation of modernity seems to have established itself only during the final years of the nineteenth century, and ultimately to have arrived at a terminus in the late twentieth century. Baselitz opposed such conventional conceptions of historical contexts through the development of his own pictorial practice. That which began as an empathetic intuition, an unconscious stimulus rather than a well-founded position,

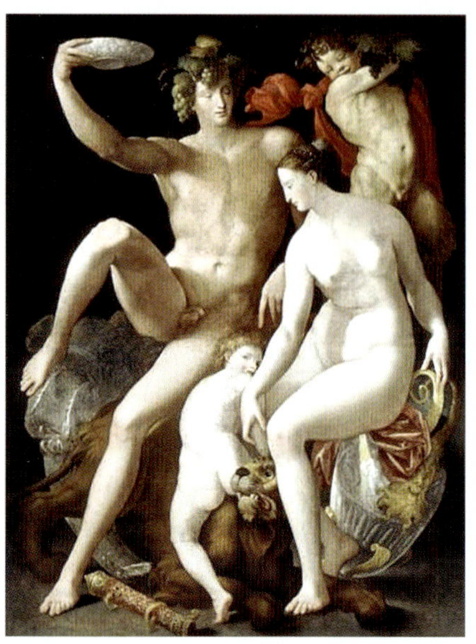

Rosso Fiorentino, *Bacchus, Venus, and Cupid*, 1530–31

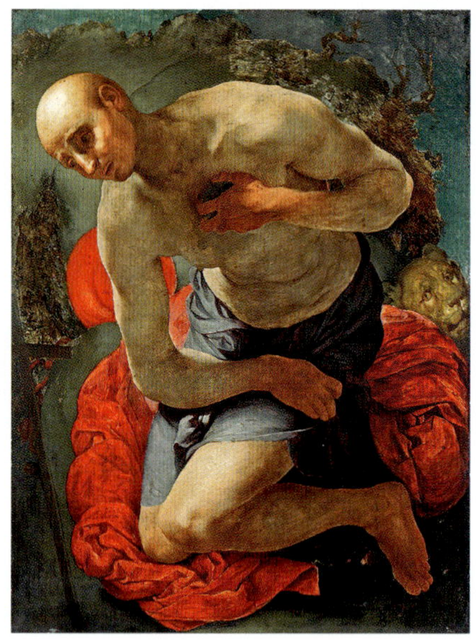

Jacopo Pontormo, *The Penitent St. Jerome*, ca. 1528–29

evolved after the vivid experiences of his first stay in Italy, in 1975, into an ideational elective affinity.

Baselitz's relationship to the epoch and the artists of mannerism is not displayed in an obvious way through artistic quotations. Instead, he perceives himself as being linked to them through a kind of elective affinity: although they occupied a pre-modernist habitus, the artists of the sixteenth century turned away in more or less radical ways from the ideals of a "classical" form of language, thereby rejecting the fixations of a canonical pictorial art they regarded as obsolete.

The painters of the first generation of mannerists in Florence, among them Rosso Fiorentino and Jacopo Pontormo, were described by Giorgio Vasari in *Lives* as erratic and extravagant characters who became artistically radicalized.

Of special interest to Baselitz was the adoption of a peripheral, distanced perspective through which the mannerists liberated themselves from the restrictions of their era, thereby bypassing the standards established by the geniuses Michelangelo and Raphael.

And not least of all, there existed parallels between extreme temporally-conditioned crisis situations that liberated the kind of instinctual forces capable of supplying painters with the preconditions for thrusts of innovation.

To be sure, the backgrounds formed by such comparative historical moments shape fateful and militant confrontations that result in far-reaching societal upheavals—whether in the sixteenth or the twentieth centuries.

Between 1494 and 1559, the territories of what is now Italy to a large extent formed the battlefield for a series of confrontations that entangled many of the more powerful European states. Also decisive were the Reformation and

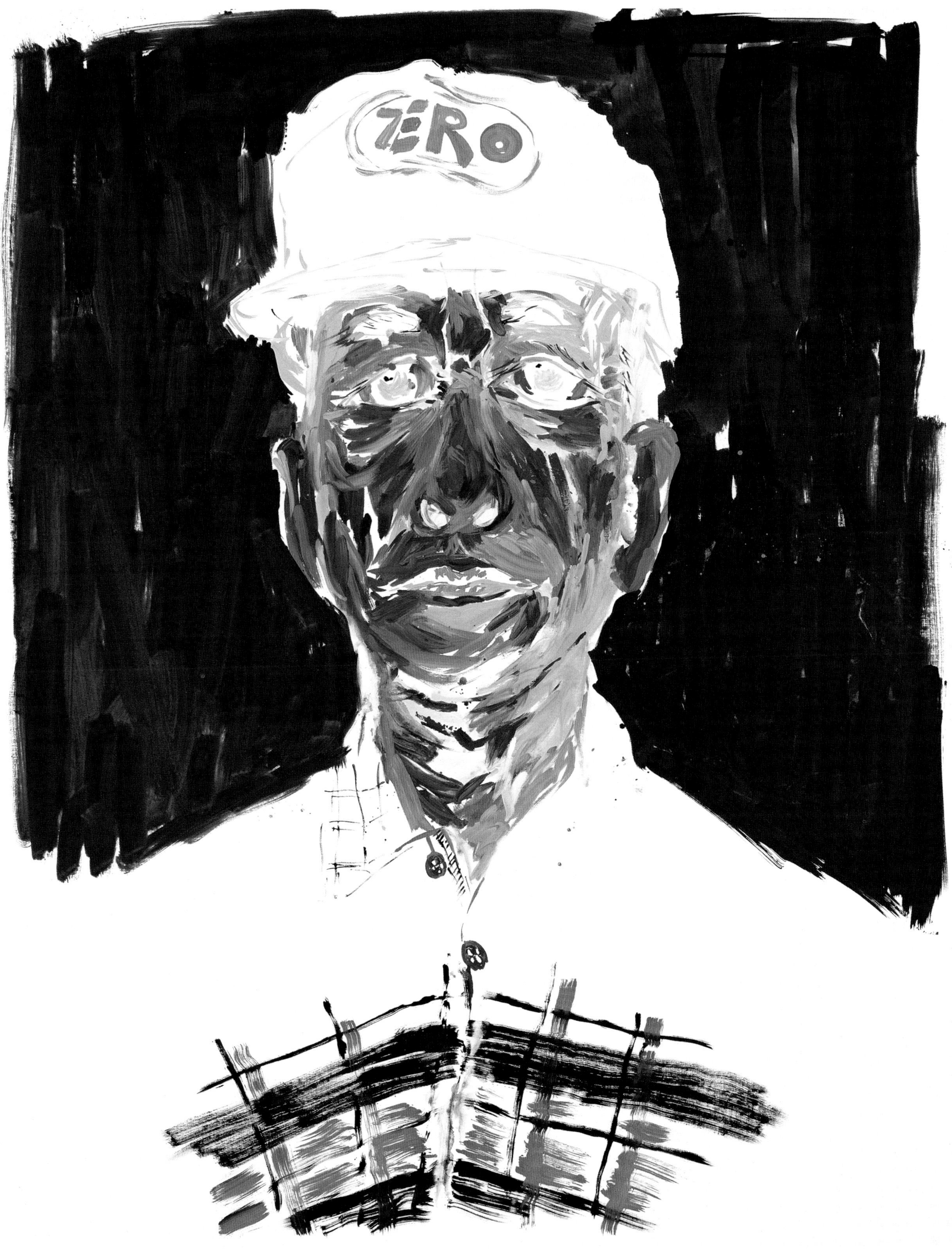
ZERO

Counterreformation that accompanied the waning of the Renaissance, whose rupturing of the hardened system of beliefs were decisively strengthened by the epochal shift toward the Copernican worldview that displaced the earth from the center of the universe to its periphery.

In contrast, the twentieth century ushered in a far-reaching reorganization of the political landscape from a monarchical to materialistically determined civic systems whose claims to supremacy were fought out in the "primal catastrophes" of two world wars. At their center was the antagonism between the totalitarian ideologies of communism and fascism, which led after the collapse of National Socialism to the division of a now totally destroyed Germany, which therefore became the boundary for the emerging Cold War.

In the confrontation of this postwar order, Baselitz—who was born shortly before the outbreak of the Second World War—sought a liberating orientation without predetermined models of thought. Around fifty years later, he described this state of loss and disillusionment, which was preserved in him as a belief system of sorts: "There are no ideals today. I was born into a destroyed order, a destroyed landscape, a destroyed people, a destroyed society. And I didn't want to re-establish an order: I'd seen enough of so-called order."[2]

While he has always contested the presence of formal quotations, he detects an affinity between the decentered subject of modernism and the impulse to destroy the classical ideal, which the mannerists perceived as the only path available to them.

The process of the positive revision of the mannerist epoch—long dismissed as anti-classical—had two highpoints: one in the early twentieth century,

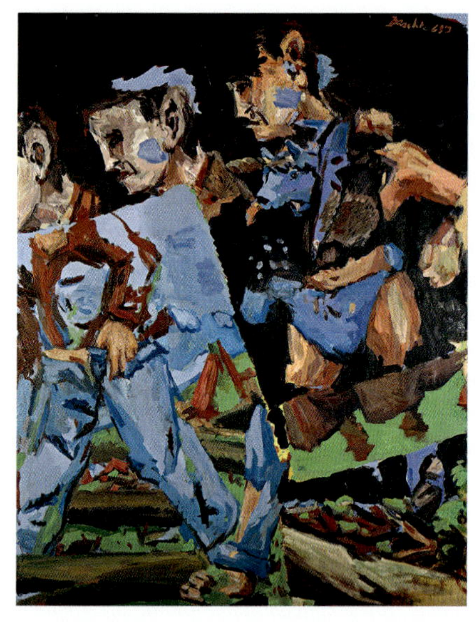

Georg Baselitz, *Meissen Woodsmen*, 1969

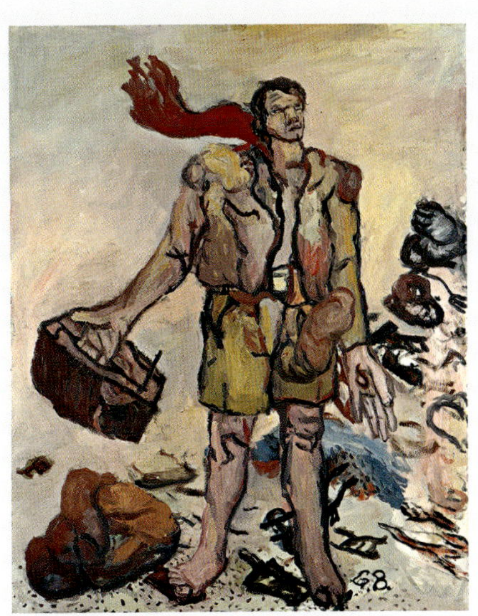

Georg Baselitz, *The New Type*, 1966

the other in the nineteen-fifties, when Baselitz sought a new artistic beginning. Decisive in particular was Gustav René Hocke's *Die Welt als Labyrinth* (*The World as a Labyrinth*),[3] which develops a conception of mannerism and its impact all the way up to modernism.

During Baselitz's stay in Florence, this stimulus was further intensified by his viewing of original works by Rosso Fiorentino and Jacopo Pontormo. Here, the concept of *maniera* must be accorded an essential function. Its ambivalent meaning in the sense of a dialectic attitude and style seems close to Baselitz's self-image as an unaffiliated artistic existence. When it comes to oblique formal and contextual quotation, Baselitz himself perceives them in the work group known as *Helden* (*Heroes*), produced exactly around this time, with their disproportionate figures in bleak, abandoned landscapes. In his still remarkable study of Baselitz's collection of mannerists prints,[4] a text of great importance for this work group, nonetheless, Thomas Röske relativizes this aspect, but on the other hand emphasizes Siegfried Gohr's remark[5] on compositional analogies. In fact, these references seem to open up decisive access to the perspectival densification of the pictorial space that is traceable via the *Fracture Paintings* all the way to the artist's current production of the *Negative* and the *Black Paintings*. In them, pictorial space seems to be constituted not as a perspectival construction or as a space of action, but instead as a compressed space for static and frozen configurations—in ways highly congruent with Rosso's conception.

Moreover, as Röske explained, Baselitz's attempt to establish a new approach to figurative depiction strives to "dissolve" academic conceptions of representation and abstraction, "In a form of representational painting that for the most part preserves the independence of material shaping (in the spirit of *Informel* painting) vis à vis the motif."[6]

Baselitz was inspired—as indicated in the "Pandemonic Manifesto"—by the mannerist "obsession with exaggeration" and by the "demonstrativeness" of their body language, because these did not result solely from a hyper-artificial erosion of connectedness to reality, but instead even more from reflections on the existing pictorial ideals that they sought to overcome. With this conception of "manner" and "mania" (both words are contained in the subtitle of Hocke's *The World as a Labyrinth*), Baselitz took up a stance that corresponded to his own conception of the encrusted conventions of established artistic practice, prescriptions he deemed absurd, hopelessly obsolete. In Hocke's "suprahistorical concept of mannerism," Röske perceives an essential incitement for the general flaring up of interest (on the part of art historiography and theory) in this period, as well as in the tendency toward the abnormal that emanated from it, one that erupted in the context of the critical tendencies of the nineteen-sixties because it manifested such striking parallels with present-day challenges to the ideological system, accompanied by debate about military rearmament and nuclear deterrence. These hitherto outsiders of European high art were also reevaluated by André Breton, who among others invoked the representatives of the School of Fontainbleau as "precursors of surrealism," and as Röske points out: "If Baselitz was genuinely unaware of this provenance, then this testifies to an astonishing subterranean communication between cultures in the postwar era."[7] In fact, it was only in Florence that Baselitz arrived at the insight that "The attitude I had adopted was completely false,"[8] thereby singling out the preoccupation with mannerism as an aspect of an

essential learning process through which he passed during the nineteen-sixties, the period during which he broke new ground with his manifesto.

In the context of twentieth century modernism, the interrogation of the abstract in its relationship to representation was a groundbreaking affair, one pursued along various main and subsidiary lines. Strategies of destruction and construction led from opposed directions toward the overcoming of depiction and the creation of contents that emerged exclusively through formal resources.

The art of the postwar era—the context in which Georg Baselitz grew up—was characterized by a radicalization of inherited assumptions about the image, which were formulated programmatically in America, however with an impact that was felt simultaneously in Europe as well. Abstract expressionism (Jackson Pollock, Willem de Kooning, Barnett Newman, and Mark Rothko) and *Informel* (Wols, Georges Mathieu, Bernard Schultze, Karl Otto Götz) shared the intention of abolishing the panel picture as a formal totality in order to extinguish all allusions in favor of an explosive expansion of the delimiting frame of the painting into the external space, or of an implosion of the plumbed outer boundaries into an fathomless interior. Pollock's dissolution of the figure-ground relationship into a seemingly chaotic web of lines, one that spreads itself without compositional hierarchy, was complemented by Newman's unbounded colored areas, heightened to the point of vastness by a one-dimensional guiding of the gaze. These were confronted with Wols's poetic self-renouncing creations, whose figurative organisms dissolves the material in favor of a structural center, and by the exhibitionistic appearances of Georges Mathieu, who stylized the painterly action as a performative pictorial invention.

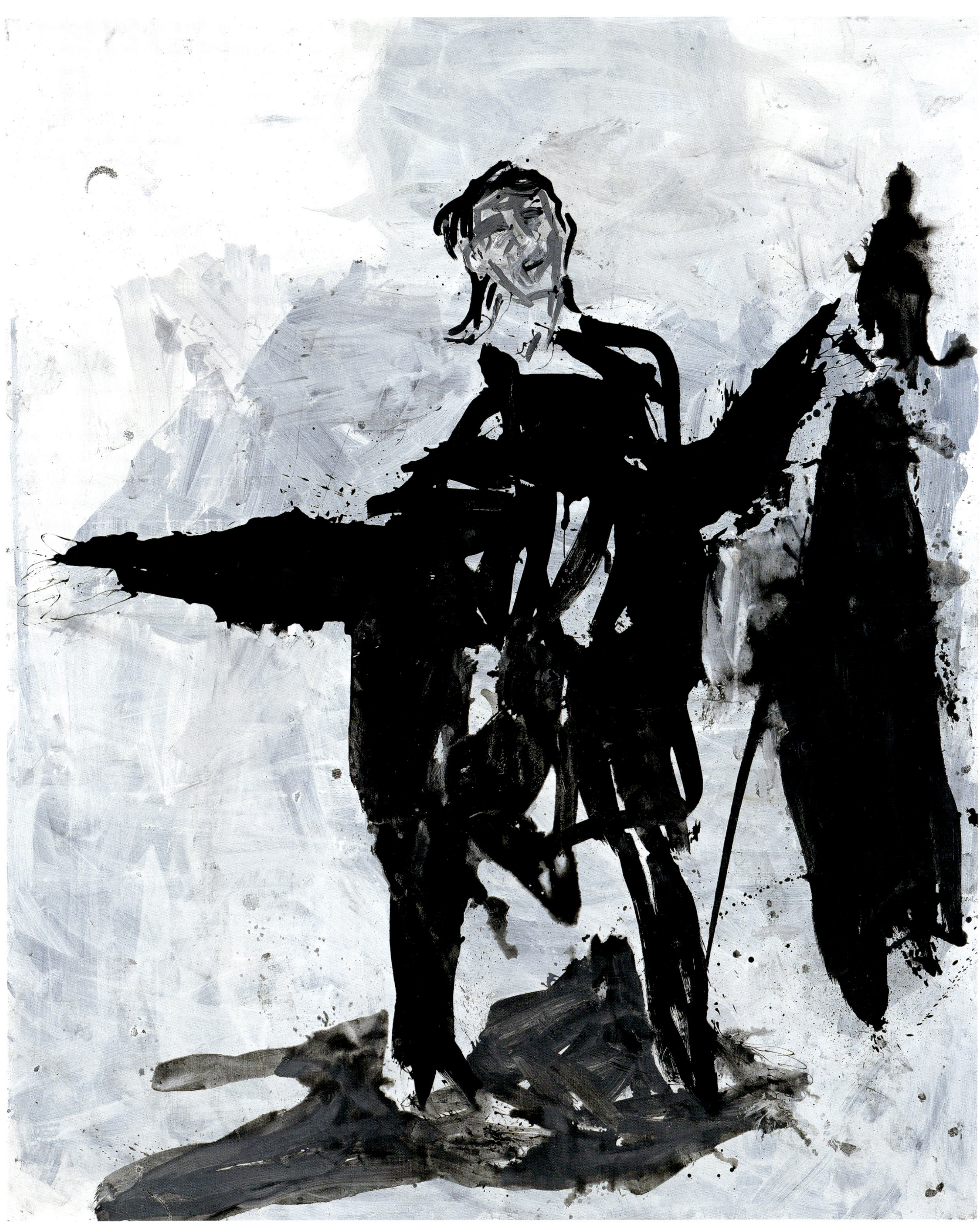

In 1958, an exhibition took place at the Hochschule für Bildende Künste in Berlin under the title *Die neue amerikanische Malerei* (*The New American Painting*). This propagandistic overview, organized by the Museum of Modern Art in New York, which traveled to a number of European cities and remained in Berlin for four weeks, featured eighty-one works by seventeen painters, among them, the main representatives of abstract expressionism mentioned above. For the young Baselitz, this encounter amounted to a shock that confronted him with a hitherto unfamiliar attitude, one based on a notion of freedom that seemed limitless to him: " … There were no doubts about Pollock or his paintings. Nevertheless, at the academy, Pollock had very little influence, particularly with the younger students. De Kooning had much greater influence because his painting was European, or of European origin, and its means of depiction were more easily comprehended. The most important aspect of the de Kooning pictures at that time was expression—the caricature of a woman which had been painted—her horrible expression. She was showing her teeth, and that was decisive."[9] For Baselitz, at the same time, this experience triggered a sense of frustration, since all conceivable possibilities for linking up with this art seemed obstructed:

"I found those pictures so overwhelming, so totally unexpected, so different from the experience of my own world at the time that I felt totally desperate, because I thought I'd never stand a chance of doing well compared to those painters."[10]

The propagandistic function of the Berlin exhibition was confirmed in an obvious way by the choice of an art academy as venue. The show mirrored the confrontation of two social systems based onto opposed ideologies respectively, each claiming to serve as a legitimate countermodel on German soil for the overcoming of the fascist past. For each, assertions of superiority were staged on all socially relevant fields (economics, science, space flight, culture). Baselitz, who was born during the reign of National Socialism and grew up in in the GDR in a socialist worker and farming community, was so appalled by this ideological confrontation with the German past and by the present of the postwar era that he was never really able to free himself from; instead, he admitted to being continuously shaped by it: "I lived through seven years of war. After 1945, the part of Germany I grew up in was occupied by the Russians; then I was sent to the part that was occupied by the Americans. It was as though the children were being punished for the stupidities of the fathers."

Ultimately, Baselitz held this situation responsible for his aversion to "accept[ing] dictates from above" and to the aggressiveness that drove him for so long: "In Germany those dictates changed from one part of the country to another, but they were still dictates—supposedly to create a new society, but they just weren't my kind of thing."[11]

Notwithstanding the powerful impression it doubtlessly made on him, Baselitz explored the exhibition against the background of the stylization of the discourse—conducted under the aegis of an escalating Cold War doctrine—about the fundamental question of abstraction and representation as a confrontation over the autonomy of art. The one-sided Anglo-American orientation of the art market and current tendencies in painting served the propagation of "abstraction as a world language," exalted now to a synonym for freedom as such, while representation was equated with the functional appropriation of

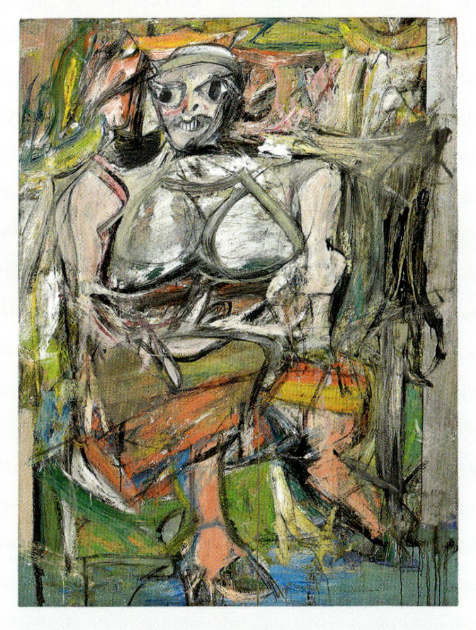

Willem de Kooning, *Woman I*, 1950–52

art through a political system of one type or another. In abstraction, Werner Haft-mann perceived "The most direct confrontation with reality and with the facts of existence … of which the human species has ever been capable," while on the other hand, "The entire domain of confrontations with the optical appearance of the world of objects is able to generate only feeble impulses."[12]

Clement Greenberg went even further, regarding the highpoint of the radical reshaping of self-referentiality and autonomy as having been surpassed already by midcentury. For Greenberg, then, the "the essence of modernism" "lay … in the use of characteristic methods of a discipline to criticize the discipline itself, not in order to subvert it but in order to entrench it more firmly in its area of competence."[13]

This self-criticism, on whose basis painting is said to have submitted itself to a process of self-purification, results in a purity of form and of expression, leading finally toward the following conclusion: "The purely plastic or abstract qualities of the work of art are the only ones that count. Emphasizing the medium and its difficulties, and at once the purely plastic, the proper values of visual art come to the fore."[14]

The recourse to the certainty of a recognizing vision confronts painting with the problem of how to respond to this altered perceptual practice. The question of the pictorial object was endowed with an existential significance, one that provoked a challenge to its legitimation. This affected the immanent problems of the medium, deprived now of its original depictive function. And the consequence that art around 1960 was prepared to draw from this has long since solidified as the art historical formula: "an exit from the image"—a

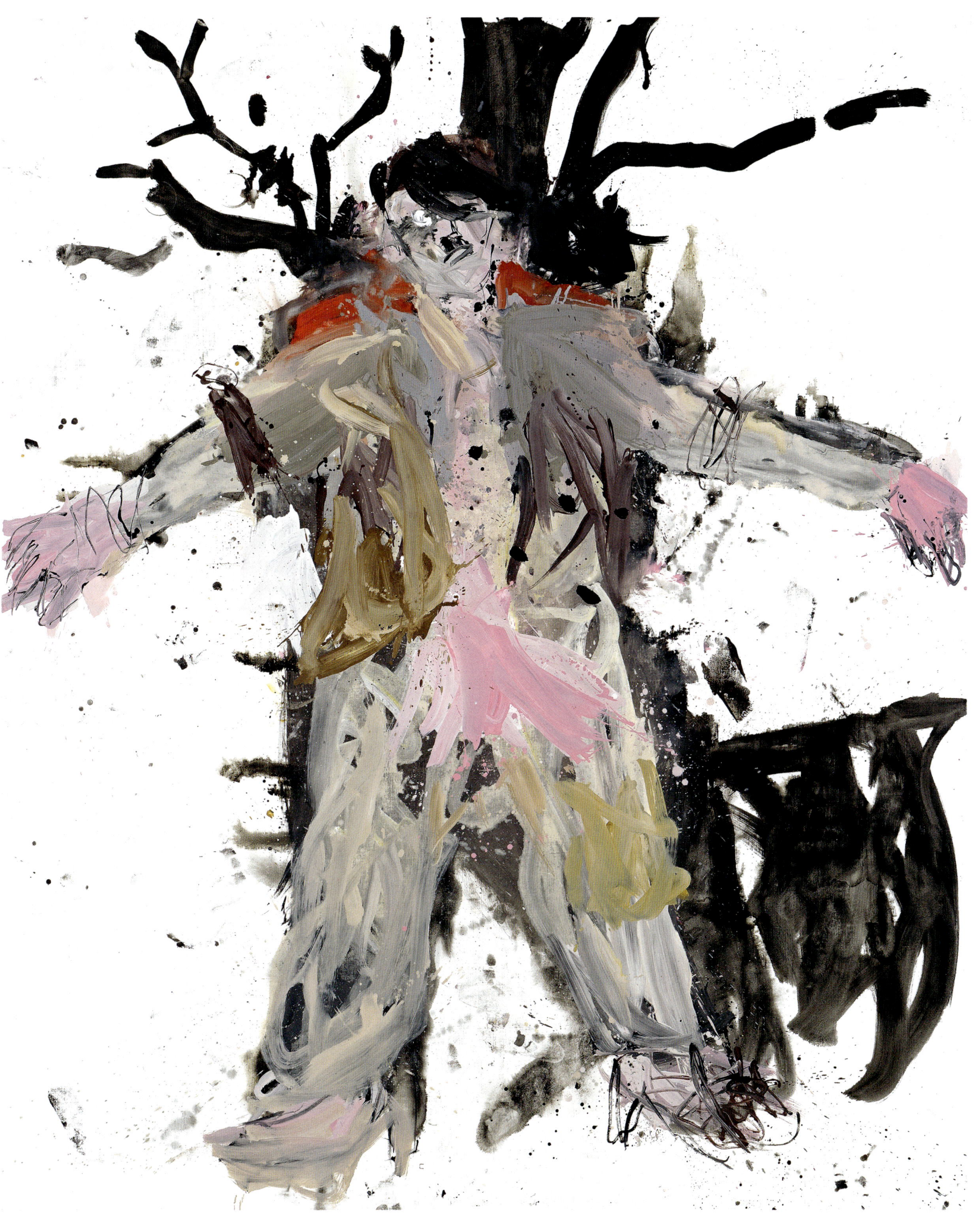

consequence that Georg Baselitz (along with a number of other artists) would reject violently for various reasons.

This public questioning of painting as a medium of contemporary art represented an extreme challenge, particularly for a painter who remained committed to figuration.

To trace the "purely plastic qualities" corresponded thoroughly to Baselitz's conception of the function of contemporary painting, and supplied a decisive impulse for his pictorial approach. But he did not accept the necessity of nonobjectivity, which was acknowledged explicitly by Greenberg's doctrine of abstract expressionism. Baselitz's conception of painting became radicalized instead precisely in relation to the theory of the image, and along the interface of abstraction and representation. It was here that he perceived the possibility of resistance against all forms of conformism as an impetus to generate new visual experiences on the basis of a contemporary attitude through which he conceived of himself as an individual and a collective being—and on whose basis he vehemently repudiated the progressive character of the absolutization of nonobjectivity as conformism with the predominant zeitgeist. The object served Baselitz exclusively as a pretext for the picture, and was not the purpose of the presentation; therefore, he regarded the motif as arbitrary.

The decision in favor of a specific pictorial object followed personal tendencies and sympathies, which however seem irrelevant to the beholder. In the foreground stand the conditions that are achieved by the picture. During the process of production, the work distances itself from the painter's intentions and achieves its own existence.

"To reinvent painting for yourself, you must address the obvious and the marginal, disrupt the predictable by using what people don't want to look at or are not familiar with."[15]

The painter must turn away from pre-existing pictures. Baselitz's method for achieving this process of elimination is the engendering of dissonances, which guide the beholder toward unknown terrain. At the same time, his pictures often astonished by virtue of their unintentional equilibrium: "Harmony: it arises as desperation. I work exclusively with disharmonies. If I paint a red dot on the left, I don't put another on the right, I put a green one instead. And if I paint a triangle in the upper left, I will guaranteed not put another in the lower right. In fact, in everything I do, I apply the principles of disharmony, of imbalance, of destruction. And the misfortune, the really great misfortune, is that harmony ensues, time and again. But if it seems like that to you, and you say my paintings are harmonious, then all I can say is—bravo. But the intention, or the route, was different from that."[16]

The present investigation is based on specific themes that, upon being developed further by Baselitz, have occupied prominent positions, and are connected with the production of the *Black Paintings* (2012–13), and of the large bronze sculptures that were produced in the same context. Those considered individually in the following are the eagle motif, the standing figure and the figural pair, the portrait, and the nude. In the foreground of the present investigation, the question is: According to which current pictorial considerations and interests—however conceived—does Baselitz decide to take up again an object he handled years or even decades earlier? When they are taken up again, Baselitz's motifs are further elaborated on the basis of their future development. This means that the motif is not only reconsidered, but also fathomed from multiple perspectives.

Five paintings from the years 1965 to 1977 define five central pictorial objects, all of which have assumed such fundamental positions in Baselitz's further development that he has become preoccupied with them again from time to time.

Die großen Freunde (*The Great Friends*) from 1965 possesses a kind of iconic significance within Baselitz's oeuvre as a whole. In the context of the *Heroes Paintings*, it occupies the position of a swan song. One cemented by the artist himself through a manifesto text, and often forms the basis in the literature for elaborate analyses: "Conveying existential loneliness in the face of historical forces, these counter-heroes take on the personae of homeless shepherds and defenseless partisans and rebels … The programmatic work *The Great Friends* endorses this reading, its scale being comparable to an altarpiece. Like Latter-day Saints set against a background of apocalyptic ruins, the two figures—their military uniforms in shreds and their flies open—show their wounds and gesture towards future collaborative and ideal creativity."[17]

The self-reflexive character that is attributed to the paintings of this period can be traced back to Baselitz's aggressive and defensive stance in relation to a repressive and conservative postwar era, one that left him no room for deviation from the consensus—whether in social or artistic respects.

The picture conveys the monumental impression of anti-heroism, of an appropriately withdrawn attitude, and one that had been internalized as a result

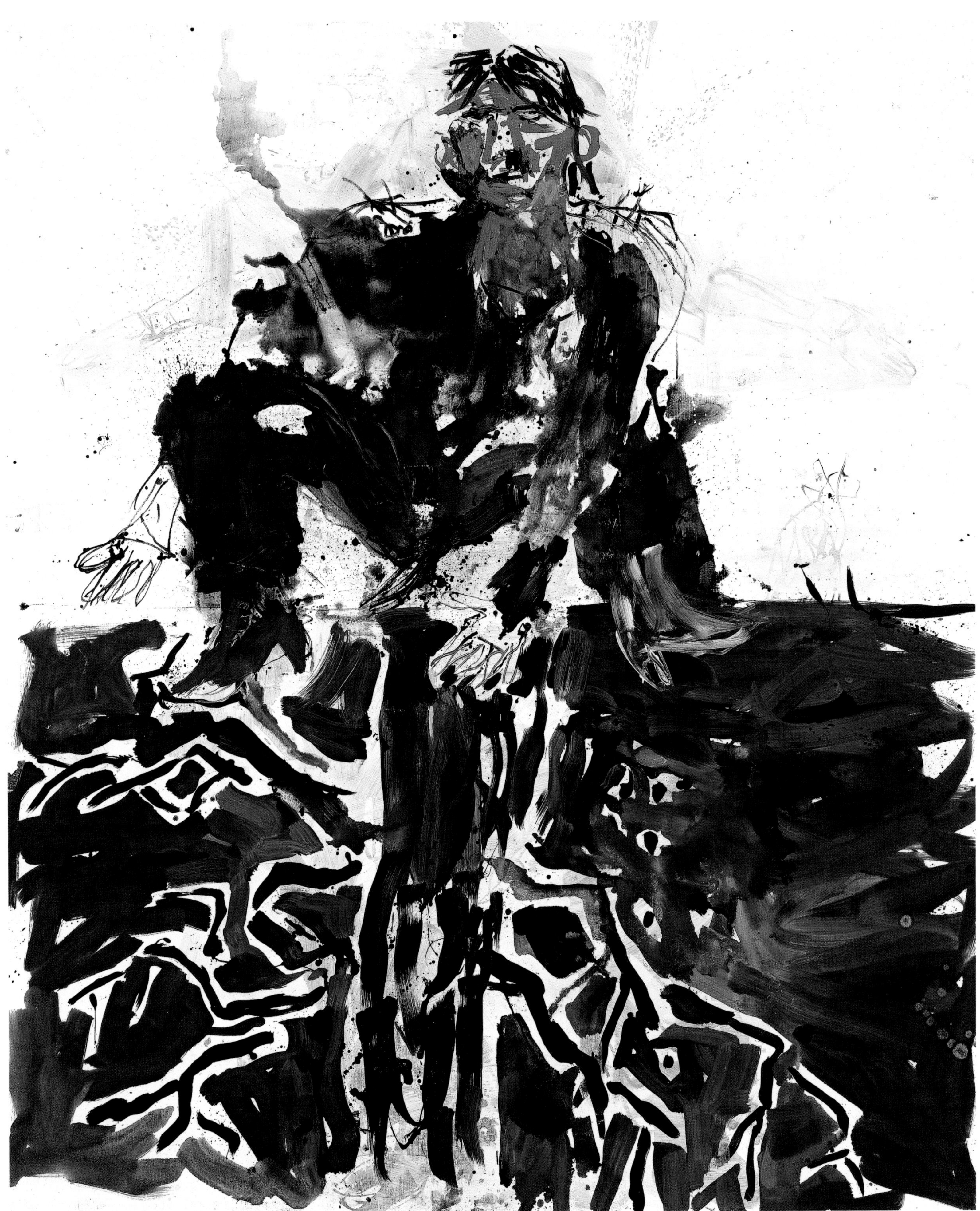

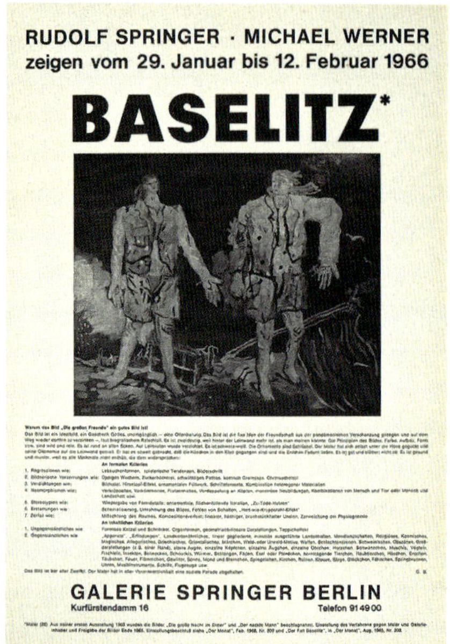

Exhibition poster and manifesto,
***Baselitz*, Galerie Springer, Berlin, 1966**

of the unspoken consciousness of guilt concerning the repressed history of the young republic. The tattered figures move in gloomy times on top of the ruins of disastrous past, and in a deeply darkened space.

In a text entitled "Why the Painting *The Great Friends* Is a Good Picture," Baselitz grounds the validity of the picture in a purely negative way via a list of those criteria that are not present in it, in order to conclude that, "The painting is devoid of all doubts. The painter, in full responsibility, has held a social parade."[18] This comprehensive list of exclusions takes considerable space, because the artist's sense of certainty (still) finds no words, or doesn't wish to. *The Great Friends* gives expression to his "farewell to anecdote and statement" and opens the path toward a freedom in which "The picture is simply a picture and is nurtured by the history of pictures."[19]

This also required a turn toward simple motifs that were as traditional and conventional as possible, and which would therefore not distract the artist from his painterly task.

The *Porträt Elke I* (*Portrait of Elke I*; 1969) is the first portrait that Baselitz painted of his wife. It is perhaps no accident that it dates from the period when Baselitz began painting his pictures standing on their heads. Aside from this feature, the portrait is perfectly conventional, and sets the model in front of a monochrome blue background that does not open up into space beyond the depth of the paint. The perspective is frontal, the pose respectable, it is restrained both physically and psychologically. The inversion of the motif, achieved earlier, created the precondition for painting portraits because this practice endowed the personal aspect with the necessary neutrality, since

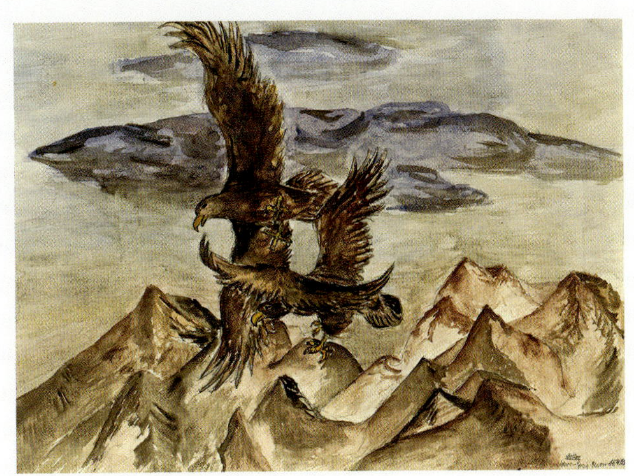

**Hans-Georg Kern [Georg Baselitz],
Two Fighting Eagles, 1953**

individual expression would interfere with the painting's impact. *Schlafzimmer* (*Bedroom*; 1975) and *Akt Elke* (*Elke Nude*; 1976–77) interpret intimate subjects, with Baselitz and his wife modeling in the nude. They are staged in easygoing, relaxed poses that testify to the absolute trust of a long-term relationship. This thoroughly positive atmosphere is heightened by the clear, bright color tones, and its impact is troubled to some degree only by the gray of the female form.

Subsequently, Baselitz varied both of the individual figures presented here motifically a number of times, in both paintings and sculptures, which were extended medially beginning in 1979. Back then, his decision to present his *Modell für ein Skulptur* (*Model for a Sculpture*)—his first three-dimensional work—at the Venice Biennale on the occasion of his appointment as Artist of the Federal Republic of Germany testifies once again to Baselitz's confident refusal of expected attitudes.

Fingermalerei—Adler (*Finger Painting—Eagle),* which dates from 1972, is his first depiction of this motif—at least if we disregard *Zwei kämpfende Adler* (*Two Fighting Eagles*), painted by Hans-Georg Kern around 1953 when he was about fifteen years old. It shows two birds in flight with outspread wings against a stark, mountain landscape that is set beneath the cloudy sky, and was derived from a plate from a pattern book for hobby painters authored by the master electrician Aschenbach.[20] This image conveys no hint at all of the allegorical character of the eagle as a symbol of strength and power, even immortality. It is the unpretentious depiction of an adolescent who takes pleasure in the striking sight of two raptors observed in playful battle above the landscape. Two decades later, this fascination has barely diminished; now, however, the rendering of the motif is far more evocative. Despite Baselitz's deliberate strategy of rejecting any virtuoso painterly manner, the painting captivates by virtue of a pictorial design within which figure and ground interlock with one another harmoniously. In the context of its further development, the artist's absorption by (or predilection for) this motif led to a consistent preoccupation that reveals its current, contemporary significance for Baselitz's. None of the animal motifs that are incorporated into his iconography are depicted more frequently or multifariously.

Here, in light of the dynamism and bodily control of the raptor in flight, the inversion seems to have been designed almost in unison with the motif. Its painterly realization emphasizes the motif's heraldic and symbolic force—and yet it is the *Eagle Paintings* in particular that to an unusual degree challenge the antithesis between a subjective perception or personal interpretation of the motif on the one hand and objective pictorial reality on the other.

The preoccupation with the eagle motif during the late nineteen-seventies, involving varying degrees of abstraction and experimental-formal approaches to the object—ranging from compression to the disintegration of its pictorial presence—is symptomatic of Baselitz's painterly attitude during this period. This attitude is characterized by a darkening of the palette with differentiated gray and blue tones, which generate a cloudy atmosphere, as well as through powerful brushwork, which allow the coarse concreteness of the painted motif to emerge with greater expressive force. Effects of contrast involving powerful white accents are carried to such an extent that the forms appear to be punched

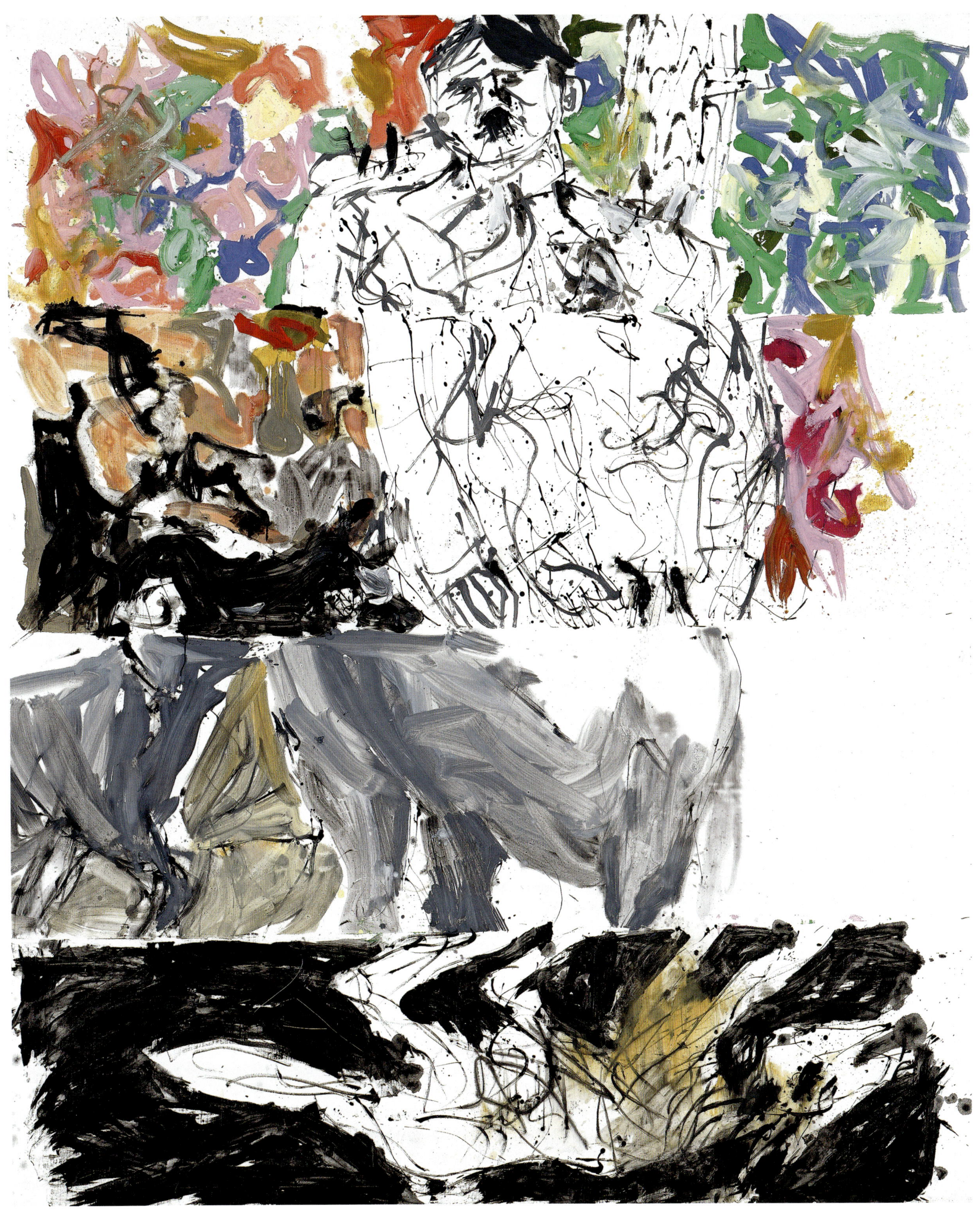

out like negative stencils by the white highlights. This is especially noticeable in *Kopf—Elkeprofil* (*Head—Elke in Profile*; 1977) and *Stilleben* (*Still Life*; 1976–77). In formal terms, these images achieve a highly vigorous synthesis of pictorial structure and painterly contents. The attributes of concreteness and abstraction are densified on the pictorial surface to form a complex figure-ground relationship. Caldwell's characterization of *Still Life* can be applied to the paintings of this period in general, such as when he writes:

"… Here, the dark shapes of the objects merge with the dark elements in the background, and the picture as a whole tends to flatten into abstraction. The subject is hardly legible; this is partly because the scale of *Still Life* is very large. But it is also due to the pronounced painterliness with which the work was done, in very large, gestural strokes and in colors that mix with others underneath and alongside them."[21]

The series of *Remix Paintings*, begun in 2005, performs a temporal leap in the direction of the developments of the latter part of the previous decade. On the one hand, Baselitz here cites works from the *Heroes* in a paradigmatic fashion, or in *Ein Neuer Typ* (*A New Type*), through which he returned to a preoccupation with monumental figural depictions during the nineteen-sixties. *Vorwärts Wind* (*Forward Wind*) appears here in a relatively analogous approximation. The depiction of a figure in front of a naked tree stump is taken over, while the painterly structure is dissolved and the wan coloration is accentuated through the red epaulets and the pink fleshy hands and genitalia. In the new *Remix* versions, in contrast, *Moderner Maler* (*Modern Painter*) and *Schwarz* (*Black*) are associated with swastika motifs in the style of Piet Mondrian, with the symbol's iconic

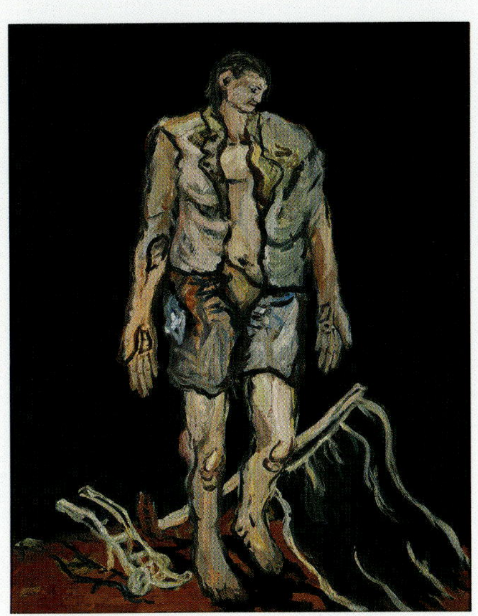

Georg Baselitz, _A New Type_, 1966

significance in modernism in some sense "compensating" for its ideological investment during the National Socialist era. These compositions again stand paradigmatically for the contentual emptying out of the object in favor of an abstract conception of form as the autonomous function of the image.

Since the _Remix Paintings_, it has rarely become a habit for Baselitz to turn back to preexisting pictorial motifs that have an apparently special significance for him. Manifesting itself instead is an essential renewal of "image control." In Baselitz's work on the image, Theo Kneubühler detects an "aesthetic of rupture" that "always [refers to] the existent in order to render the difference visible." Only afterwards, when it exists in its difference from the recognizable, can the work arrive at full autonomy. Baselitz's pictorial approach, then, is based on the interplay of "calculation" and "control": "Calculation pertains to the analytical prerequisites of the conception; the result is the aesthetic of rupture. Control refers to the act of making, to work on the image; in this connection, the inverted motif assumes an important control function. Without a high degree of calculation and control, it would be impossible to render the world visible, to create it in an exemplary manner."[22]

The development of the "pictorial method" is subjected to an acceleration of formal resources, one that permits a completely new access to the themes: "Today, an image that would earlier have often been developed gradually on the canvas through agonizingly interminable working phases is often the result of just a few hours. Even earlier, the working out of a functional pictorial method took place (perhaps in an equally time intensive way, albeit on a different level) in 'the head,' the method is entirely conceptual. It becomes possible with seemingly somnambulistic assurance to arrive at a self-evident synthesis of representation and abstraction, of a precisely conceived compositional scaffold and spontaneous expression. Nonetheless, the work does not become placeless or lacking in specificity. It remains … bound up with definite historical and biographical coordinates."[23]

The self-confident exploration in the *Remix Paintings* of the artist's own working history and his position in the contemporary art context led Baselitz along various formal paths, which he embarked upon in a highly experimental fashion. In an interview with Thomas Wagner, he commented on this issue: "I paint a picture and then I realize it's got all sorts of mistakes. So I paint it again. And again it's got mistakes—and again and again. At some point there's an end to it. It just won't work. An important aspect of my work is a sort of uncontrolled frenzy … Of course, I have always said that repetition is laziness. It always seemed to me that repeating my own things would be fatal. But now I have a concept and can legitimize what I'm doing … I take photographs of my paintings and then paint them once again. Of course to do it better. It's a form of protest."[24]

The monochromatic depictions of *Modern Painter* (*Remix*) and *Die Rote Fahne 65* (*The Red Flag 65* [*Remix*]) in graphic black-and-white followed their usual form, heightening abstraction. But Baselitz does not restrict himself to simply improvising upon a pictorial template; instead, he often unifies various motifs and methodical approaches to form a new synthesis. Baselitz continually has recourse to fracturing—a form of structuring the image that breaks open the unity of the object, both formally and in terms of content. Brought to bear in its drive toward the destruction of representational unity is both the dismemberment of the motif,

Jump (Remix), 2007

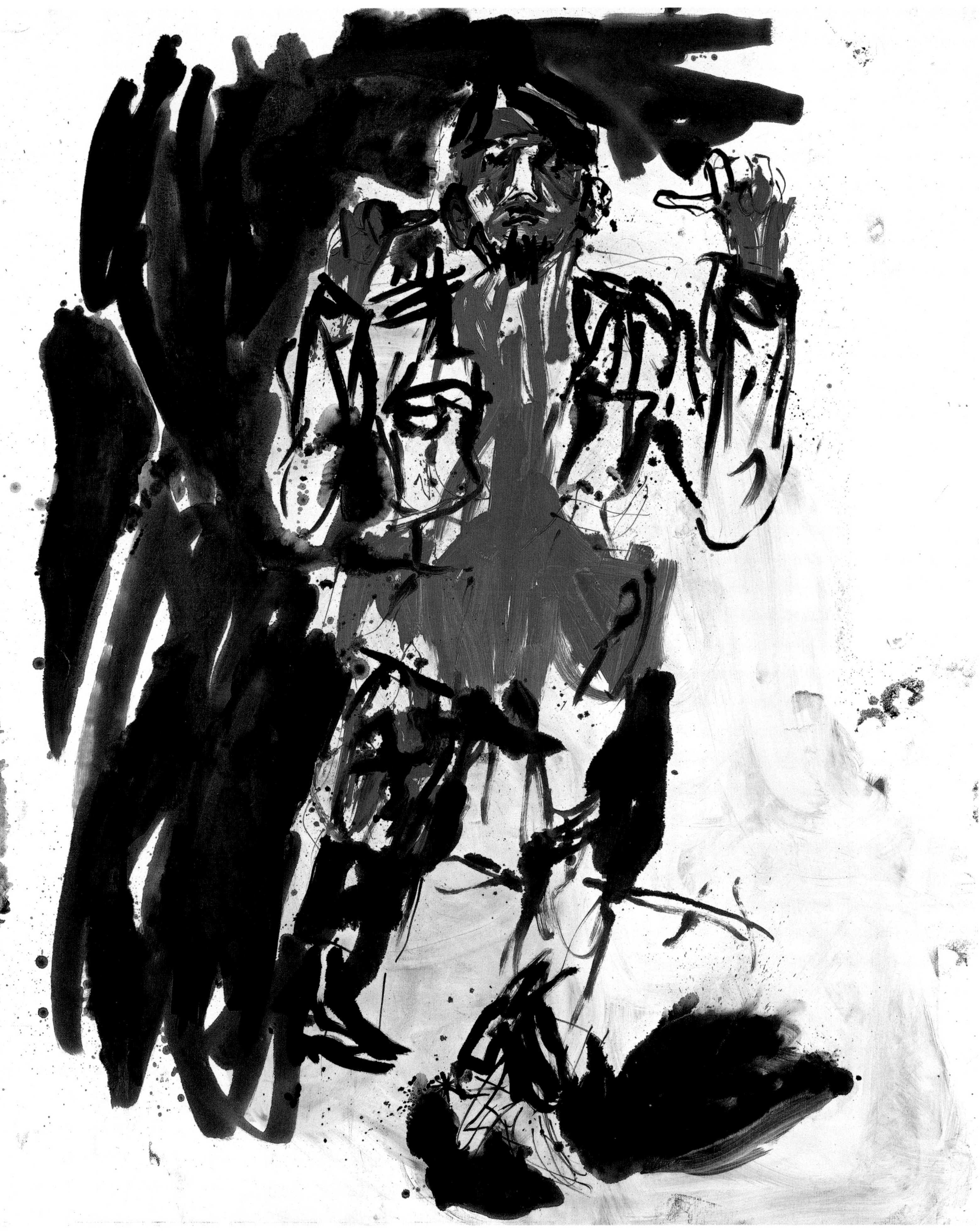

as well as the confrontation of various motifs. As a formal resource for the overcoming of representational meaning in favor of the autonomy of the image, the *Fracture Paintings* immediately precede the inversion of the pictorial motif.

The monumental vertical format of recent years integrates various aspects of the artist's early development. Their fractures cite fragments that refer to *The Great Friends*. The semi-profile of the heads and the arm positions are subjected to radical abstraction. Corporeality is almost completely dissolved in rapid, coarse smears characterized by high transparency. Moreover, physiognomic details are almost corroded by nervous, dribbling lines in the *Remix* manner. Striking here is the parallel, downward-hanging hands in *Die Flügelhornistin Gracie Irlam* (*The Flugelhornist Gracie Irlam*), which resemble raw, burnt flesh. The person in question is drawn from W. G. Sebald's short story "Max Aurach," in which the figure of Gracie Irlam encounters the hero in various personae, initially as a hotel owner, later as a painter's model, and as also as a flugelhorn player. A multiple personality that Baselitz allows to emerge through the sketchy, tentative weave of autonomous linear configurations.

The pictorial emphasis of recent decades points towards a formal interpenetration of the image's painterly values with an increasingly free handling of pigment flows and brushwork to create more motifically open structures. As though liberated now from any tectonic stabilization in the construction of the image, the orientation is now more toward the material properties and conditions of the pigments. Baselitz detaches these connections from representational givens in the literal sense in favor of configurations that "propel" themselves around the pictorial surface, thereby developing freely.

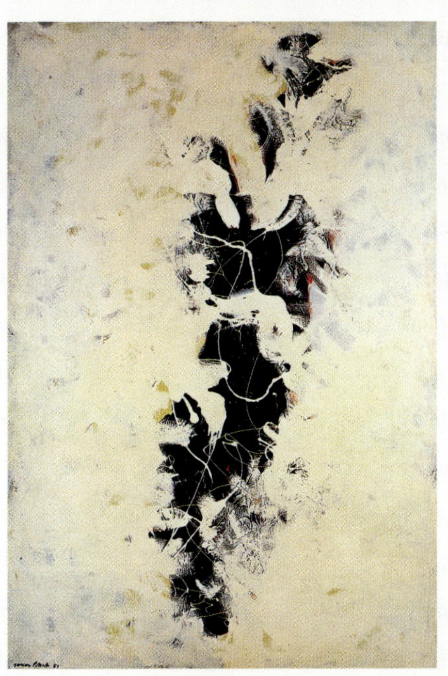

Jackson Pollock, *The Deep*, 1953

At the same time, Baselitz unleashes memories that recall the period of his ambivalence between East and West, of ideological and artistic strife. Baselitz has never denied that de Kooning's paintings left a deep impression on him in the late nineteen-fifties. And in particular the powerfully expressive persiflage of the dictates of contemporary ideals of beauty embodied in *Woman I* (1950–52), seen by Baselitz in 1958 in Berlin at an exhibition at the HBK (where it was shown together with Jackson Pollock's *Number 12* [1952], among others).

"When as a young man you want to become a painter, imagine discovering at your own university painters from a nation that, up until then, you thought was superficial and only interested in the quest for money," he says. "A few of my co-students tried to paint in the style of de Kooning but it wasn't possible … I said to myself, 'Be done with studies, be done with painting' and asked myself what would happen if I started back from the beginning."[25]

After nearly sixty years of creative production, Baselitz is again facing this challenge in a particularly intensive way. In this painterly confrontation, he focuses in particular on color and applies it to his own, personal iconography.

Once again, the eagle is one of the central motifs. It is clear that he has reconsidered this familiar subject a number of times in recent years. *Bei Willem* (*With Willem*; 2009), the bright colors, inscribed generously and rapidly to the picture field, and delimiting the figure within it, with a free drawing that essentially takes possession of the motif by searching out its own course of development.

In *Oh, ein Schatten, ach* (*Oh, A Shadow, Alas*; 2010), in contrast, Baselitz approaches de Kooning as a model more directly, although its subject is, on the other hand, familiar to him through his own thematic history. The comparable palette of colors, which are handled completely differently, formed the background for a seated female figure which however seems to have been scenarized far more rigorously by de Kooning, while Baselitz has embedded it far more gently in the chromatic space. The otherwise nude figure, whose head is hidden by a brutal cast shadow, is accentuated by white pumps, which give her appearance a frivolous touch.

The *Black Paintings* form the thematic center of this investigation; together with the monumental, black-painted bronze sculptures, they supply the iconographic focus of the conception. These works—in identical vertical format with the exception of two horizontal paintings—subtly differentiate the eagle motif in such a way that their identifying traits are all but concealed. Although the depicted motif is submerged in a light-absorbing darkness, the paintings are by no means colorless. Instead, the inverted image of an eagle in flight is executed in a chromatic sonority of dark tones consisting of blue, brown, and gray ranging to black.

In his study on the *Black Paintings*, Michael Semff aptly demonstrates that through them, Baselitz has augmented his pictorial language with a further radical turn, one that aims toward the "elimination of all visible contrasts."[26] At the same time, he refers to the fact that the eagle motif has so to speak obtruded itself into this renewed displacement of the relationship between representation and abstraction in the boundary zone toward complete non-objectivity. "With these paintings, he has achieved the culmination to date of his artistic potential, which attains unforeseeable areas of the unknown, far beyond the controllable intelligence of his pictorial thought."[27]

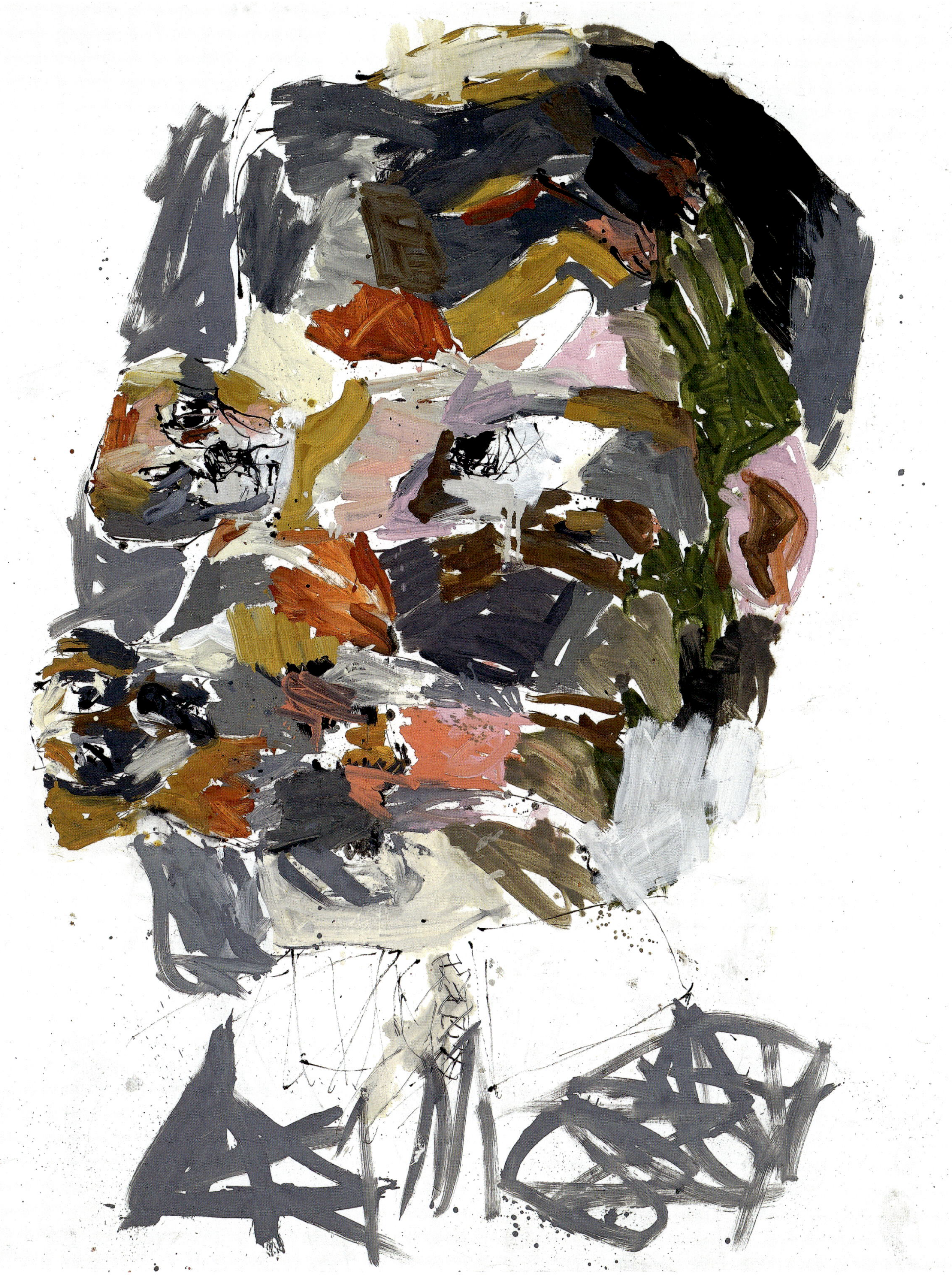

Through this powerful execution, Baselitz generates a painterly texture "in which ground, motif, and brushwork arrive at an equilibrium, canceling one another out."[28] Appearing all the more strongly are the filigree details which signal minimal nuances within this thematic diversification. At times, thin white threads are spun through the densely wrought pictorial surface, or red accents emerge, albeit without generating effects of deep space. Evident here instead are affinities with the graphically-oriented pictorial model pursued by Baselitz in a series from the early nineteen-nineties, where the figures are rendered through an extremely freely flowing network of colored lines against a black background. *Bilddreizehn* (*Picture Thirteen*) again takes up motifs of fractured "heroes" whose unusual horizontal shift is probably due to the fact that the two half-figures are joined at their centers not unlike playing cards, thereby manifestly annulling the formal inversion of the motif. *Bildsechzehn* (*Picture Sixteen*) refers directly to the double portrait of *Schlafzimmer* (*Bedroom*).

Here, the graphic handwriting on a black background already evokes the impression of the transparency of a photographic negative, whose effect of reversal between light and dark Baselitz had appropriated by the middle of the first decade of the twenty-first century, both in relation to black-and-white and color representations. It is not difficult to perceive the function of the photographic negative as a pictorial template as a vivid formal analogy with the inversion of the motif that has been a distinctive feature of Baselitz's conception of the picture for more than four decades.

"This manipulated alteration of the color codes produces a stage towards abstraction, essentially undermining the construction of the images and their

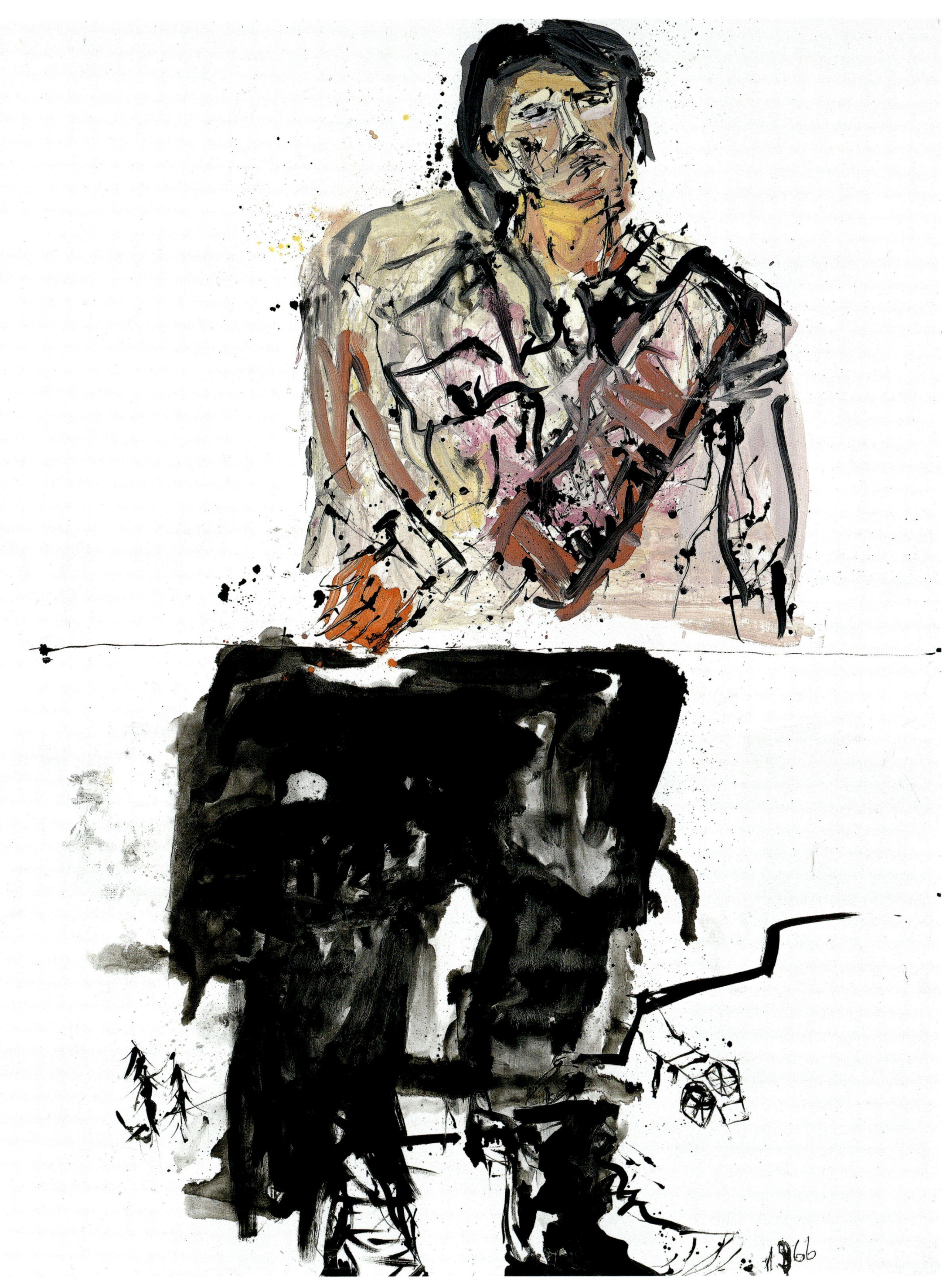
1966

arrangement between ground and figure, by rendering interchangeable the dimensions of positive and negative, of fullness and emptiness between unfathomable black and blazing white."[29]

In the series of works known as the *Negative Paintings*, Baselitz not only inverts the represented object, but tonal values as well. This presentation as a photographic negative enacts an additional reversal of the image in relation to a "natural" perception of the motif.

The black-and-white *Negative Paintings* already heighten the degree of abstraction in three respects. Baselitz, then, has come close to exhausting the potential for the alienation of the object's external appearance and its possibilities of pictorial representation.

The self-portrait *Zero* (2004) shows the artist in frontal symmetry. Only the cap sitting somewhat askew on the sitter's head and bearing the lettering "ZERO" loosens up this rigidity. This simple, unpretentious view is rendered in strong, serene brushstrokes containing a mixture of differentiated gray values. The collar and the pattern of the shirt, on the other hand, are sketched delicately. It is no accident that the aforementioned cap appears frequently in Baselitz's paintings and sculptures alike. In *Sing Sang Zero* (2011), the lettering is not inscribed in the sculpture itself, but appears instead in the title. Regardless, the figural group would be readily identifiable as a double portrait through the familiarity of the expressive gesture of the linked arms. Needless to say, the word "zero" suggests a variety of interpretations, and Baselitz enjoys alluding to this ambivalence through the cap: "A promotional gift from a painting supplies firm that has meanwhile gone bankrupt."[30] In his discussion of the most recent

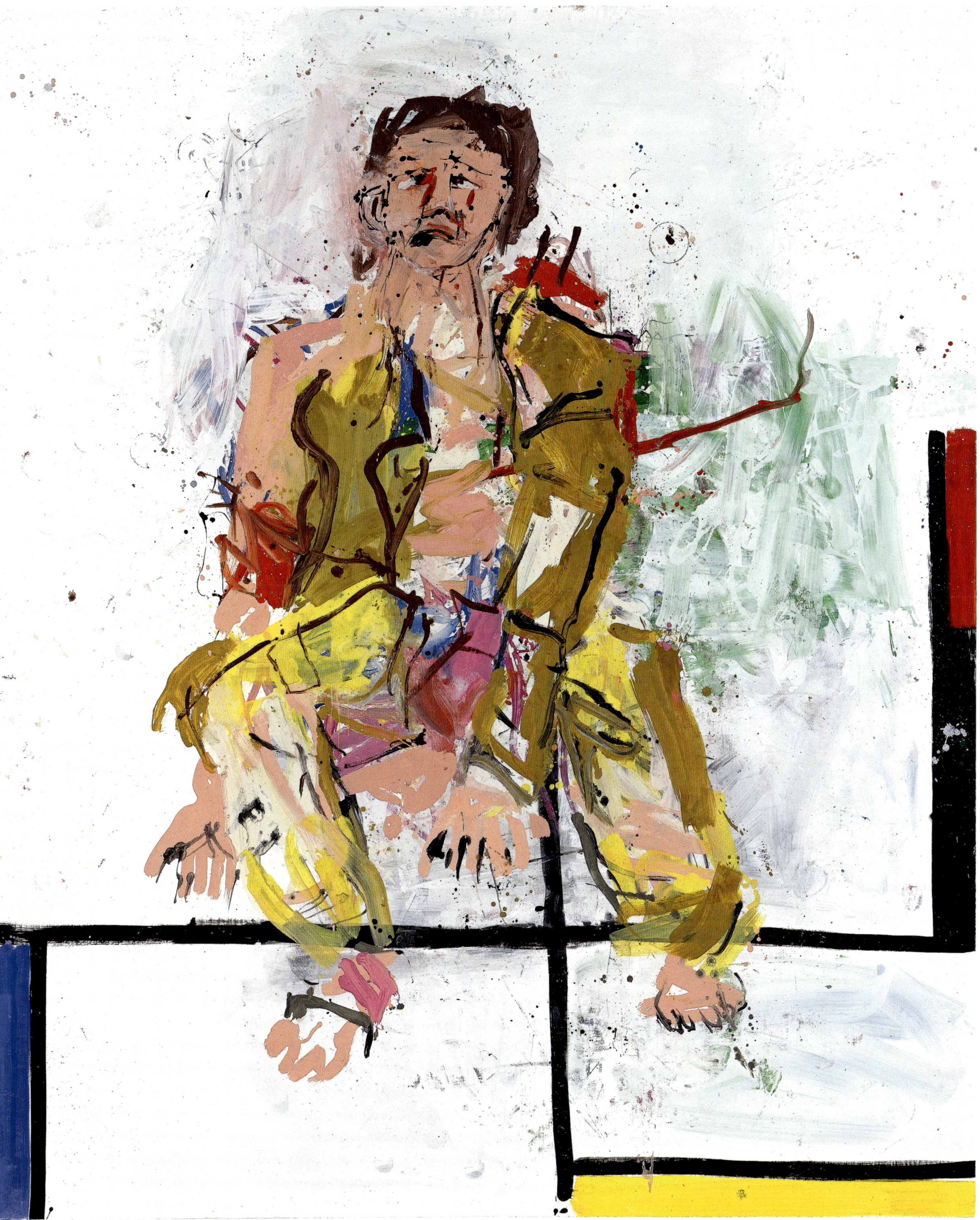

bronze sculptures, in contrast, John-Paul Stonard refers to the cap's biographical and historical implications, which he derives from its appearance in an earlier sculpture: "The cap worn by the figure in *My New Hat* is taken from a photograph of a war veteran who claims to have unearthed a *Pimpf* cap, of a type worn by the *Pimpfe*, the youngest section of the Hitler Youth, aged from ten to fourteen. Membership of the Hitler Youth was compulsory after 1939. As a child Hans-Georg Kern would have liked to be a *Pimpf*, but in 1944 he was too young as he sat on the fence watching the girls go by, arm in arm."[31]

With the formally analogous work *Negativ weiter links* (*Negative Further Left*; 2004), Baselitz turns back to *Elke I* (*Elke I*). The work shows a half-figure that is displaced slightly from the center. As a consequence, her attitude is relaxed, her slightly inclined head resting on her hand. With the pattern of the Norwegian pullover and the heightening contrast of the negative view, the motif gains temperament and expressive power in comparison to the static fixity of the self-portrait. Baselitz varies the same photographic prototype in *Elke negativ blau* (*Elke Negative Blue*; 2012), which brings the characteristics of the black-and-white version to resonance even more incisively. In a vivid commentary, Baselitz describes the derivation and application of this motif: "Here, we are at the very beginning again. I've taken up this Elke picture from 1969 again and again. Around ten years ago, I painted it as a negative in black and white, and finally made a new photo, almost in the same pose, but with a knitted pullover displaying a Norwegian pattern. I asked my grandson Hans, who is very good with computers: 'Can you convert it into a colored negative?' It worked, and if you reconverted the painting today, the blue skin of the negative would become flesh-colored. Of course, you

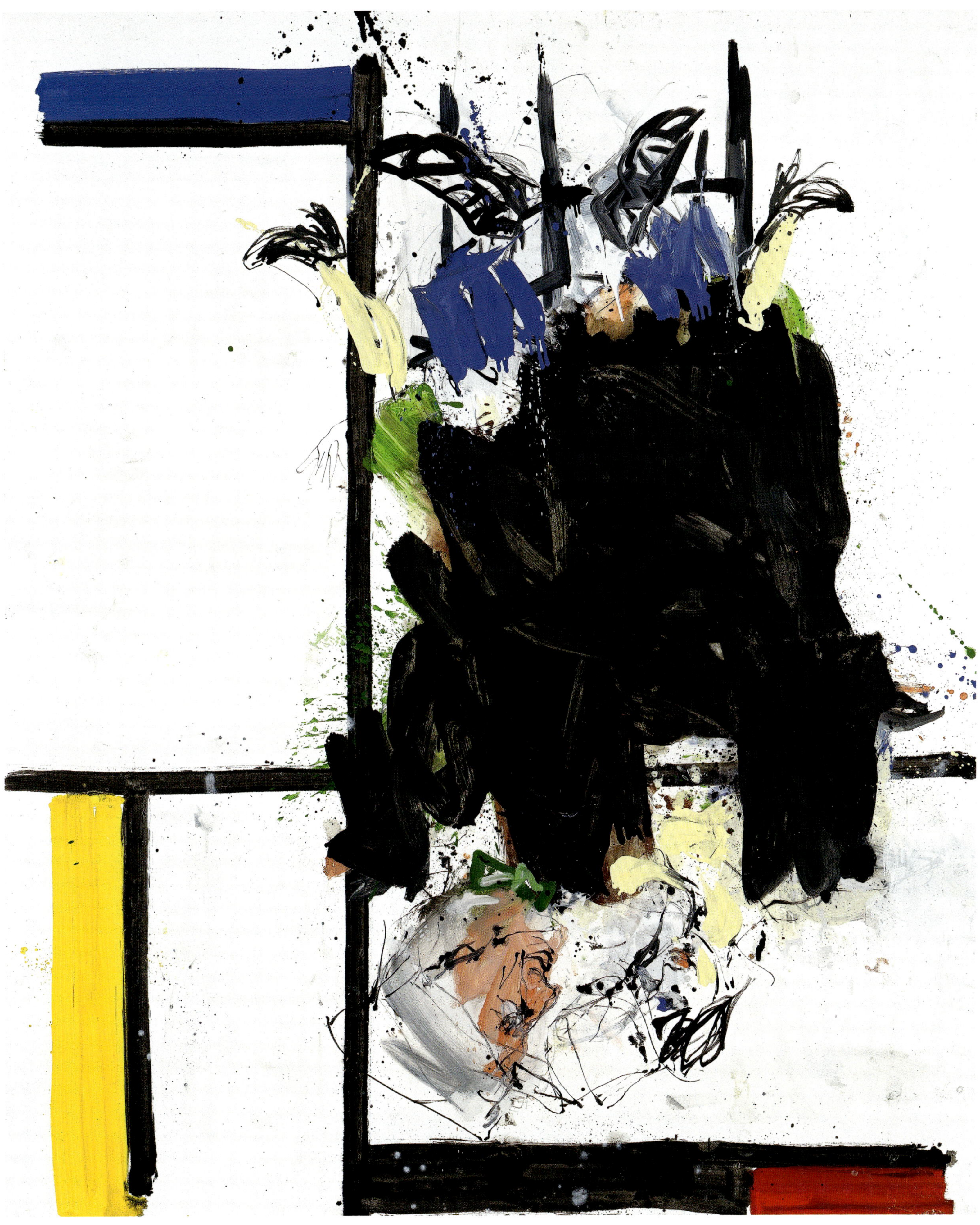

could say that this is mere gimmickry—but for me, this work is very serious, even over a period of months or years. And most importantly: There is now a new [type of] picture. For I don't yet know any pictures like it, I've never seen one before. And I'm well-versed in art history, I even run off to the library to try to find out whether anyone has done anything like it before me."[32]

Accordingly, the extension of the negative motif to color reversal schemes heightens the degree of abstraction, since the complementary colors obscure recognition of the depicted object more emphatically than a black-and-white image. In the case of the portrait, this affects in particular the facial expression of the subject, whose state of mind is no longer legible. This demonstrates once again that Baselitz is interested neither in physiognomic characteristics nor in psychological traits. He is stimulated instead by the painterly possibilities of a newly available procedure, in whose context he is by no means concerned tenaciously with physical principles exclusively, but also with investigating the visual leeway they offer him. This leads toward pictorial ideas that open up expanded coloristic and tonal possibilities, and which propel him to explore the reversal of negative and positive according to a variety of criteria. In pictures such as *Vorwärts im Mai* (*Forward in May*; 2012), *Komplementär bräunlich* (*Complementary Brownish*; 2012), and *Das gelbe Kleid* (*The Yellow Dress*; 2012), he seems to be concerned exclusively with the color design as a relationship of contradiction between local and symbolic colors—in their function for the representational subject as such on the one hand, and for the sake of the organization of the picture as a whole on the other.

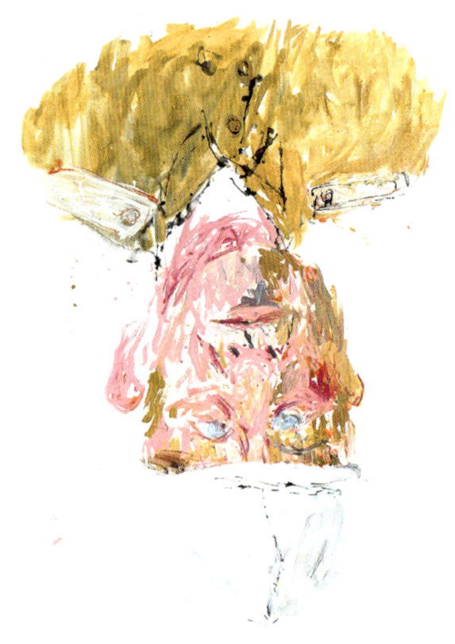

Georg Baselitz, *My New Hat*, 2001

Also bound up with this play of illumination and obfuscation, recognition and ignorance, are the wordplays that serve as the titles of the *Black Paintings*. The anagrams Baselitz invents are more-or-less simple to decipher. Nor is their significance ever concealed. It is instead the process of encryption itself that he pursues in what one might perhaps call a "quirk," perhaps a linguistic analogy to Baselitz's pictorial conception of abstraction: the object is estranged in its clarity without its integrity being dismantled.

The painting that initiates the series of *Black Paintings* bears the title *Dunkel age schwarzim* (*Dark Age Blackim*; 2012), which is relatively easy to decipher, although it plays on words in two different languages: it is composed of the words "dunkel" (dark), "Schwarz" (black), and "image." These are so to speak the programmatic terms that prescribe the theme of the entire series, which of course culminates in the eagle. The significance of these paintings—also outstanding for their biographical associations—for the development of Baselitz's oeuvre is suggested by the subject as such as well as by the exceptionally large number of versions: twenty in all. A special status must be accorded to the pair of versions having horizontal formats, since they directly invoke the above-mentioned model, namely *Zwei kämpfende Adler* (*Two Fighting Eagles*). The presence of historical reflexivity is confirmed as well by the titles *Niemandsland* (*No Man's Land*) and *Ne ne ne nu nu nu dif dif duz züg*, even if the latter comes close to (nonsensical) Dadaist onomatopoeic poetry.

The monumental bronze sculptures produced since 2011 display formal and contentual references which, alongside figurative allusions, simultaneously relativize the pictorial function of the figurative and photographic reversal.

These sculptures, all of them bearing a black patina, appear just as "obscured" as the *Black Paintings*, produced at exactly the same time.

"The crudely-carved, unrefined forms might at first sight seem like monumental folk art—or 'pop folk art'—but the range of personal associations and the interrelation of the figures create a depth of meaning that takes these works far from the world of carved and painted toys, religious charms or makeshift fetishes."[33]

The sculptures invoke figurative themes that were coined in Baselitz's paintings; they allude to art-historical and biographical fields of reference. An especially plastic link is detectable in the *BDM Gruppe* (*BDM Group*; 2012), in which Baselitz mixes iconographic references with personal motifs. The space of meaning of the three figures is overlaid by recollected experiences, in relation to which the tradition of The Three Graces appears in contrast almost preposterous in formal terms: the figural group makes reference to Baselitz's memories of his sister, who was a member of the BDM (Bund Deutscher Mädel), the female branch of the National Socialist Youth Organization. It was in this period that the image of three young women standing alongside one another with linked arms solidified in his memory. It is a nonpolitical memory that conjures illusions of a carefree childhood remote from the horror of the regime and the war: "What has survived, from a memory that must have been filtered a thousand times, is the motif of the linked arms. Not hands held, but arms linked; a rare motif in the history of art; one thinks perhaps only of *Tobias and the Angel*, and then only in painting. Canova's *Three Graces* embrace one another with full-armed sensual intimacy. Linked arms are a more sober gesture of solidarity and friendship,

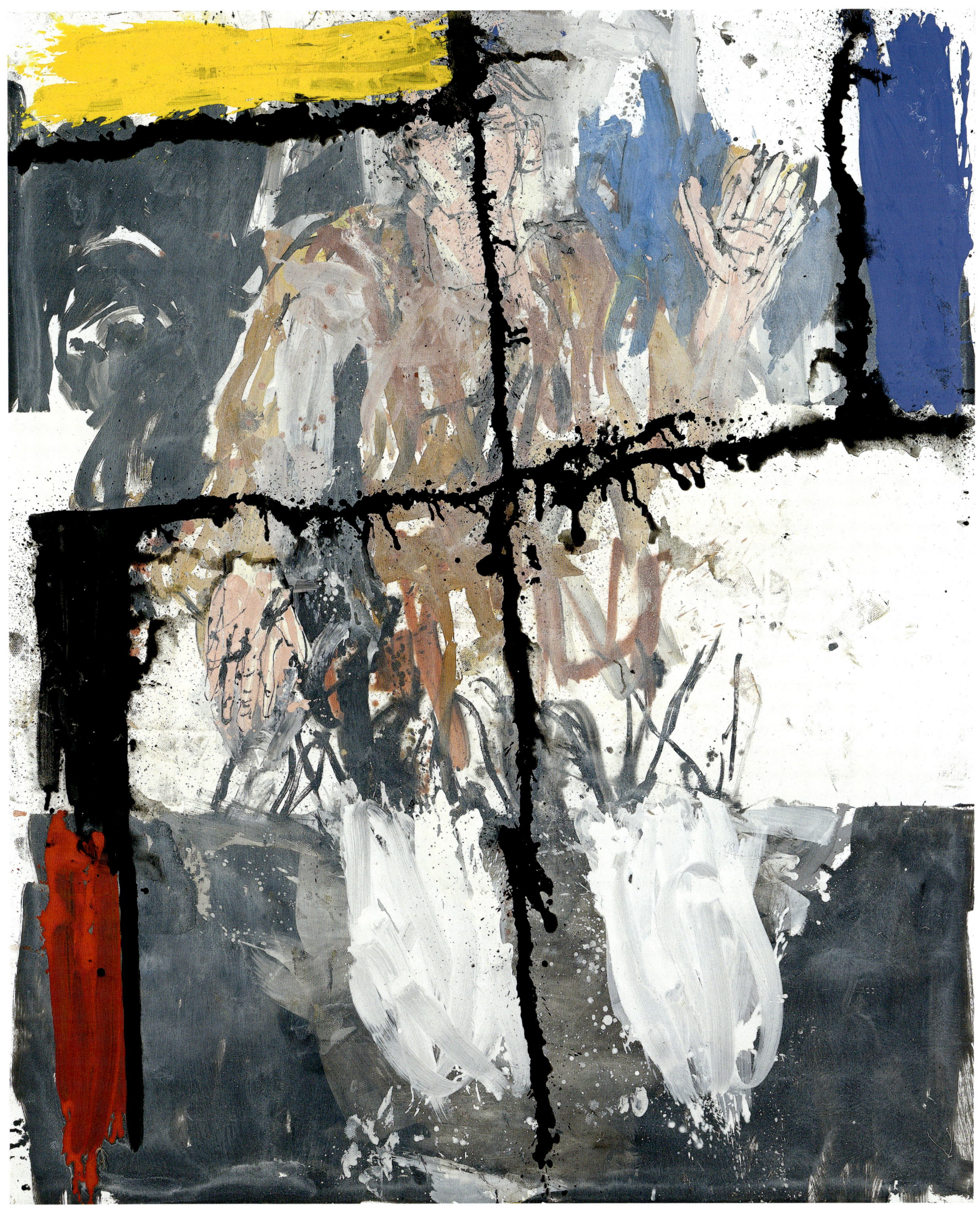

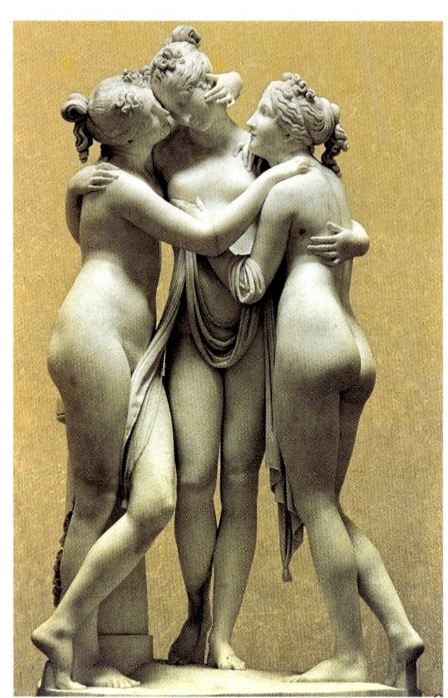

Antonio Canova, *The Three Graces*, 1812–16

a sense of common belonging—which in the case of the BDM girls can only appear now, with the benefit of hindsight, as a matter of extreme pathos."[34]

The gesture of the linked arms is still observable today when teenage girl-friends stroll together. And it was not the gesture itself, but instead its connection to the work's title that led to Baselitz being pressured to suppress the title during a temporary installation in the garden of the Victoria and Albert Museum in London. "I was told by [the V&A] museum that the sculpture's title was unacceptable.... So I said, 'OK, let's call it "Forbidden Title."' They said that was too cynical so, instead, we settled on 'Untitled.' Clearly this shows that people still don't want to acknowledge that the BDM existed but, like the Hitler Youth Movement, it is a historical fact."[35]

Once again, Baselitz had stirred up feelings of resentment that oppose his understanding of memory and contemporary history—the posing of which has always been a decisive aspect of his personal stance, even in the face of stiff resistance: "If I want to look back at a part of history in a non-critical way, then who is to tell me I can't? Should I simply say that my sister did not belong to the BDM? If the system is evil and suspicious, does that mean everyone who was a part of it is evil and suspicious? It might seem that way from the outside but from the inside it is not the case."[36]

This anecdote testifies to the fact that diametrically opposed readings become possible when we deal with historical experiences. The taken-for-granted way in which Baselitz takes up this theme and the reaction it is capable of triggering, highlight the powerful impact of a work that is hardly based on ideological motifs, although the artist was probably aware of its potential

The Forgotten Second Congress of the Third Communist International in Moscow 1920; on the Right of the Picture Ralf, Next to Him Jörg, 2008

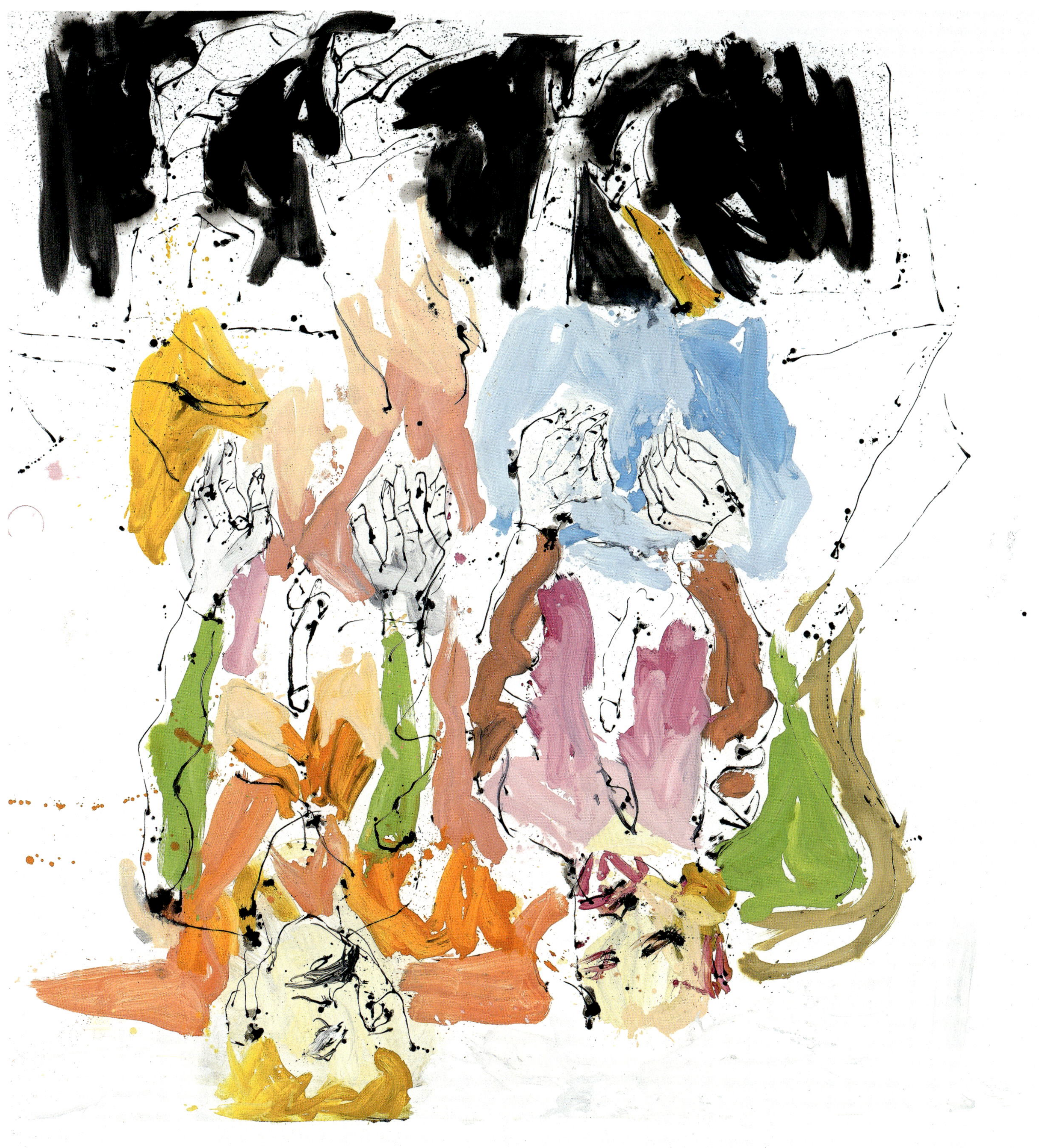

for provocation. By renouncing the correct titling of the *BDM Group*, Baselitz has expanded the discourse. His concern was to show just how fragile our consideration of the work can be, how dependent upon placement. Baselitz lived through the historical context invoked by the sculpture as an eyewitness, and visualizes it here as a personal recollection. At the same time, he withholds any value judgment concerning his sister's membership in a National Socialist Youth Organization. What interests him is the gesture of friendly attachment, one that in *Sing Sang Zero* evokes the normality of a personal history, one that reaches far back to a shared youth, and which Baselitz narrates little by little in his double portraits. Nor does he shy away from drawing on his own biography. As in the aforementioned *Komplementär bräunlich* (*Complementary Brownish*), the work *Das gelbe Kleid ist blau geworden* (*The Yellow Dress Has Become Blue*; 2012) refers back to Otto Dix's second version of the *The Artist's Parents*, which dates from 1924, and which shows the elderly couple, who can look back on a shared life, are shown seated side-by-side on the sofa in intimate togetherness. In his interpretation of this subject, Baselitz isolates the figures in an indeterminate black pictorial space. For the most part, he draws on the color scheme of his prototype. The faces and hands of the sitters, which Dix renders so incisively in his painting, are emphasized by Baselitz as well, albeit in a way that endows the figures with the negative image of beings that are perceived already in the state of dissolution.

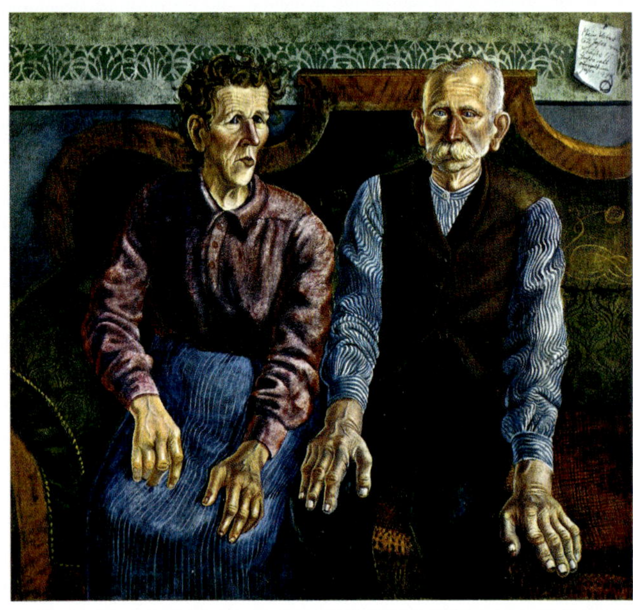

Otto Dix, *The Artist's Parents II*, 1924

A painting that is unusual in every respect is *Hembel* (2004). The negative depiction of the death's head reinforces the *memento mori* effect to the point of hopeless finality. In this unspectacular black-and-white painting, Baselitz reduces the motif to its simplest element, to which nothing can be added. This painting is closely associated with the most recent bronze sculpture, *Zero Ende* (*Zero End*; 2014). Here, the skulls are linked together in a form that resembles a dumbbell that is surrounded by seven rings, as though even in death, they cannot be parted from one another.

"To dream oneself to the other end of the world was a childhood wish. I have dug, drilled, and trenched in the sandpit in order to come out again on the other side. Then later, years later, to find the past, the eon, the things from people who have been here before us, I have excavated at the same place for urns … The game was not to lift oneself out of any old bad time into a better one. More than anything, curiosity propelled the discovery of what lay hidden in there, behind, and below. A good start for a painter's life, highly recommended."[37]

1 *Elke*: Georg Baselitz in Conversation with Michael Auping," [1996] in *Georg Baselitz: Collected Writings and Interviews*, ed. Detlev Gretenkort (London: Ridinghouse, 2010), 251ff.
2 "Goth to Dance: Georg Baselitz in Conversation with Donald Kuspit," [1995] in *Georg Baselitz: Collected Writings and Interviews*, 242.
3 Gustav René Hocke, *Die Welt als Labyrinth: Manier und Manie in der europäischen Kunst—Beiträge zur Ikonographie und Formgeschichte der europäischen Kunst von 1520 bis 1650 und der Gegenwart* (Hamburg: Rowohlt, 1957).

4 Thomas Röske, "'Unglaublich unseriös und bizarr': Druckgraphik des Manierismus, gesammelt von Georg Baselitz," in *Georg Baselitz: Das große Pathos—Gemälde, Zeichnungen, Graphik*, exh. cat., Hamburger Kunsthalle Hamburg (Hamburg, 1999), 25–33.
5 Siegfried Gohr, "Ein Bild ohne Stil" [1976], in *Über Baselitz: Aufsätze und Gespräche, 1976–1996* (Wienand: Cologne, 1996).
6 Röske, "'Unglaublich unseriös und bizarr': Druckgraphik des Manierismus, gesammelt von Georg Baselitz," 26.

7 Ibid., 27.

8 Johannes Gachnang, "Ein Gespräch mit Georg Baselitz am 6. November 1975," in *Georg Baselitz*, exh. cat., Braunschweiger Kunstverein (Braunschweig, 1981), 70.

9 "Georg Baselitz in Conversation with Henry Geldzahler," [1983] in *Georg Baselitz: Collected Writings and Interviews*, 114.

10 "Georg Baselitz: Raw Views of a Painful Past," *New York Times*, February 26, 2014, http://www.nytimes.com/2014/02/27/arts/international/Georg-Baselitz-Raw-Views-of-a-Painful-Pastnt-to-the-end.html?r=0.

11 "Goth to Dance: Georg Baselitz in Conversation with Donald Kuspit," in *Georg Baselitz: Collected Writings and Interviews*, 242–43.

12 Werner Haftmann, foreword to *II. Documenta '59: Kunst nach 1945—Malerei, Skulptur, Druckgraphik* (Cologne: Dumont, 1959), in Laszlo Glozer, *Westkunst: Zeitgenössische Kunst seit 1939* (Cologne: Dumont, 1981), 196–203.

13 Greenberg, "Modernist Painting" [1965], in *Art in Theory 1900–2000: An Anthology of Changing Ideas*, 2nd. ed. Charles Harrison and Paul Wood, eds. (Oxford: Blackwell), 774.

14 Clement Greenberg, "Towards a Newer Laocoon" [1940], in *Art in Theory 1900–2000*, 566.

15 Michael Auping, *Georg Baselitz: Portraits of Elke*, exh. cat., Modern Art Museum of Fort Worth (Fort Worth, 1997).

16 "Georg Baselitz in Conversation with Heinz Peter Schwerfel," original German publication in *Kunst heute*, no. 2 (Cologne 1989), reprinted in *Georg Baselitz: Collected Writings and Interviews*, 148.

17 Shulamith Behr, introduction to the catalogue plates, in *Baselitz*, exh. cat., Royal Academy of Arts (London, 2007), 65.

18 Georg Baselitz, "Why the Painting *The Great Friends* Is a Good Picture" [1996] in *Georg Baselitz: Collected Writings and Interviews*, 31.

19 Baselitz and Schwerfel, *Georg Baselitz: Collected Writings and Interviews*, 146.

20 Georg Baselitz, "What It Is," [2001] in *Georg Baselitz: Collected Writings and Interviews*, 254.

21 John Caldwell, "Baselitz in the Seventies: Representation and Abstraction," *Parkett*, no. 11 (December 1986): 88.

22 Theo Kneubühler, "Georg Baselitz," in *Georg Baselitz: Biennale di Venezia*, ed. Klaus Gallwitz, exh. cat., Städel Museum (Frankfurt am Main, 1980), 9.

23 Carla Schulz-Hoffmann, "Verdunkelung," in *Georg Baselitz: Verdunkelung*, exh. cat., Galerie Thaddaeus Ropac (Salzburg, 2009), 11ff.

24 "Painting Was Never Dead, It Was Prohibited: Georg Baselitz in Conversation with Thomas Wagner," [2006] in *Georg Baselitz: Collected Writings and Interviews*, 308.

25 Tobias Grey, "Georg Baselitz's Black Period on Show at Thaddaeus Ropac," *Financial Times*, October 12, 2013.

26 Michael Semff, "The Dark Side: Reflections on Georg Baselitz's New Paintings," in *Georg Baselitz: Le Côté sombre*, exh. cat., Galerie Thaddaeus Ropac (Paris, 2013), 61; (cf. pp. 185–195 in this catalogue).

27 Ibid., 63.

28 Ibid., 61.

29 Ibid., 58.

30 "Sammlerstück: Georg Baselitz—Mein Leben, meine Bilder," *Art: Das Kunstmagazin*, no. 2 (2013): 31.

31 John-Paul Stonard, "Baselitz Black or History as Background," in *Georg Baselitz: Le Côté sombre*, 29.

32 Baselitz, "Sammlerstück: Georg Baselitz—Mein Leben, meine Bilder."

33 Stonard, "Baselitz Black or History as Background," 29.

34 Ibid., 28.

35 Grey, "Georg Baselitz's Black Period on Show at Thaddaeus Ropac," 15.

36 Ibid.

37 Georg Baselitz, "Appropriation: Back Then, In Between, and Today," [2010] *The Art Bulletin* vol. 94, no. 2 (June 2012): 167–69.

Forgotten at Some Point—Sand Pond Dam, 2009

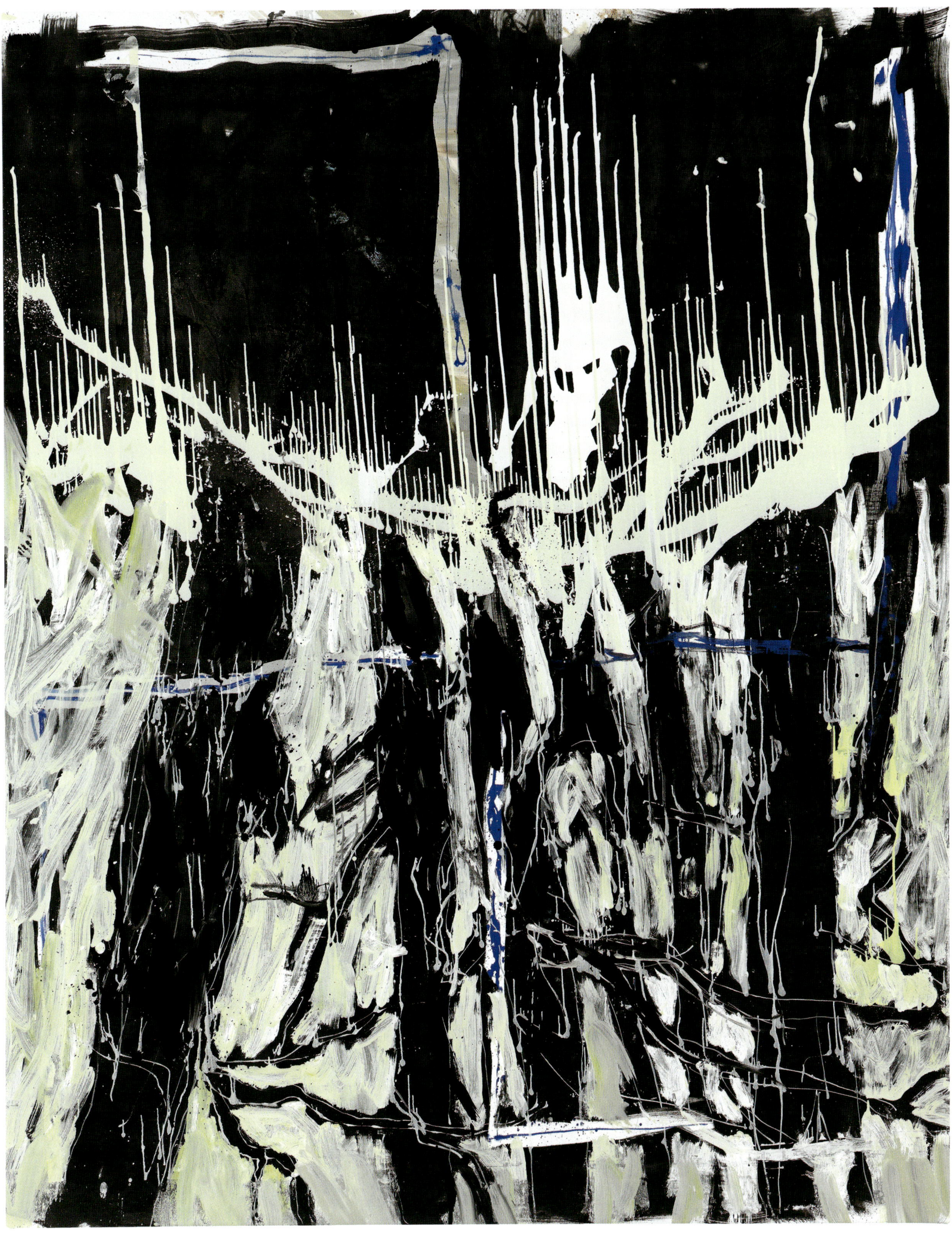

Bedroom, 2009

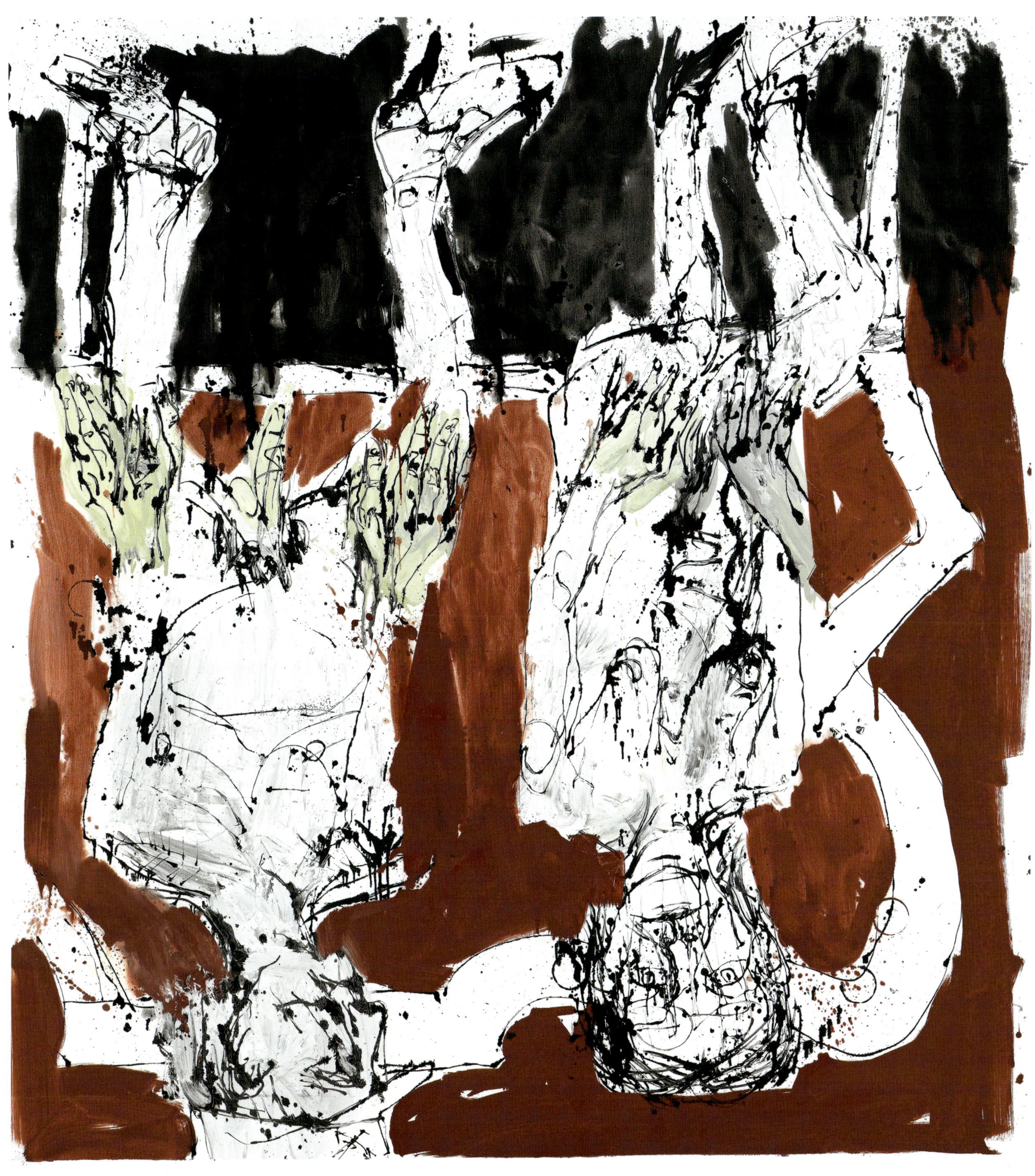

Unforgotten Then, 2009

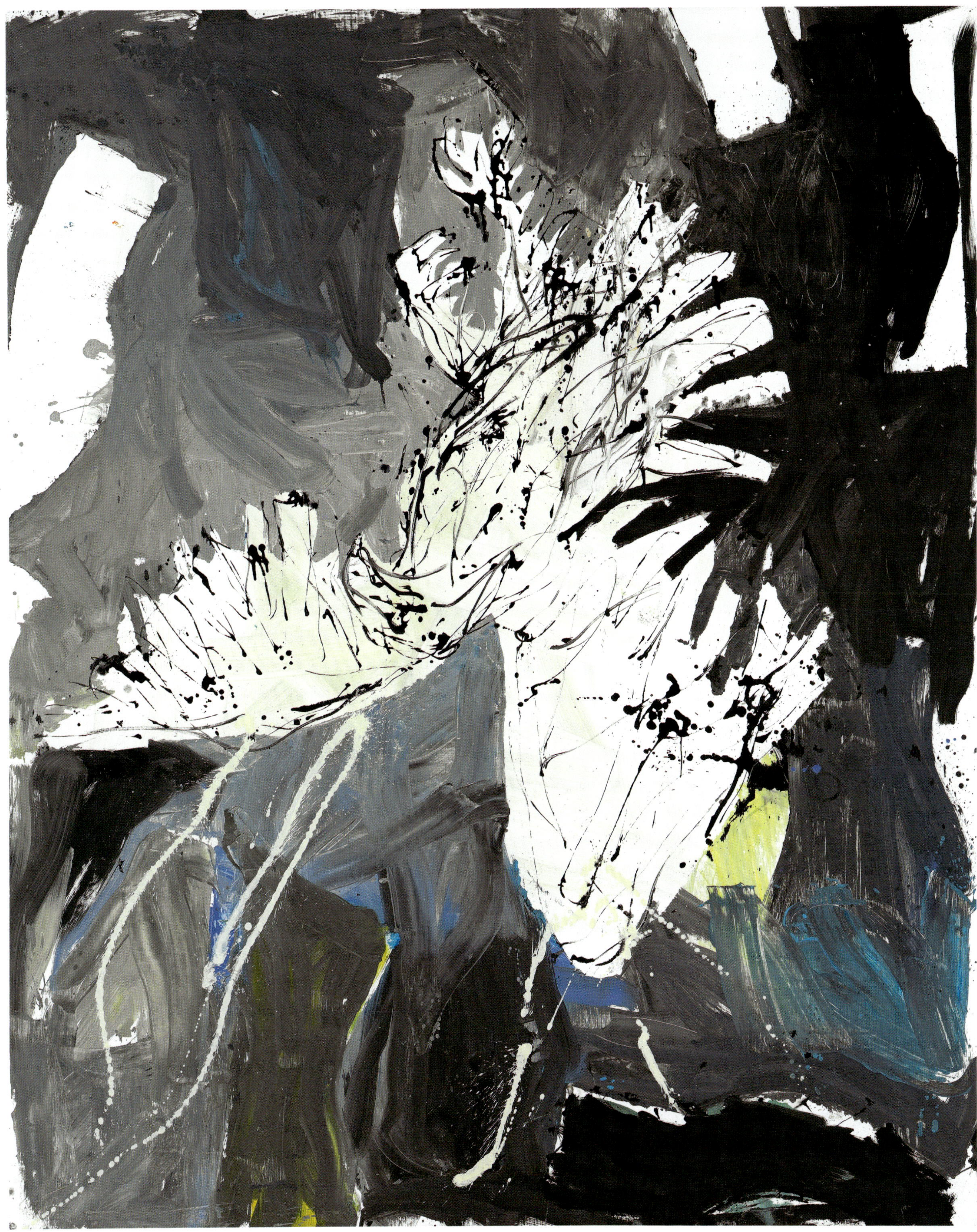

Willem Above, 2009

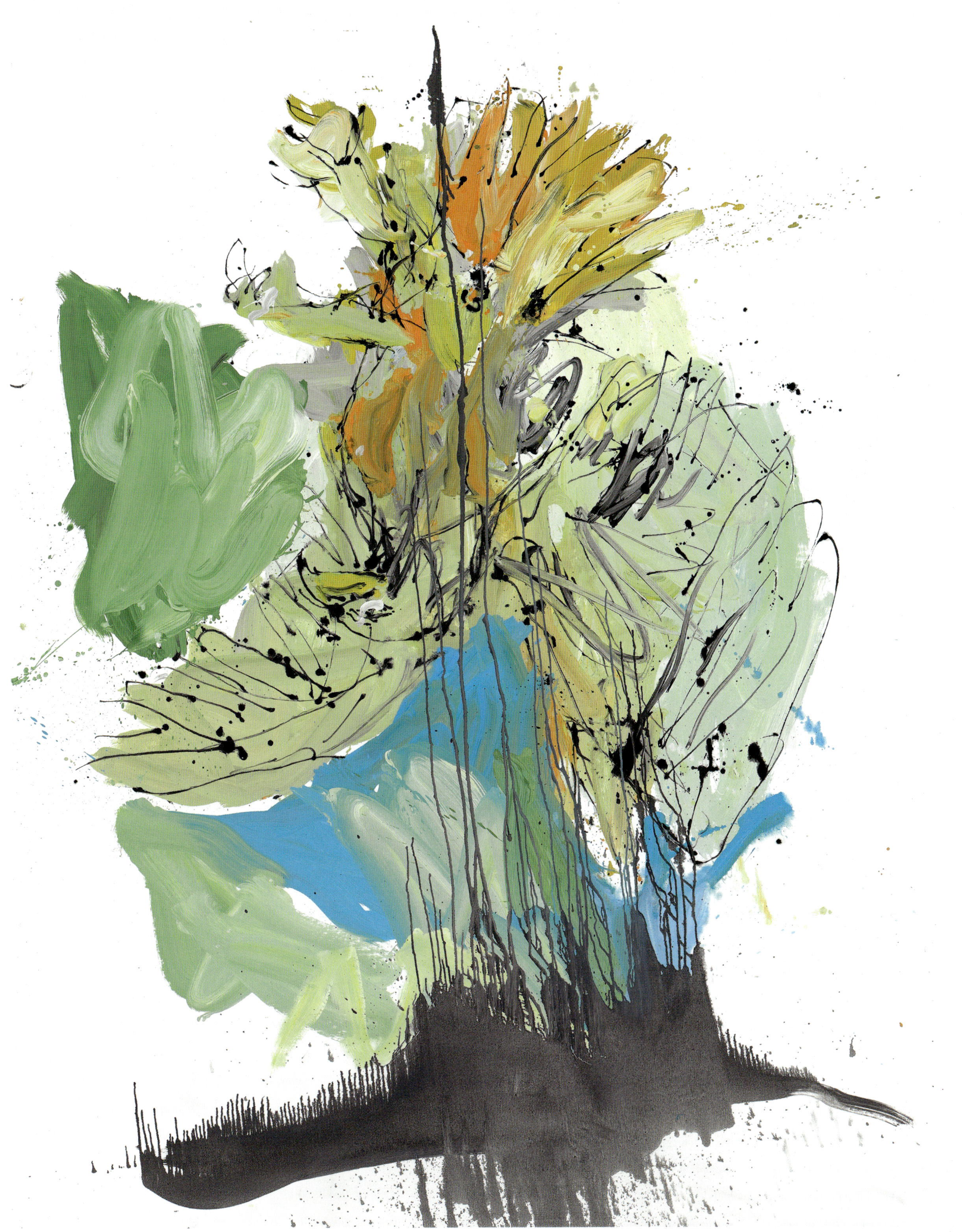

With Willem, 2009

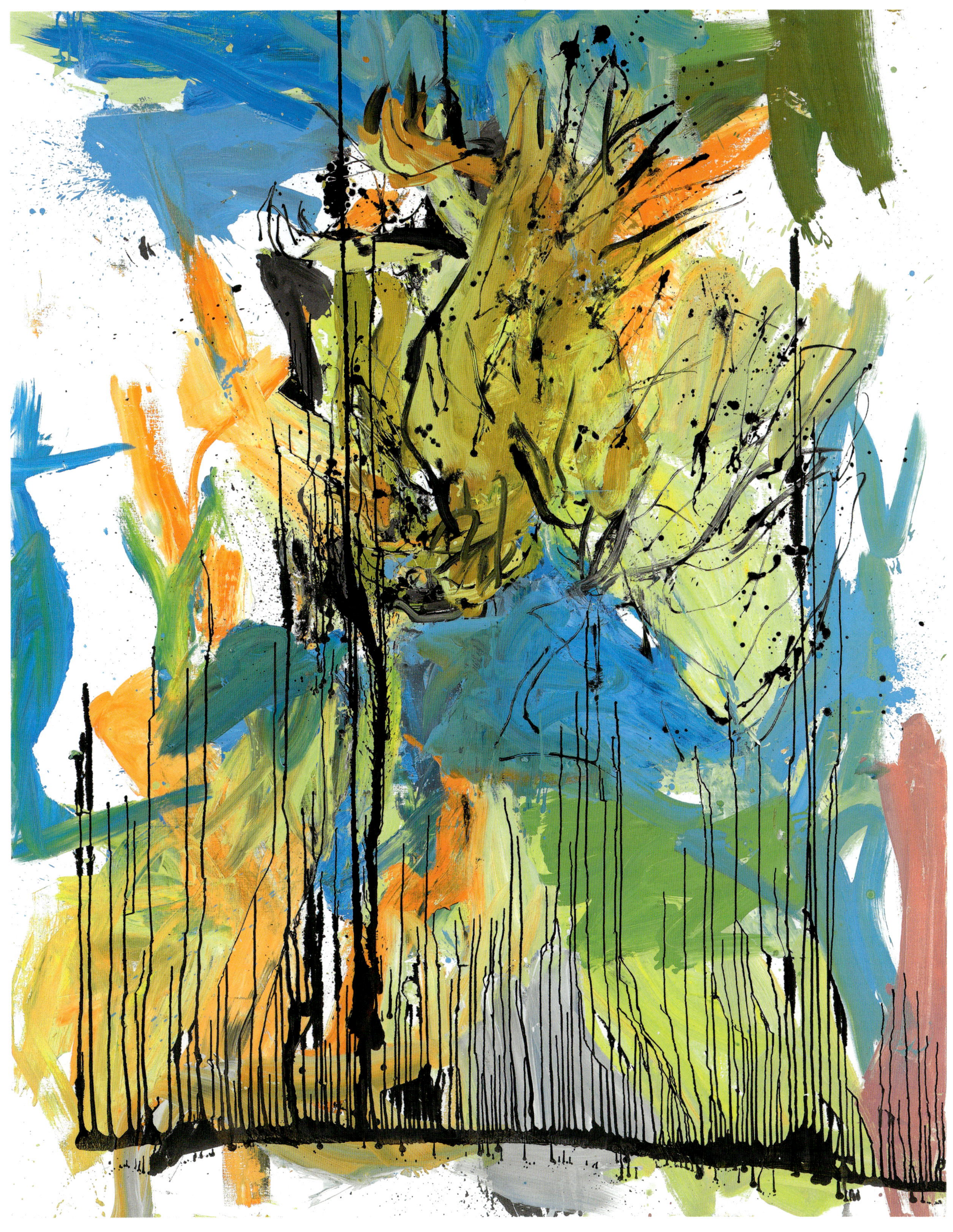

Two Black Russians, 2010

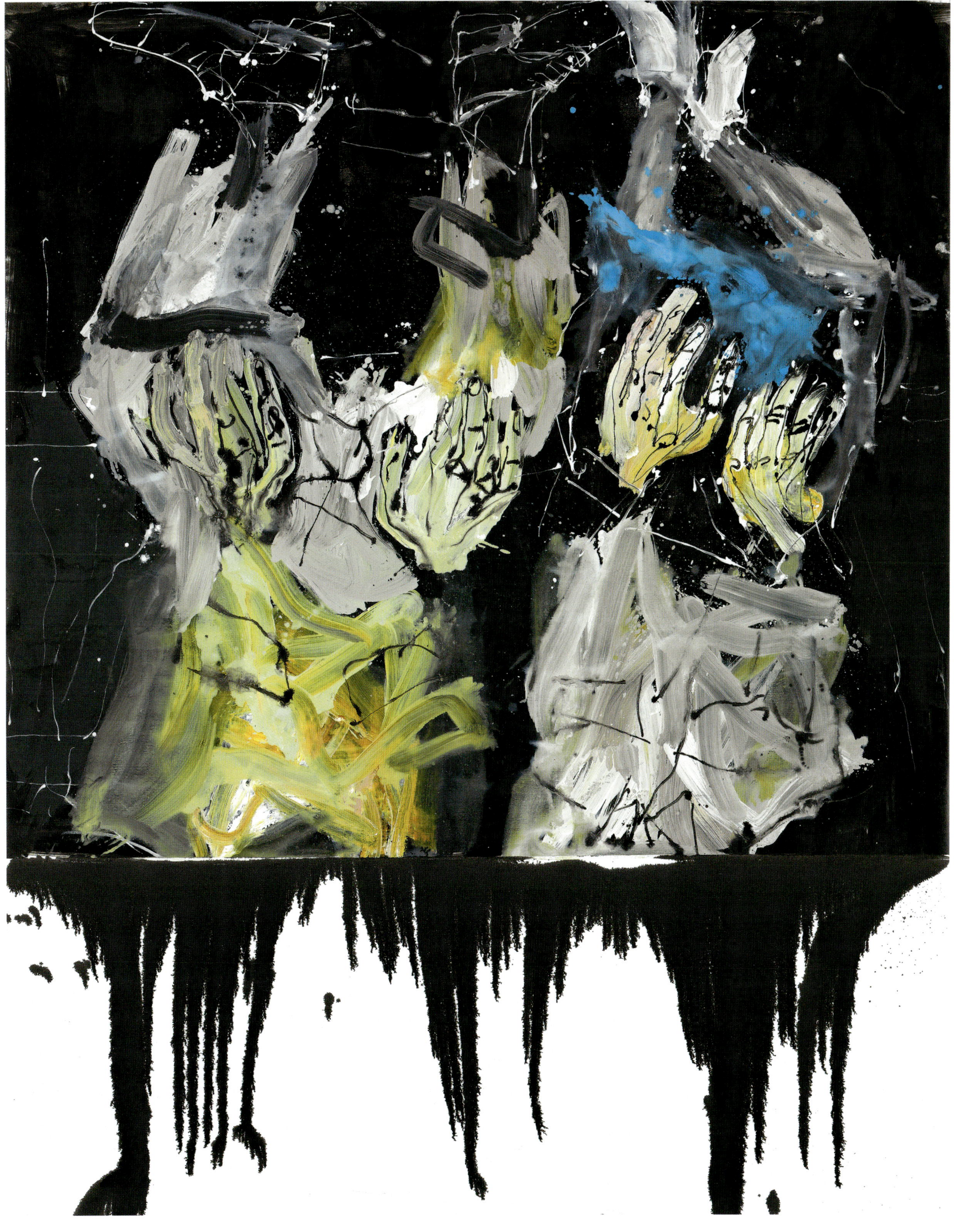

Oh, a Shadow, Alas, 2010

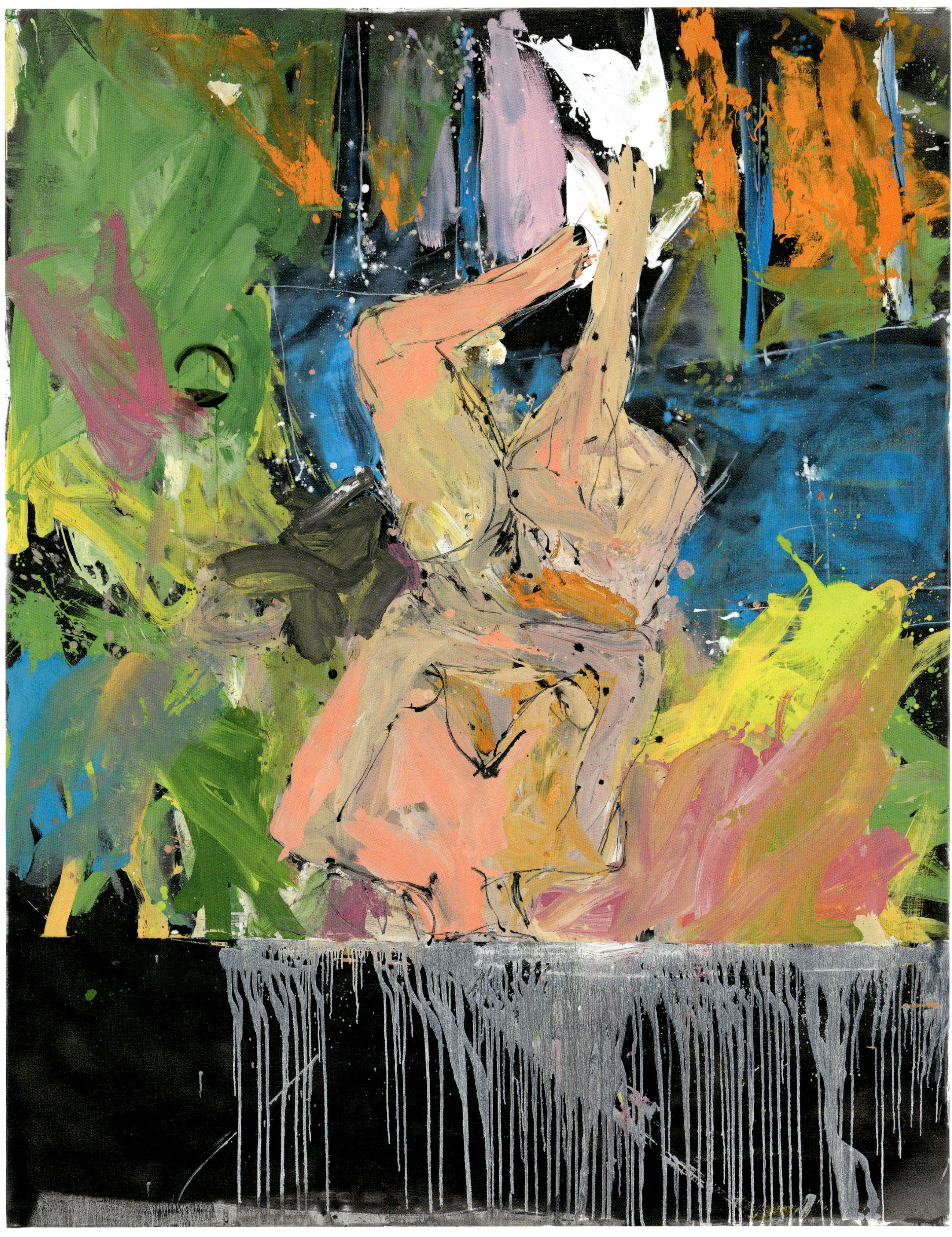

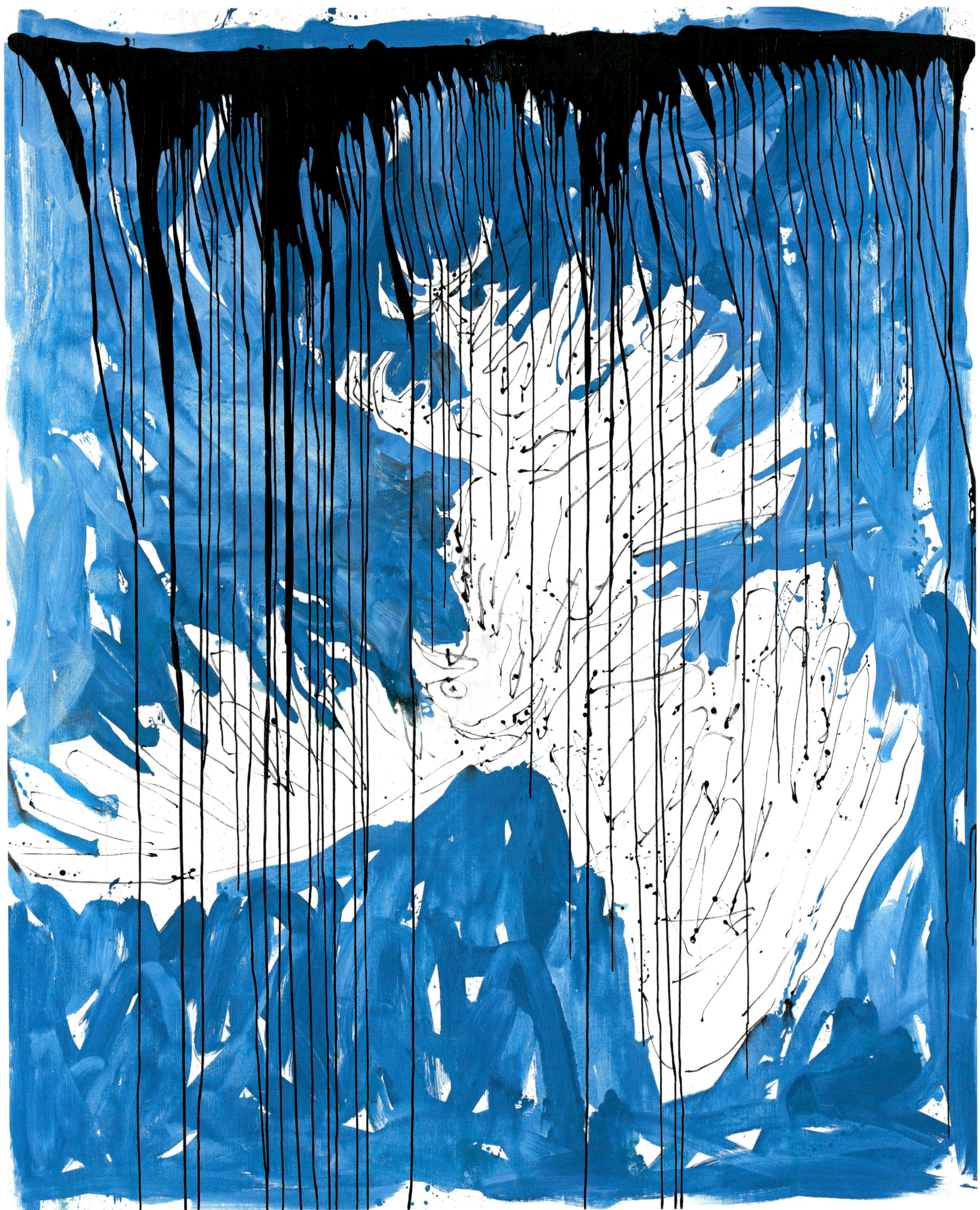

As a young man, Georg Baselitz couldn't be a modern artist; as an older man, he has often been asked whether he and his work are "contemporary."[1] What did and does that mean? During Baselitz's time in Berlin, the art school hosted twinned touring exhibitions of American art—a Jackson Pollock retrospective and *The New American Painting* group exhibition. Baselitz immediately felt that the paintings on view—by Pollock, and even those by the most "accessible" of the artists, Willem de Kooning—would come to define the modern for his moment. And while the art itself was expansive, the definition it embodied was quite narrow: "modern" meant large in scale, abstract or broadly symbolic, allover in composition, and above all, American. Baselitz knew that his paintings were not any of these things. And so the young artist gained a "desperate insight": "I'd lost the ambition or the interest in becoming a modern person. In effect, of becoming contemporary. That was so overwhelming that as a young person one couldn't just say: 'I'll go along with it. I'll become an American,' and so on. I told myself: 'No, it's over. You don't stand a chance.'"[2] Despite the efforts of his teacher Hann Trier "to make me a modern artist," modern was something other than what Baselitz did and someone other than who he was.[3]

Yet the art that Baselitz went on to make throughout the nineteen-sixties, the *Heroes* and *Fracture* series, and the inverted subjects of the end of the decade, were all clearly independent, different from what came before—all criteria for the modern. So how is it that Baselitz failed to be modern? It was a commonplace failure of synchronization, an artist's inability or unwillingness to be in the right place at the right time, to align with factors chosen and

Katy Siegel

DOUBLE POSITIVE:
NOT FOR NOT AGAINST NOT *NEIN*—
GEORG BASELITZ

privileged by external forces. Within history, the modern artist is expected to continue some designated "main" current, and, in order to be modern, also to break with its terms (a break predicated on acceptance of those terms). Within the present moment, the artist is asked to align with a recognizable, central character of his social moment—industrialization, ennui, concern for the environment, whatever. The rare moments when Baselitz appeared in harmony with external circumstances have been risky, artistically and socially—he seemed to be in tune with the wrong things. This was most true in the nineteen-eighties, when the artist was both praised and condemned for being classically "German" and (neo) expressionist, tied to a politically suspect past, and often related to a group of fashionable but weak younger artists (the artist himself played a part in this, perhaps misrecognizing what those artists were doing).[4] In these accounts, painting was a generalized practice, demanding allegiance or defeat, and the recent history of German art remained a blind spot.

As that blind spot shrinks, one subject that has emerged is the centrality for German artists, as internationally, of the dialectic of abstraction (West) and representation (East).[5] Baselitz belonged to neither place, to neither stylistic camp; although his work did not thematize the dialectic, like that of his peers Gerhard Richter and Sigmar Polke, he just as stubbornly refused the choice, the ideologies, the categories. His refusal strikes me as equally as radical a position as the ironizing performed by his contemporaries. Direct rather than distancing, affirmative rather than didactically critical or parodic, Baselitz's work nevertheless revealed his intuitive understanding that in a polarized

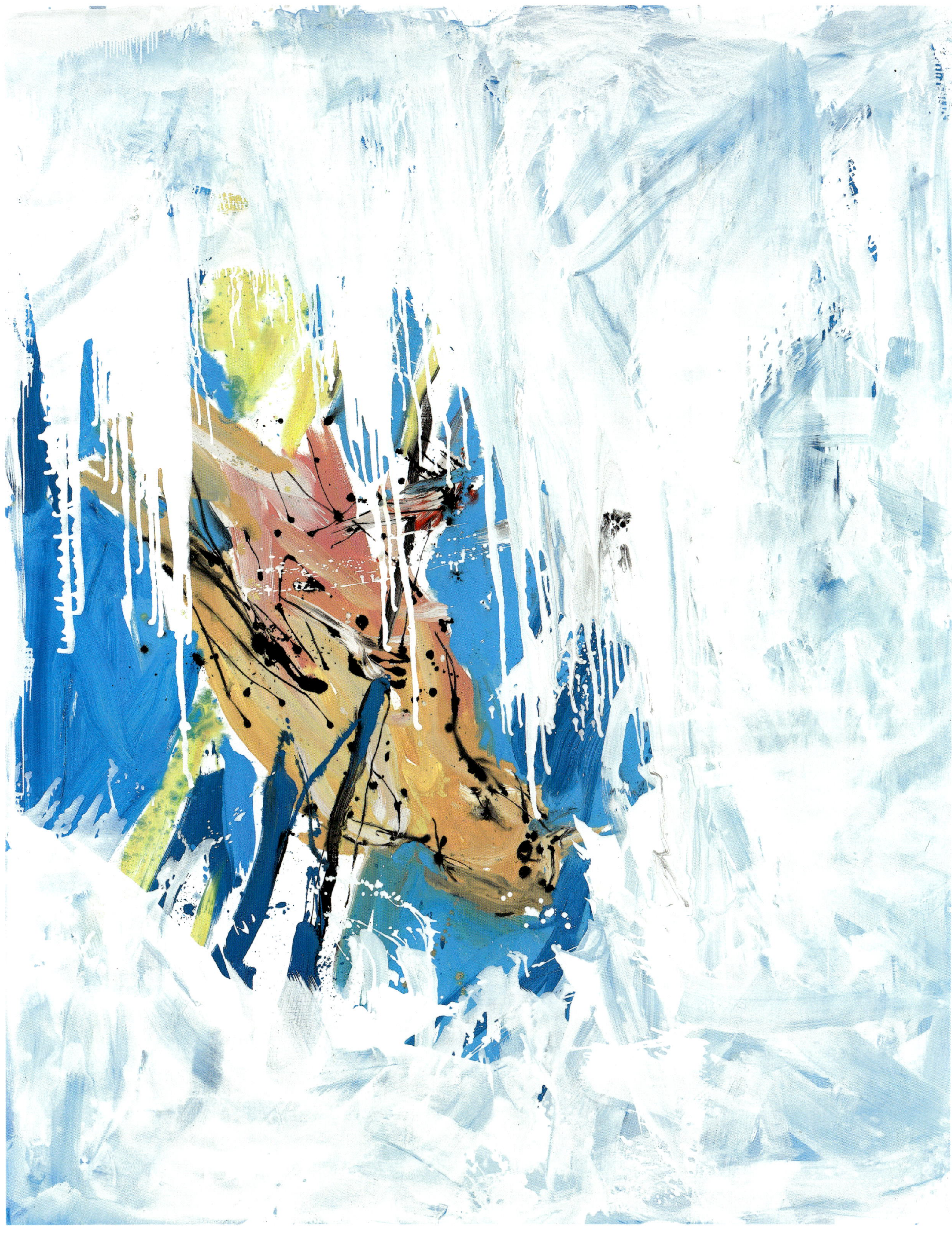

situation what appears to be the correct choice (in this instance, abstraction) is a false one.

Baselitz refused not just the artistic but also the political split between what critics insisted on labeling progressive, regressive impulses. The failure to choose abstraction, or at least to perform representation with a clear critical distance (like Richter, who would later praise the other artist's "directness"), put Baselitz at risk of being considered regressive, even as West German officials confiscated his work for provocation. His asynchrony with critical fashion hides interesting symmetries with major iconic figures of that fashion, who themselves align less perfectly than we imagine. Theodor Adorno, for instance, while of course rejecting Hans Sedlmayr's sympathy with the Third Reich, found value in his postwar critique of abstraction's idealism as an insufficient response to the "riven" nature of modern life.[6] Or, as Gerhard Richter, another favorite of the official avant-garde, said, the political charge of postwar art left a kind of artistic center missing between the given alternatives.[7] What was lost? The ability to connect to the longer sweep of painting through the centuries, as well as a relation to everyday lived existence. And what was gained was by no means secure; as Adorno famously wrote in *Minima Moralia*, wrong life cannot be lived rightly—allegiance to a particular ideological solution (political or artistic) can never be the answer.[8]

After several years in Berlin, in 1966 Baselitz left for the countryside. It's easy to see the work he embarked on there and then—the spectacular *Fracture* series—as being about familiar motifs of the countryside—dogs, hunters, cows—even a glorification of land and *Volk*. Or we could talk about how the pictures are painted—the images broken, canvases divided into tiers—and

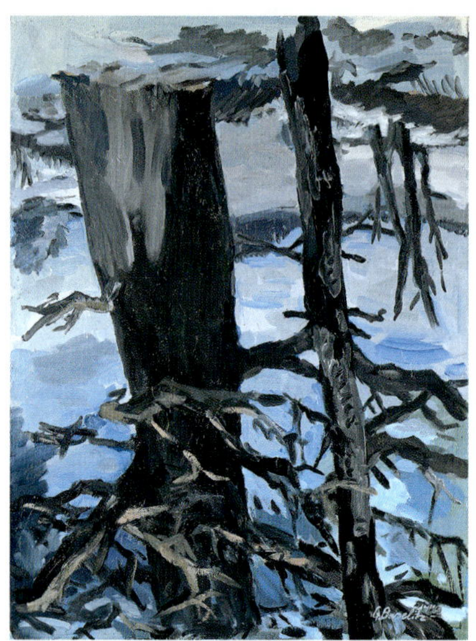

Georg Baselitz, *The Wood on Its Head*, 1969

see them as formal experimentation. The latter would seem to be the more elevating understanding of these images—as "modern"—seeing them as in fact abstract, with the traditional pastoral subjects only there to provide Baselitz with an anodyne pretext for making a painting. In the past, the artist himself emphasized solely the material aspect of the *Fracture* series, and his emphasis wasn't wrong (although perhaps ironic, given his rejection by and of abstraction). But as the previous critical privileging of abstraction begins to fade, finally, it seems increasingly apparent that the representational image plays a specific and important role in this work. The pastoral motifs—familiar, general, repeatable—of the *Fracture Paintings* highlight the extreme contradiction and interference of the breaks, inversions, and irruptions of the painted surface. (And despite the critical criteria of formal innovation in the nineteen-sixties, the radicality of Baselitz's invention in the *Fracture Paintings* was not at the time, and remains today, inadequately acknowledged.) The friction of this impossible coexistence of representation and abstraction energizes the *Eagle Paintings*, particularly the work from 1972. The most iconic possible political representation, the eagle was chosen for its role in the symbolic order by Marcel Broodthaers, who asked Baselitz to paint the work for his large, ongoing art project, *Musée d'Art moderne (section XIXe siécle) Département des Aigles* (*Museum of Modern Art [19th Century Section] Department of Eagles*). In response, the artist rendered an eagle with his fingers, the most direct and even primordial kind of mark making.

The eagle is upside down (at least from our perspective). At the end of the *Fracture* series, in 1969, Baselitz inverted the entire representational scene

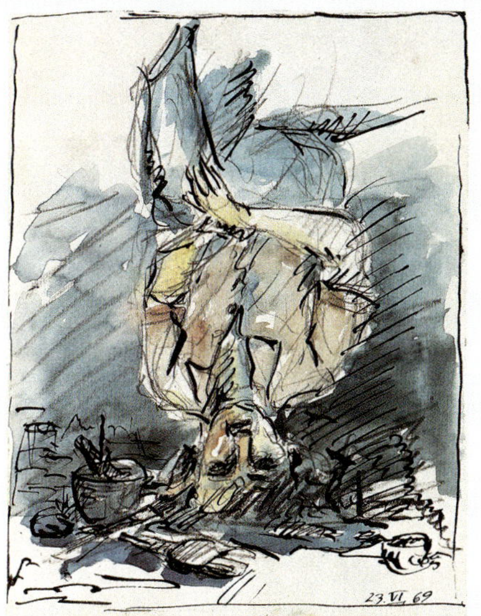

Georg Baselitz, *Painter*, 1969

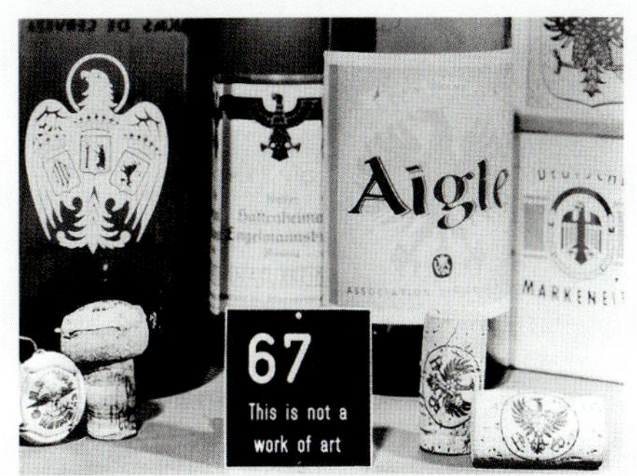

Marcel Broodthaers, *Musée d'Art moderne Département des Aigles* 1968–1972

in the famous *Der Wald auf dem Kopf* (*The Wood on Its Head*; 1969). The first inversions were, however, not quite complete. In June of 1969 he made *Maler* (*Painter*), a gouache and charcoal work on paper that depicts an apparently seated male figure, legs crossed but without feet (presumably cut off by the top of the picture), who hovers over an artist's work table, with brushes and a coffee cup. We could see *Painter*[9] as an unresolved, transitional work, but the painter's upside-down perspective on a conventionally oriented setting suggests something more interesting, that the inversions do not solely negate or abstract content, but also create a friction with representation, not as simple figuration, but as a received convention. Francis Bacon understood that it was not fidelity to nature per se, but "illustration" in service to an external idea that threatened figurative painting. Or as Baselitz put it, "The more [artists] participate because they can't help themselves, the more harmoniously they will illustrate—because they are asked—whatever people need."[10] Society is, after all, an authority with which Baselitz is much more aggressively in conflict with than he is with nature, with which he has always felt a strong affinity.For some artists, like Willi Baumeister, breaking with social tyranny meant painting abstractly, rejecting social realism and even more, traditional art. For Baselitz, like Bacon and de Kooning, to break with tradition—the figure—was simply not the point. What would be? Let's put aside the idea of a missing center—the metaphor evokes compromise between two extremes—in favor of an aggressive refusal of opposition: a double positive.

In this regard, Baselitz anticipates the weariness of subsequent generations with the abstract/representational, progressive/regressive dialectic. Albert

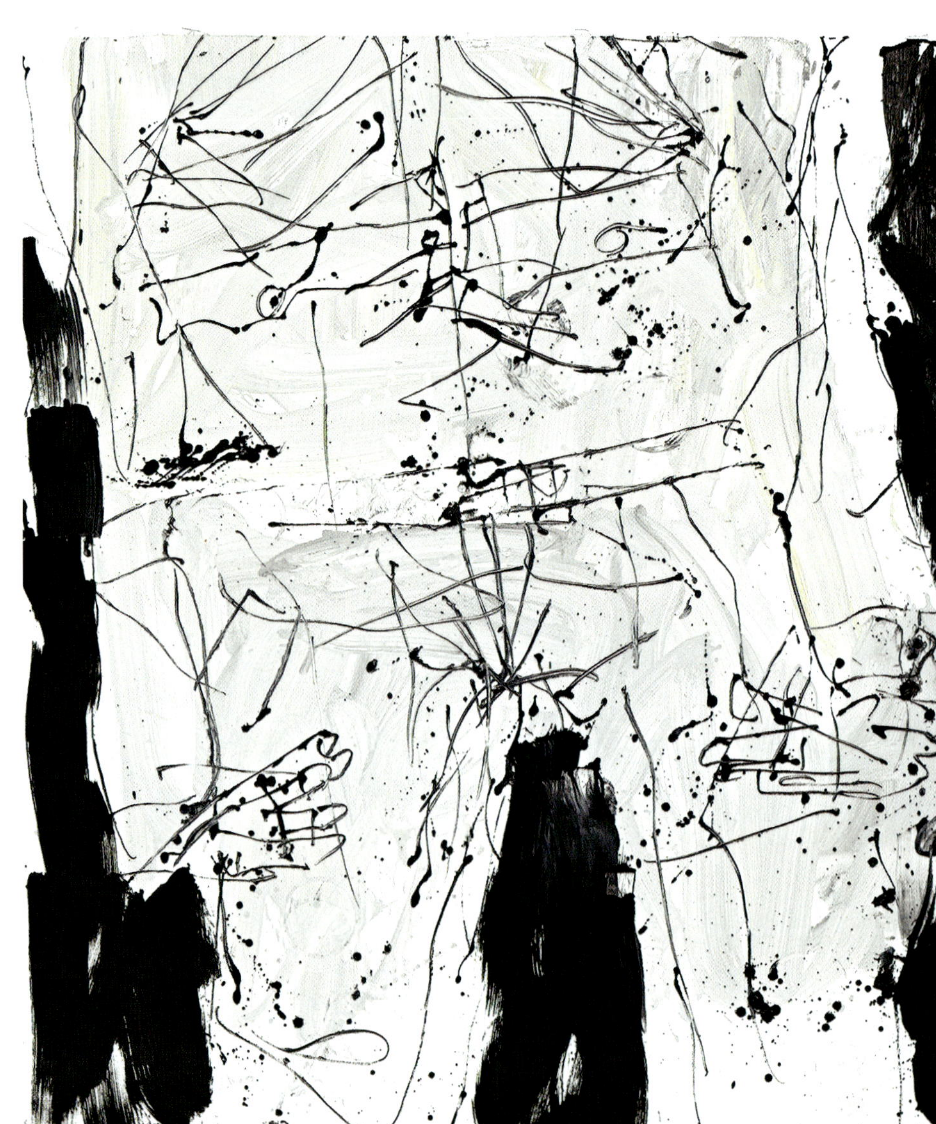

Wadi in the Evening, 2012

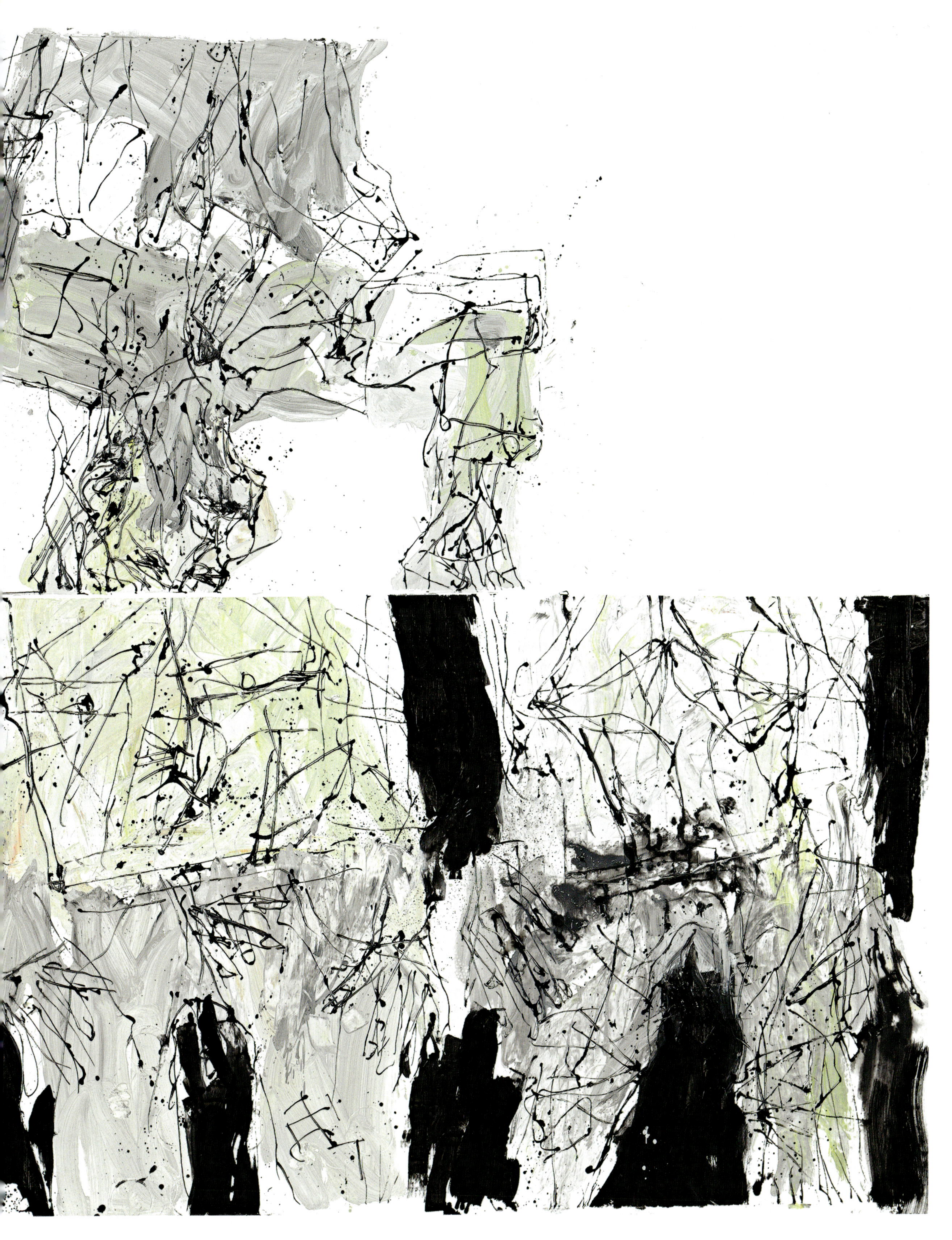

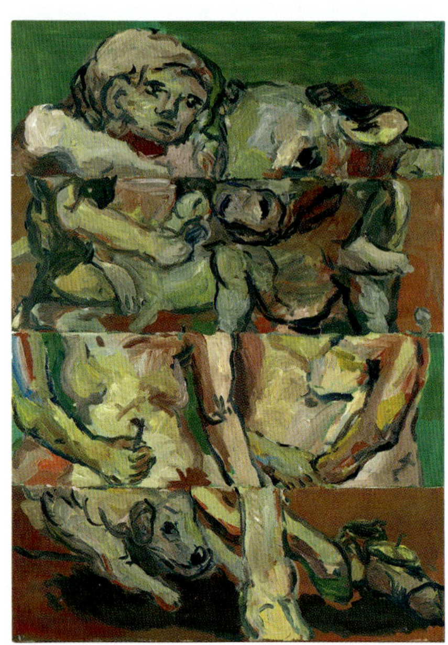

Georg Baselitz, *Four Stripes Idyll*, 1966

Oehlen, who with Werner Büttner formed the "League Against Contradictory Behavior" in the late nineteen-seventies, found as much to dislike in the official art of the leftist, conceptual avant-garde of the late nineteen-seventies and eighties as in the capering of the neo-expressionists (playfully reworking the Maoist politics of his own generation he pronounced "the enemy of my enemy is also my enemy"). His nonalignment with received positions allowed Oehlen to see other artists in a particularly clear, nonpartisan way: "The question 'abstract or not abstract,' for example, is irrelevant to me. I have a whole series of forerunners in this opinion, for example Georg Baselitz, who turned the motif upside down—a magnificent gesture, considered and courageous."[11] As we move away from the moment in which "the question" seemed real to so many people, Baselitz's obviation of categories begins to look less unsynchronized, and certainly not regressive, and more prescient, pointing to a future in which the question and the categories have begun to wobble, one in which, even if critics insist on preserving them as props, they don't matter to artists. This is how Oehlen presses painting's autonomy from illusions of political agency, aesthetic categories, and even artistic "projects." The often riotously funny syntactical conflicts in the art and even the speech of de Kooning, Baselitz, and Oehlen (who share a fondness for logical contradictions and neologisms) don't serve simply to unnerve the bourgeois art lover, or even the academic critic; rather they undo genuinely absurd social prohibitions. The artists' paintings and phrase-making are ridiculous or impossible only because we have designated as contradictory categories—a face/not a face—that can perfectly well inhabit the same pictorial world.

The Flugelhornist Gracie Irlam, 2012

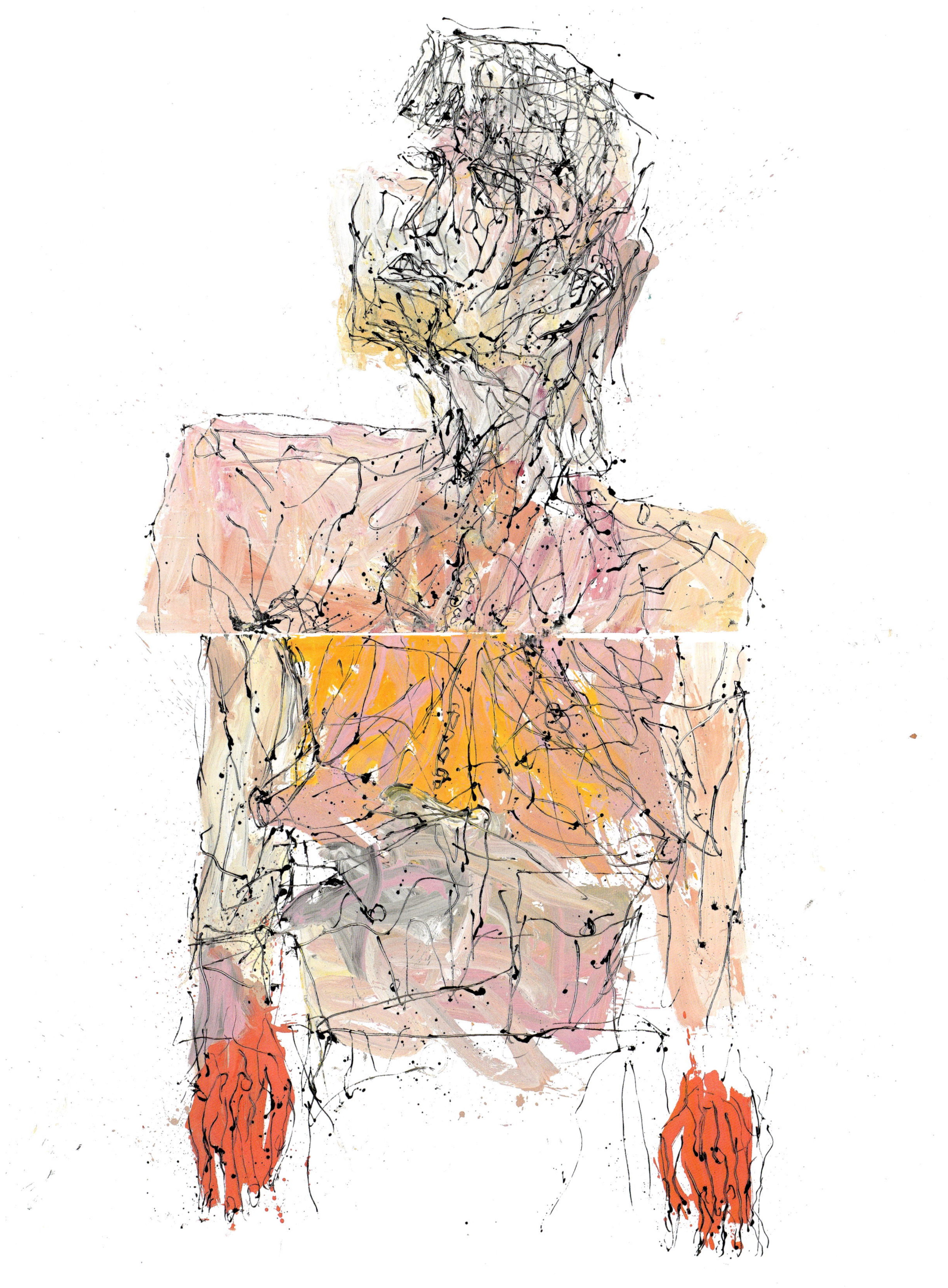

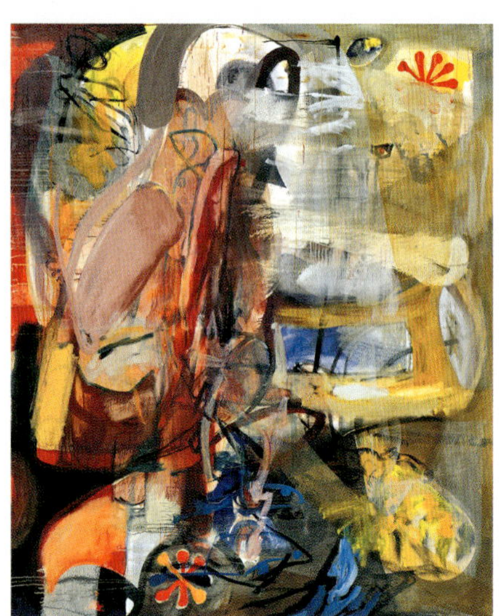

Albert Oehlen, *Check Up*, 1994

By the time of Oehlen's admiring 1994 statement, Baselitz had again changed course. Turning away from the attentions of the art world and the interest in neo-expressionism, he returned to his own history, as a painter, and as a child in East Germany. The change was prompted in large part by the fall of the Berlin Wall, which entailed the discovery of his surveillance by the Stasi, and also a sense that the door to the East, and his past, had been reopened. He began painting from family photographs, and also changed the way he worked, laying his unstretched canvases directly on the floor, painting from all sides, even from the center of the work (occasional footprints are visible on these canvases, along with telltale circles from the bottom of paint cans). In this new method, the correct viewing/making position with respect to the subject is not only inverted, it is obviated. This disorientation, or mobility, becomes the content in two paintings of paintings that closely resemble an early fabric work by Polke and a nineteen-seventies gray painting by Richter. The two depicted canvases sprout legs, bent at the knee, on each of their four sides, putting them into a spinning, running tumble (and also irresistibly evoking a swastika). There is no top or bottom, right or left, as the loaded motif spins of its own accord, set free of the painter's conscious control.[12] The device of the turning legs is less ironic yet equally rooted in the weight of the past in a series of 2005–06 paintings. In these four works, legs wander through a childhood nature scene, or perhaps more precisely, through Baselitz's teenage landscape painting of that scene. The legs belong to the artist himself (like those cut off in a late photograph of Munch in his studio, and also those in his own 1969 *Painter*). Now, even as he literally paints from all angles on the floor,

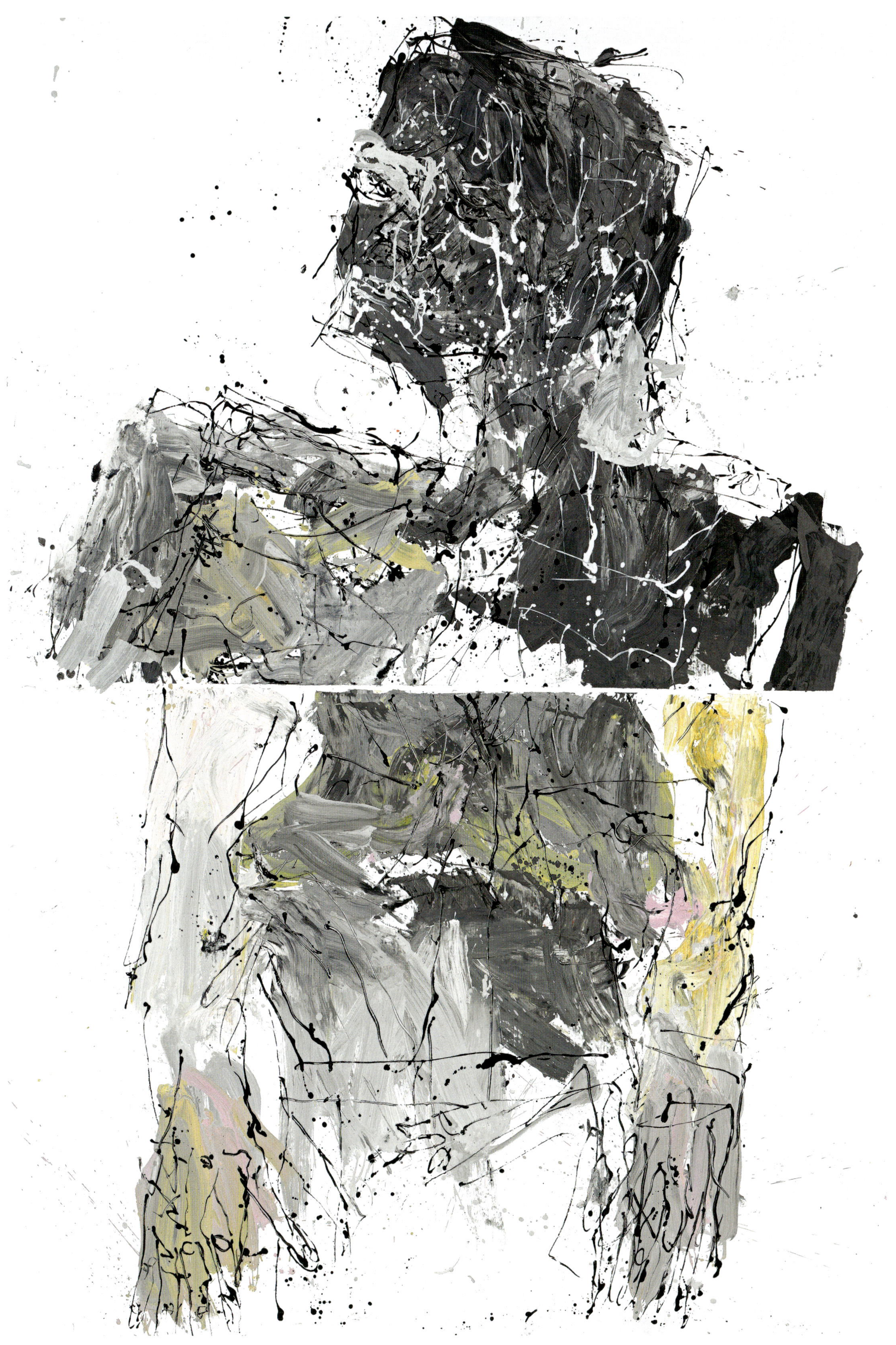

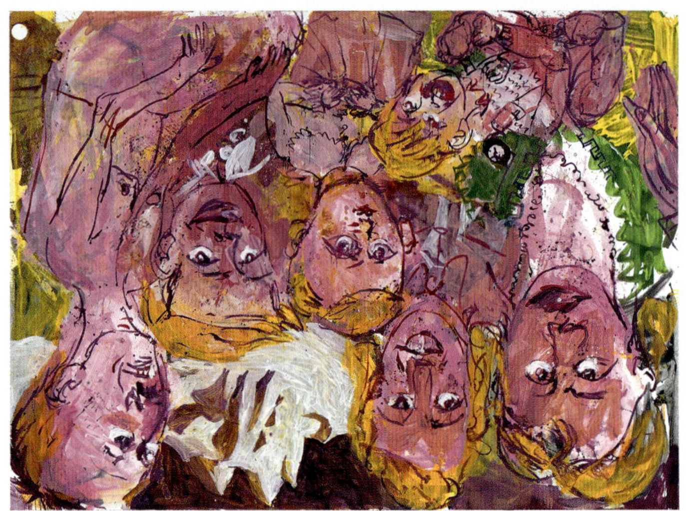

Georg Baselitz, *We Are Visiting the Rhine I*, 1996

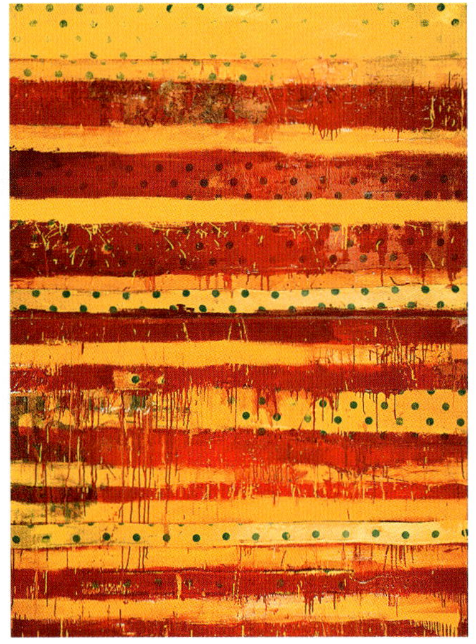

Robert Rauschenberg, *Yoicks*, 1953

he is also moving around through his own past, his own visual memories, admitting everything, without category or censorship. The pastness of the past is made physical in paintings such as *Irgendwann vergessen—Sandteichdamm* (*Forgotten at Some Point—Sand Pond Dam*; 2009): divisions in the image made using a passe-partout resemble those of the earlier *Fracture Paintings*, but here bleed drips that threaten to veil the self-appropriated imagery from the artist's own previous work.

And so we move away from the old two-sided conflicts towards a multiplicity of possiblities and realities, one that always existed, but was not available, or at least did not make itself visible, within once dominant views. Line itself is freed from the underlying fields and forms of strongly colored paint, and also from dedication to figurative drawing: "The lines are very seldom only contour lines, but rather, they are lines of growth as with plants. In medicine, there are illustrations of nerves, blood vessels, tendons, bones, muscles—my lines should be like these."[13] Organic process sits together with (self) appropriation. All of this asynchrony resonates with the woodcuts of Ernst Ludwig Kirchner and earlier printmaking, as well as with Andy Warhol's silkscreens and the artist's own wildly proficient prints. The taste of contemporary artists, like Christopher Wool, for the *Fracture* series and Baselitz's very recent work responds to the way these paintings force together materiality and image, without the demand for reconciliation, rupturing the composition of the surface image in the nineteen-sixties, and, today, creating layers that shift in and

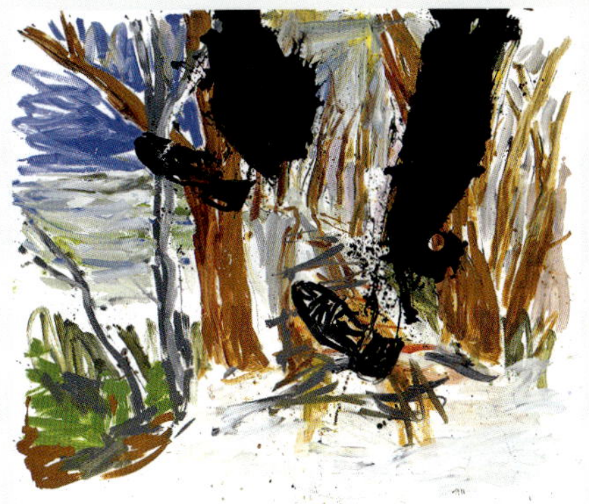

Georg Baselitz, *Ekely*, 2004

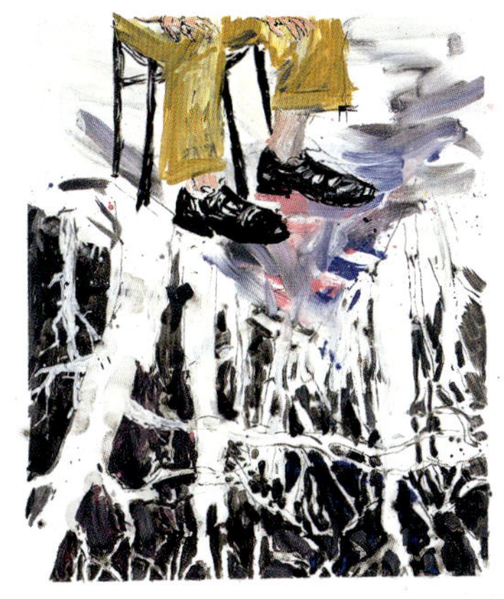

Georg Baselitz, *Sand Pond Dam 1953 (Remix)*, 2006

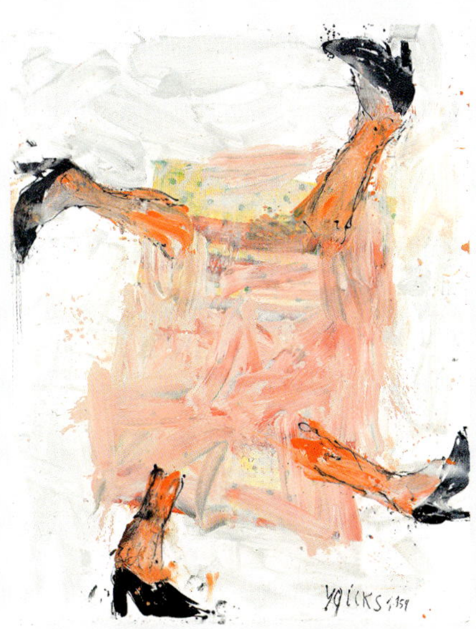

Georg Baselitz, *Yoicks (Robert)*, 2009

out of alignment. Many artists working today, including Wool, Oehlen, Charline von Heyl, Terry Winters, Mark Bradford, and others, work with this kind of depth and asynchrony, in which image and substance are treated as equally material or "real" and mutually interfering. Baselitz was quite prescient in his acceptance of both abstraction and figuration, an openness still more fully realized in his current work, with its acceptance of multiple layers, the simultaneity, multiplicity, and nonalignment of different realities, most significantly, those of interior and exterior, past and present.

Baselitz senses the change in his relation to the contemporary artistic situation. Along with it, his earlier "depression," as he very recently put it, has lifted, a depression that was the price paid by even the most aggressive, apparently self-confident artist for his failure to be in tune with society. The artist's recent lift in spirits comes specifically from his awareness of the respect of younger artists for de Kooning, and from the feeling that this respect more generally embraces a way of painting that includes himself as well.[14] Fifty years after the American exhibition in Berlin, seen from the perspective of younger artists, the two painters are no longer set against each other. Reconciled with his past through the present, Baselitz has paid tribute to "de Kooning, my master" in gorgeously loose colorful paintings such as *Bei Willem* (*With Willem*; 2009), that are often self-portraits, and yet dedicated to the late artist, drawing the two men together. Today, in what Baselitz diagnoses as a painter's paradise, it is not national identity or temporary critical dictates but painterly accomplishments and affinities that persist ("the thing that lasts is de Kooning," as Oehlen put it).[15] If there is a hint of triumph in

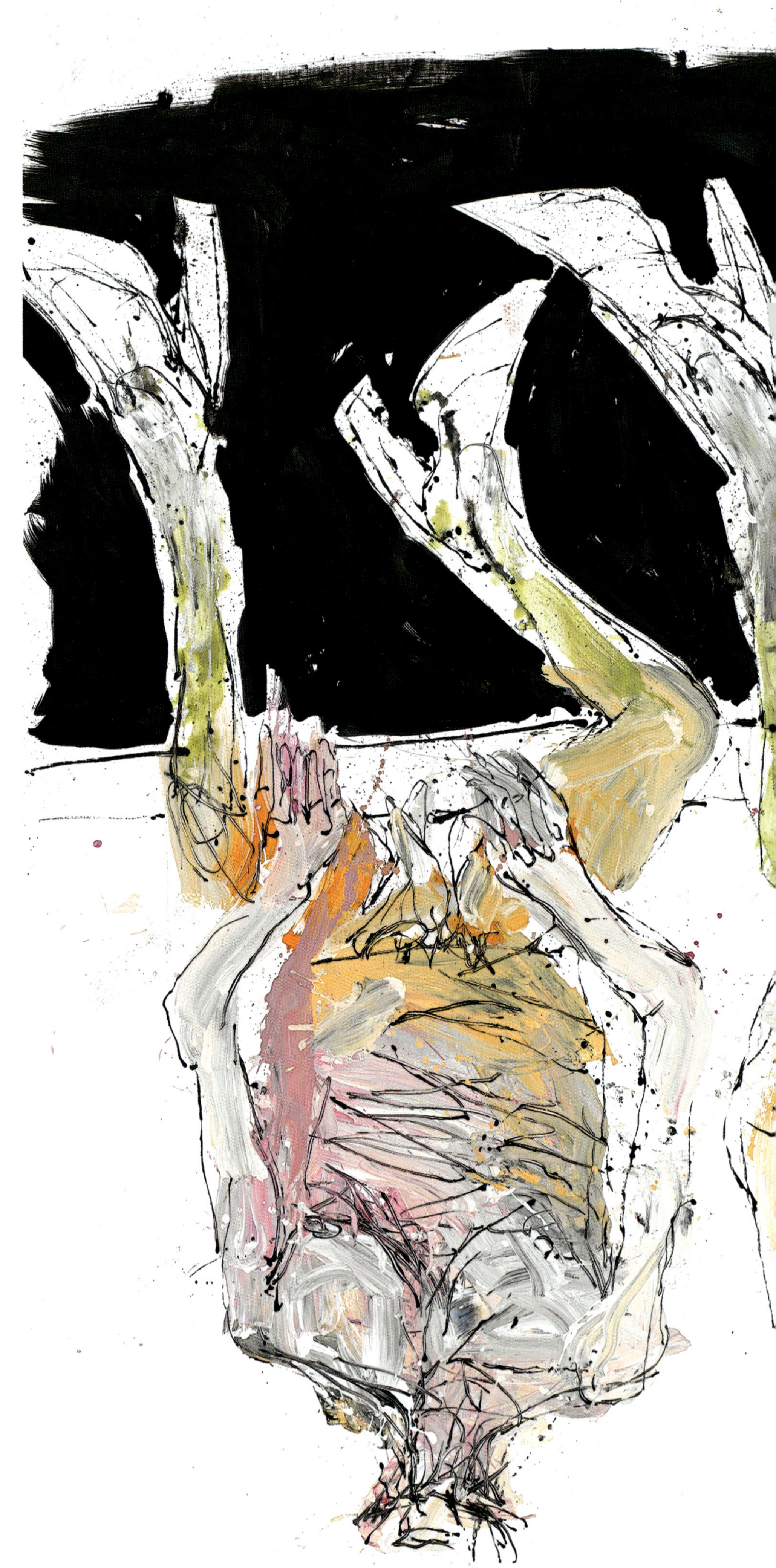

Right or Left Turn?, 2011

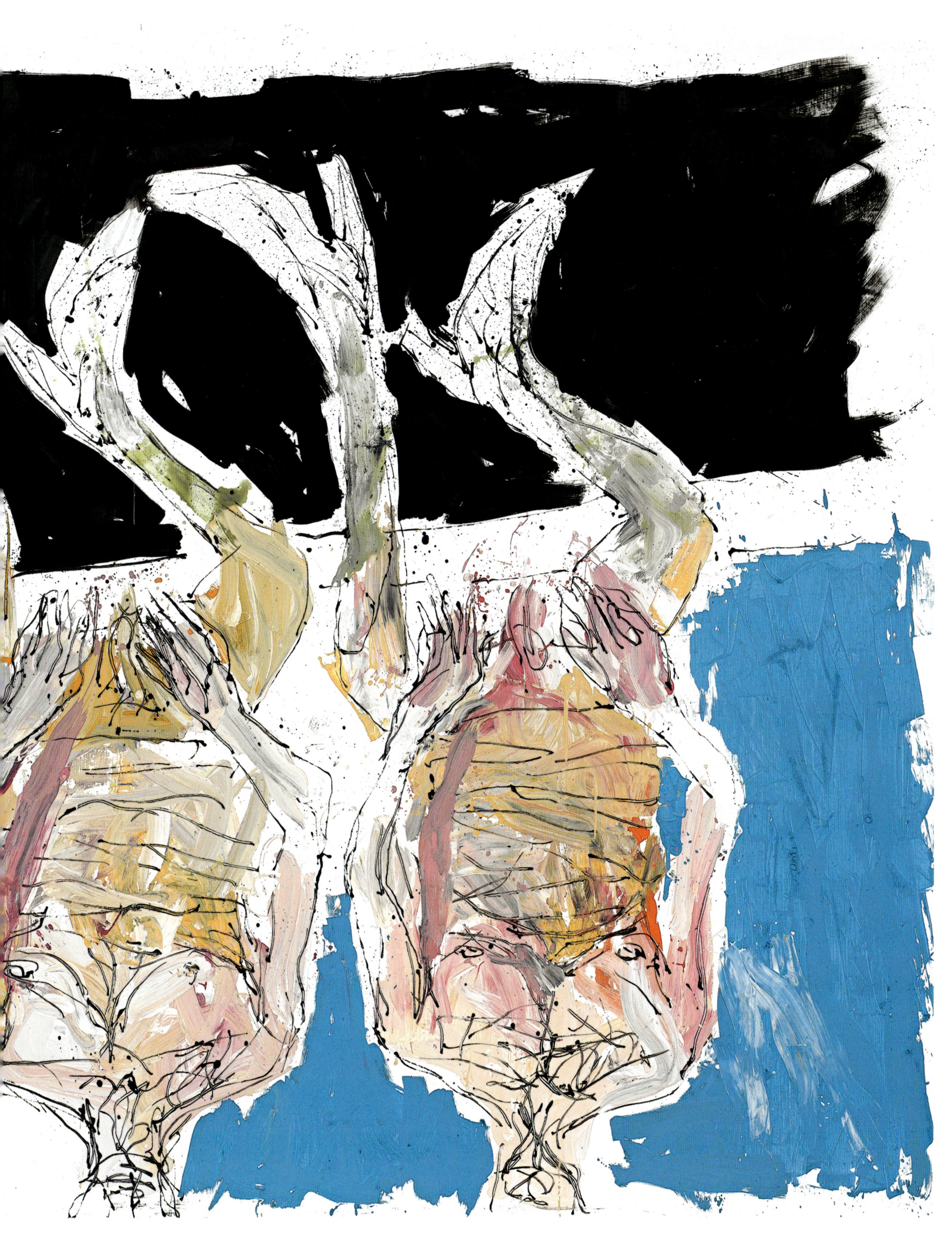

Baselitz's own survival, his expansive success in the present, we shouldn't begrudge it.

I would end here. Except that Baselitz has been working (yet again) in a new way, and one that belies an easy synchrony with current taste, with his belated triumph as a modern or contemporary painter. A recent series, the heart of this exhibition, faces us with thick black (and dark blue, gray, and brown) canvases with little value contrast and almost imperceptible subject matter, with no gap between image and materiality, seeing and touching. Even the artist cannot see what he is doing, has done, until the painting is dry; he is painting "blind" in a way sympathetic to de Kooning's drawings done with eyes closed, and also to the super-tactile Auerbach (another admired peer), who has described his own paintings as like "touching something in the dark."[16] It is as if Baselitz is no longer strolling the path around the sand pond, but going down into the pond itself, looking down into a bottomless pail or bucket, as he describes it. This diving, or digging, head down, is another kind of inversion, one that is wondrous, both introspective and almost metaphysically curious about the natural world. Baselitz: "Somehow everything is still here, perhaps just in another place, upside down, or maybe not … To dream oneself to the other end of the world was a childhood wish. I have dug, drilled, and trenched in the sand pit in order to come out again on the other side."[17] This is a matter wider than the world of art. We are in a moment in which the appeal and the endurance of nature, and the relative insignificance of cultural dictates—the temporariness of the contemporary—reveals itself. From this perspective, the anti-modern impulse is unmoored from regressive politics.

This condition puts Baselitz in sync with what feels right, as if the world finally caught up to him.

My thanks to Detlev Gretenkort and Georg Baselitz for the material support, input, and thoughtful commentary.

1 See, for example, "Georg Baselitz in Conversation with Walter Grasskamp" [1984], in *Georg Baselitz: Collected Writings and Interviews*, ed. Detlev Gretenkort (London: Ridinghouse, 2010), 80–81.
2 Georg Baselitz, "Only in Art the World Is Whole," Louisiana Chanel: Videos on the Arts, Featuring the Artists, accessed July 1, 2014, http://channel.louisiana.dk/video/georg-baselitz-only-art-world-whole.
3 Dr. Christian Weikop, "Interview with Georg Baselitz: Artist and Collector—An Interview with the Honorary Royal Academician," The Royal Academy of Arts (blog), March 28, 2014, https://www.royalacademy.org.uk/article/112. Baselitz is acute on the subject of the modern, contemporary, and avant-garde, all criteria predicated on historical timeliness. "I have come to appreciate that 'avant-garde' is a problematic term. For many years, I have looked at the work of British artists such as Freud, Auerbach, and Bacon. What is avant-garde about them? Nothing. Some years ago, I would have said that they are not contemporary artists, but the paintings that they created are contemporary and wonderful. Whereas someone such as Pechstein, very active in the avant-garde circle of the Brücke, was a mediocre artist and nobody talks about him anymore. It is a complicated matter."
4 Georg Baselitz, "Press Conference for the Exhibition *Remix* at the Albertina, Vienna, January 17, 2007," in *Georg Baselitz: Collected Writings and Interviews*, ed. Detlev Gretenkort (London: Ridinghouse, 2010), 284. Was the artist perhaps tacitly acknowledging this when he said, in 2007, "An artist should do all he can to escape the *Zeitgeist*?" *Zeitgeist* being the title of a 1982 exhibition that situated Baselitz as a neo-expressionist.
5 This includes the work of Yule Heibel, Eckhart Gillen, and Stephanie Barron. My own research over the past five years has looked at international iterations of this phenomenon. See for example, "The Luxury of Incommensurability," (lecture, Frieze, London, October 2011); the essay "Undoing Wols," in Kunsthalle Bremen and The Menil Collection, eds. *Wols: Retrospective* (Munich: Hirmer Publishers, 2013), and the exhibition series *Touching From a Distance*, held at the Rose Art Museum at Brandeis University from 2014–15.
6 Jeanne Anne Nugent, "From Hans Sedlmayr to Mars and Back Again: New Problems in the Old History of Gerhard Richter's Radical Reworking of Modern Art," in *Gerhard Richter: Early Work, 1951–1972*, eds. Christine Mehring, Jeanne Anne Nugent, and Jon L. Seydl (Los Angeles: J. Paul Getty Museum, 2010), 50–57; Richard Shiff, "Feet Too Big," *Georg Baselitz: Remix*, eds., Carla Schulz-Hoffmann and Richard Shiff, (Munich: Pinakothek der Moderne, 2006), 25–26. Nugent and Shiff make the same point about their respective subjects, Richter and Baselitz, through the vehicle of Adorno's relation to Sedlmayr.
7 Patrick Heron, "Bonnard and Visual Reality," *New Statesman* 42, no. 1081 (November 24, 1951): 588. This missing center was a theme echoed as well in British, French, and American art discourse of the late nineteen-forties through the fifties. For example, British painter Patrick Heron, also writing in 1951: "Unfortunately, these two extremes, these two aesthetic heresies, of pure abstraction on the one hand and expressionist figuration on the other, are much in favor just now; the central tradition, in which the impulse to abstract is checked

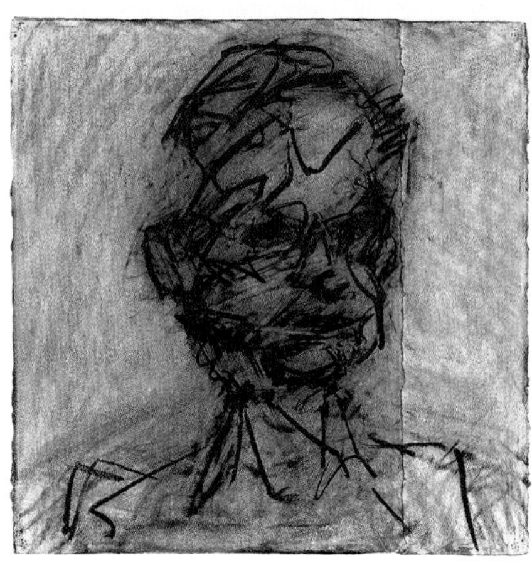

Frank Auerbach, *David Landau*, 1985

by the impulse to communicate 'a subject,' and in which that subject is divested of its fiercer emotive undertones because it has been translated into formal terms—this is neglected."

8 Theodor Adorno, *Minima Moralia* [1951] (London: Verso, 2005), 39.

9 Richard Calvocoressi, "A Source for the Inverted Imagery in Georg Baselitz's Painting," *Burlington Magazine* 127, no. 993 (December 1985): 894, 896–7, 899. The sketch is related to *Der Mann am Baum* (*Man at a Tree*), also of 1969, in which the inverted figure hangs from and against a tree, crucified upside down like Masaccio's St. Peter.

10 Georg Baselitz, "Somersaults Are Also Movement, and They're Fun Too" [1992], in Diane Waldman, *Georg Baselitz*, exh. cat. (New York: Guggenheim Museum, 1995), 242.

11 Albert Oehlen, in Diedrich Diederichsen, "The Rules of the Game: An Interview with Albert Oehlen," *Artforum* 33, no. 3 (November 1994): 69.

12 As he put it in 1992, referring to his own unwilled, repetitive drawing of a swastika, the motif is a mechanism that takes over from the painter, who merely stands by and looks on. See Baselitz, "Somersaults Are Also Movement," 242.

13 Georg Baselitz, e-mail message to the author, April 10, 2014, my translation.

14 Georg Baselitz, e-mail message to the author, April 10, 2014, my translation.

15 Albert Oehlen, in an interview with Glenn O'Brien, *Interview Magazine* (April 28, 2009), accessed July 2, 2014, http://www.interviewmagazine.com/art/albert-oehlen/#.

16 Robert Hughes, *Frank Auerbach* (London: Thames & Hudson, 1990), 86.

17 Georg Baselitz, "Appropriation: Back Then, In Between, and Today" [2010], *Art Bulletin* 94, no. 2 (June 2012): 166.

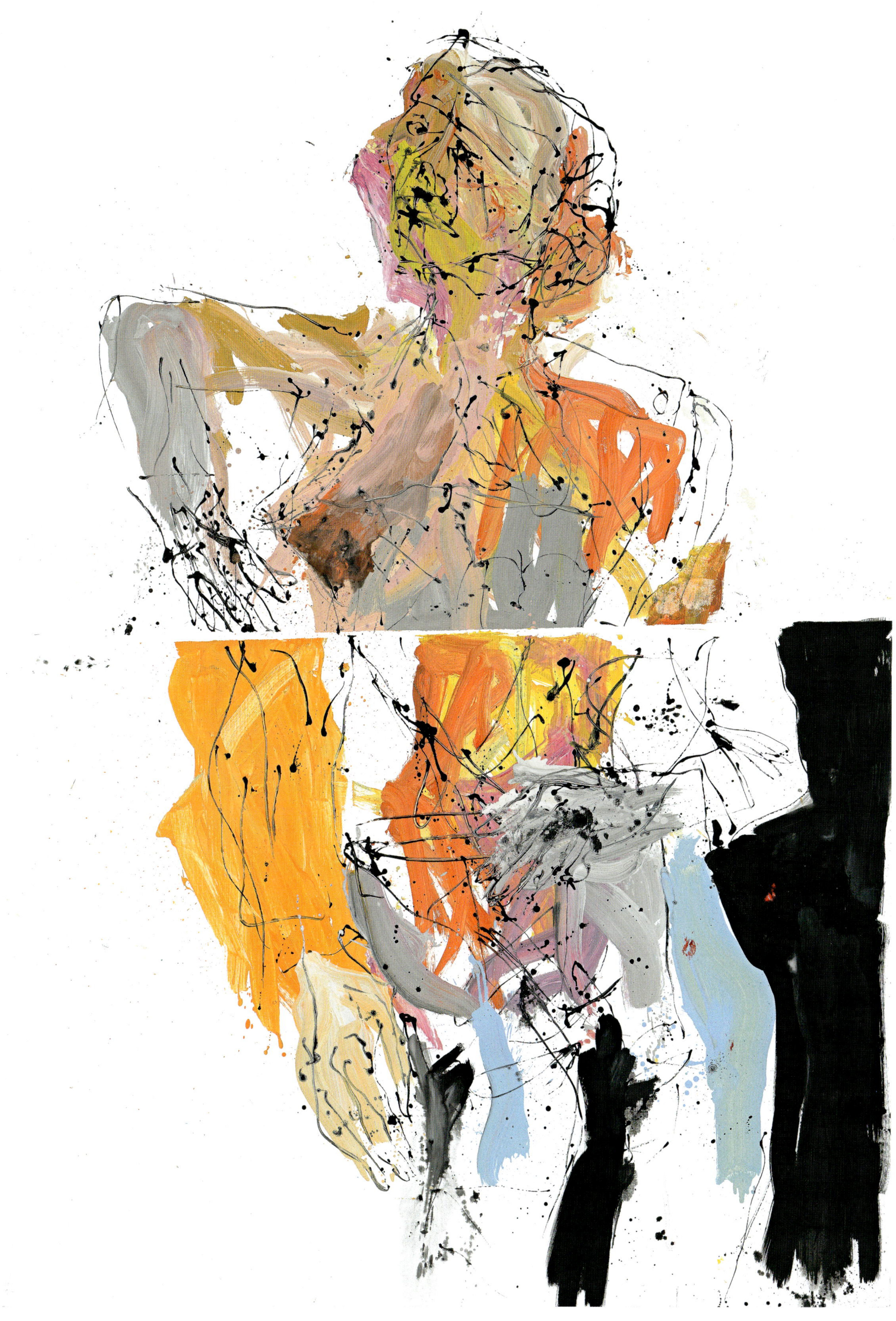

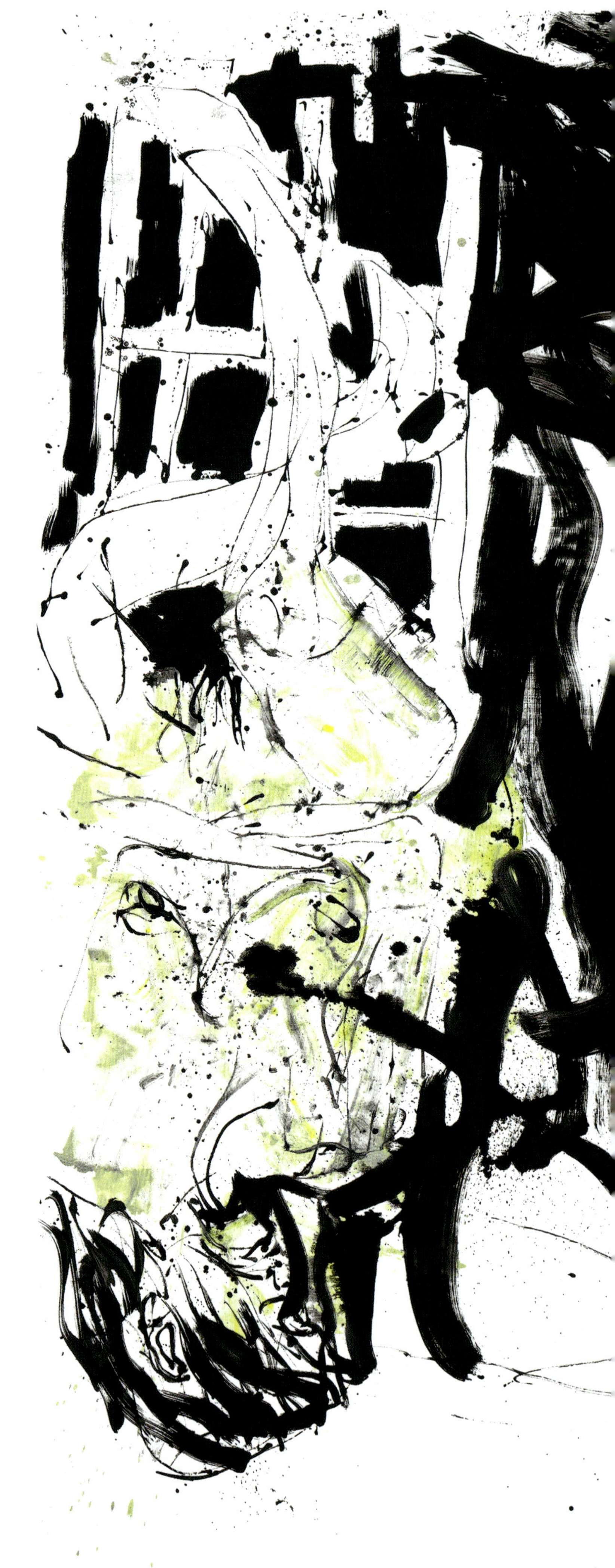

Once a Rod Like 1960, also a Stovepipe Like 60, 2011

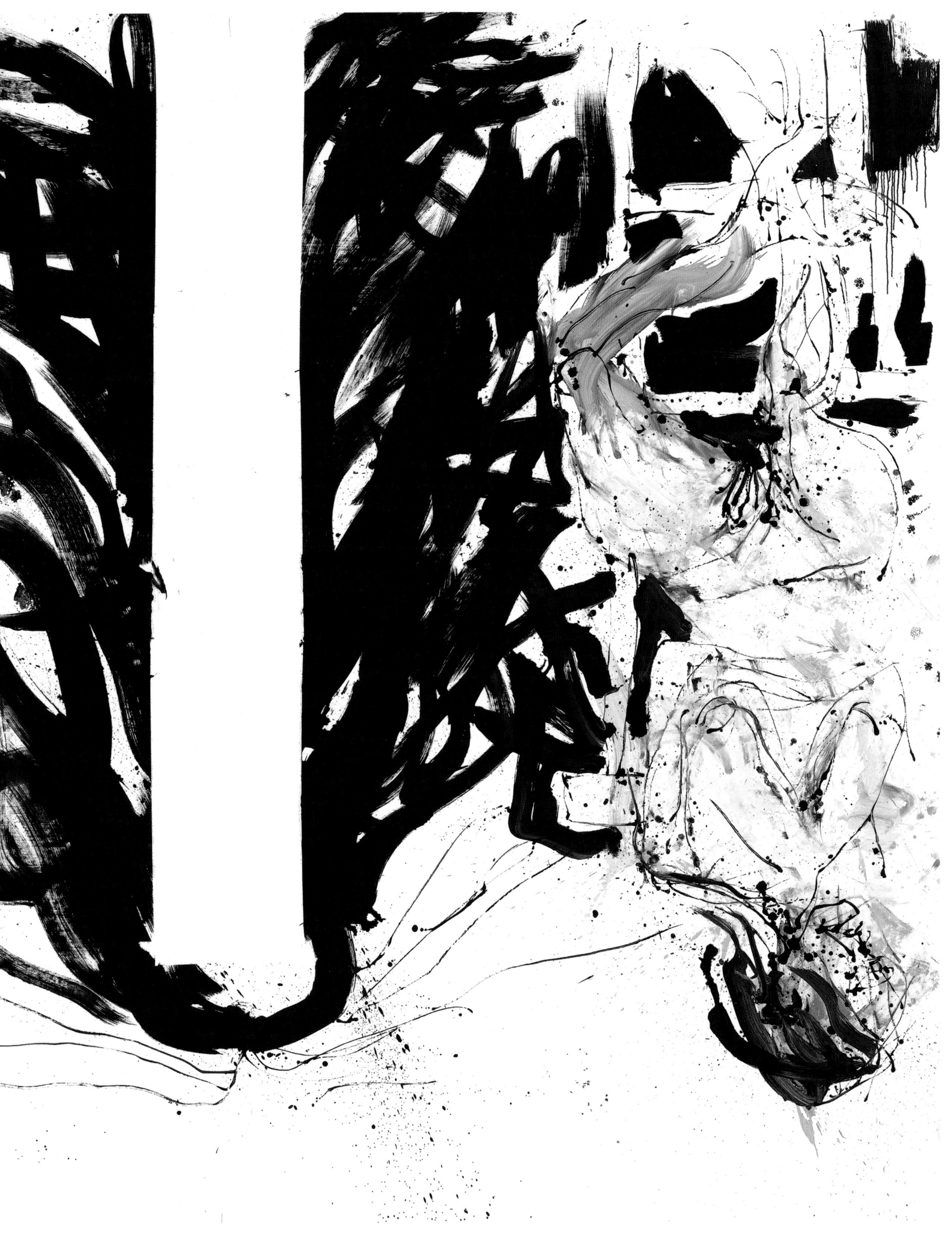

Bad Grade, 2012

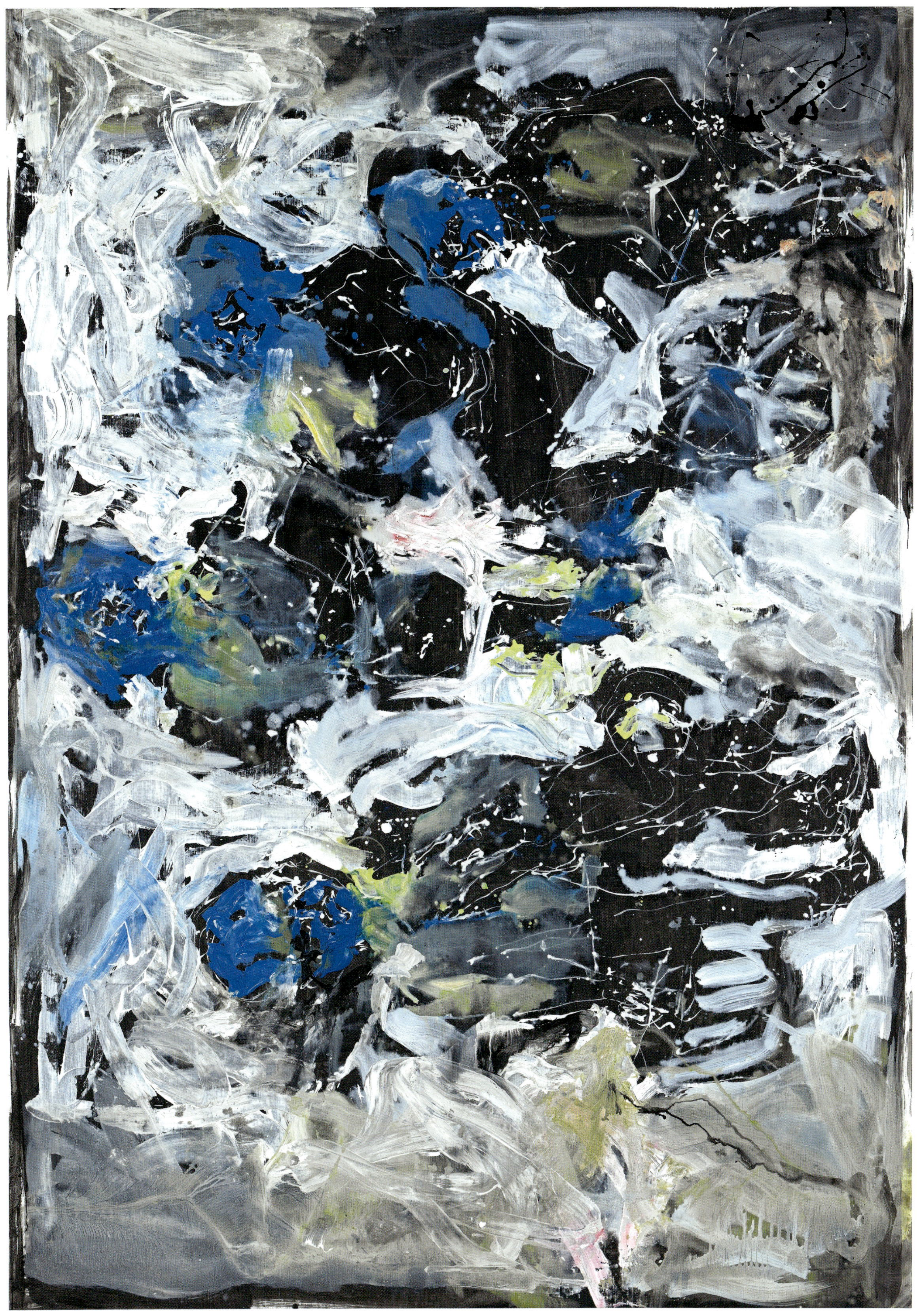

Elke Negative Blue, 2012

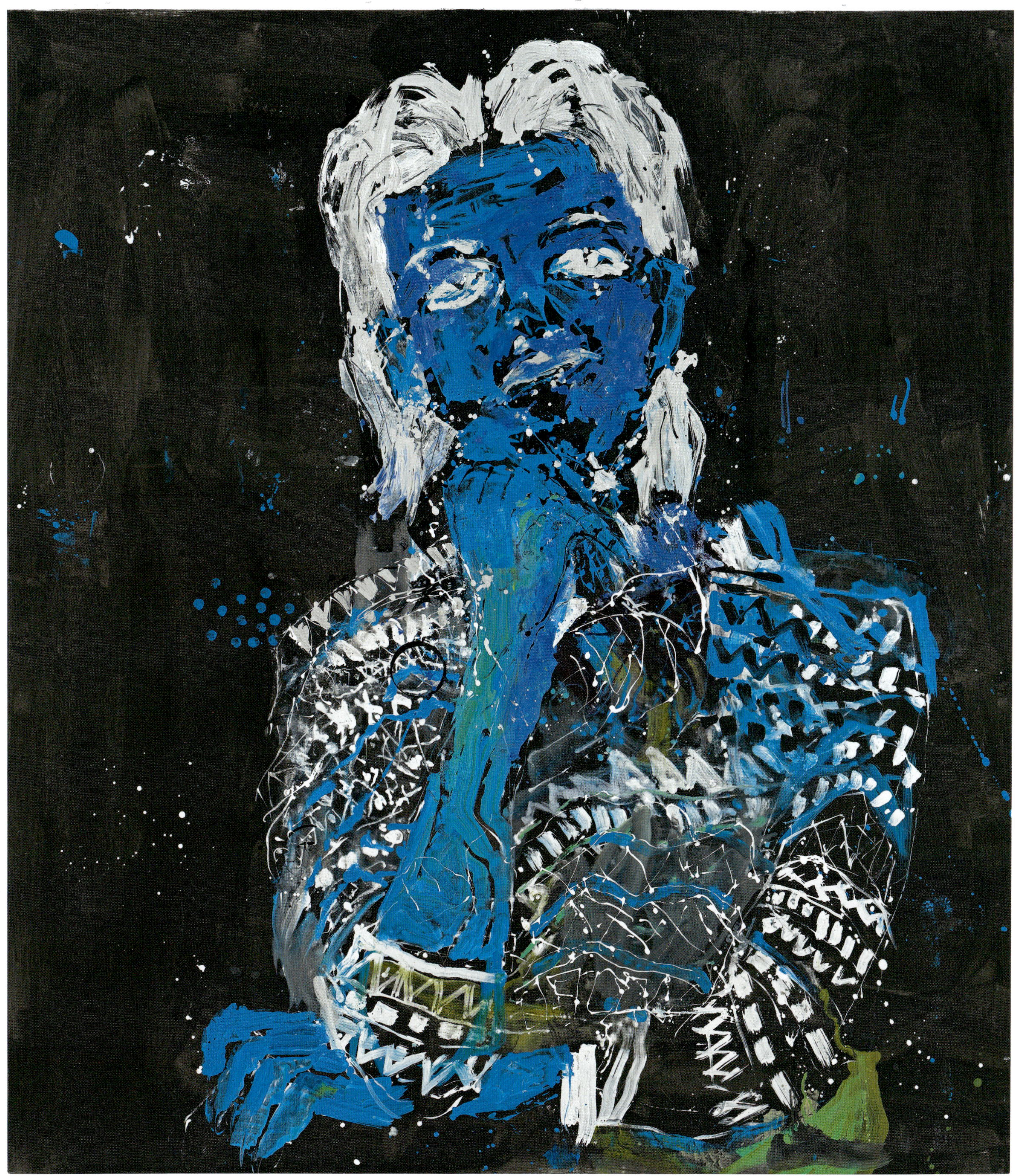

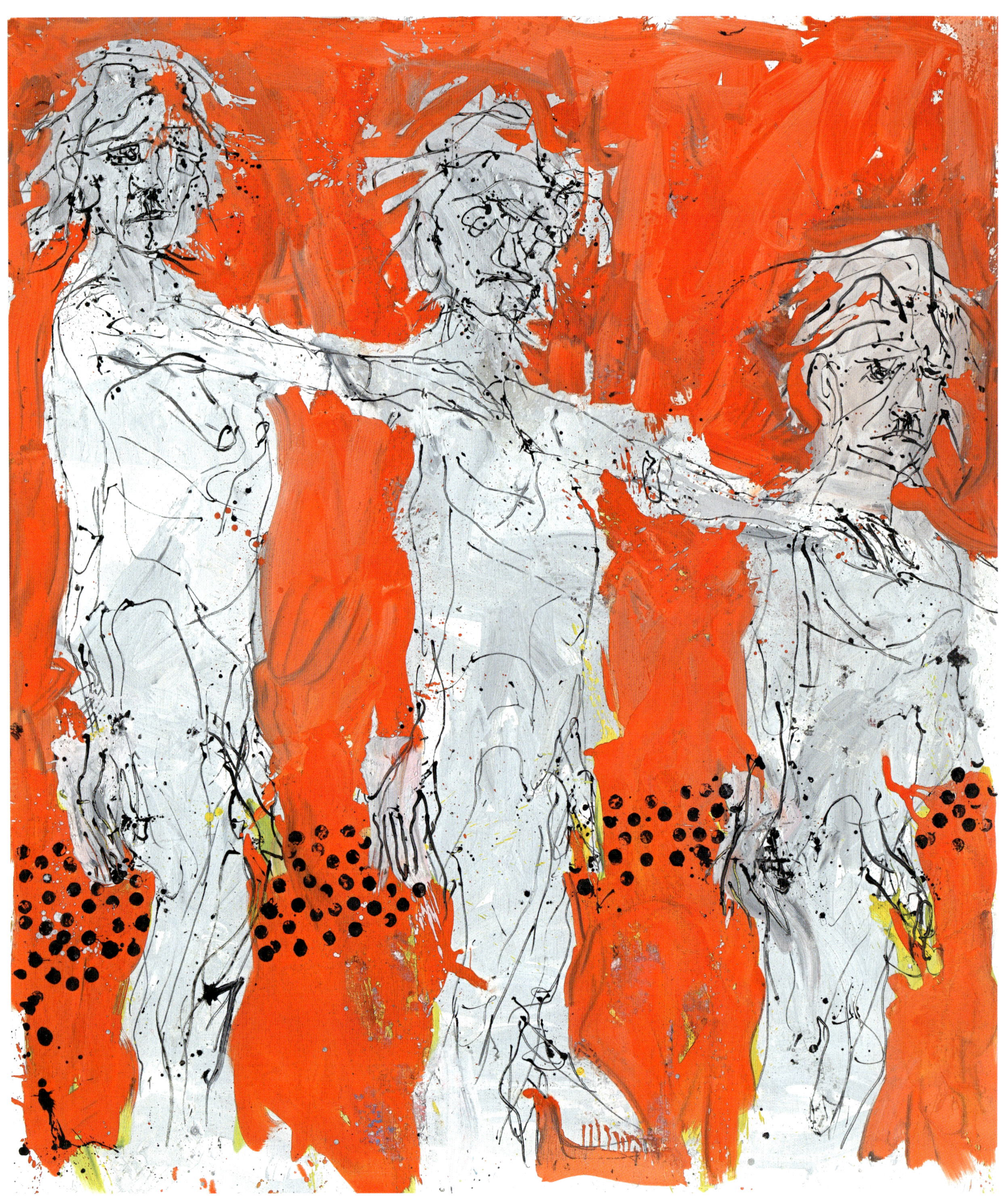

Much like *Zero Ende* (*Zero End*; 2014, ill. pp. 178–79), Baselitz's *Sing Sang Zero* (2011, ill. p. 159) does not possess a base, but unlike the former, it is erected on two pairs of legs. The sculpture's balance is not precisely ensured by a pose—since there are no poses for an artist who has always used the human body as a motif of its abstraction—but rather by a *posture* that suggests stability and, at the same time, engenders a kind of surprise, as the situation seems simultaneously banal and strange. Banal thanks to its consecrated gesture of bourgeois coupledom, and strange due to the fact that such a "natural" form of behavior—but will it seem natural for as long as the sculpture lasts, we may wonder—is expressed in surprising and unexpected conditions. We can, of course, recognize the silhouette of a man and a woman, who are doubtless the artist and his wife, but curiously, we did not quite expect to see them represented like this. At first glance, the bronze's black patina confers a kind of intensity that the wood's bareness did not. Since the legs are topped off with high-heeled, androgynous shoes, we are forced to conclude that we are not dealing with a primitive couple. Everything points to an impossible classical nudity, but also a kind of dress in the style of Azzedine Alaïa. The choice of black entails an element of distinction—it is often said that black is appropriate for any occasion—and in the sculpture, as the artist had hoped; this color tends to neutralize any anecdotal details in favor of a simplified form. However, it does not go so far as to obscure the painter's hat, a solid cap pushed down to his ears, or the famous shoes that give the whole figure a stylish but otherworldly appearance. As a result, the image we perceive is as familiar as it is incongruous; but above all, it seems to have been transformed by hardship. A hardship that was doubtless the test of time, the ordeal of the sculpture, supported by an

Eric Darragon

AVANTI PASSATO!
BASELITZ'S *BLACK SCULPTURES*, MEMORY, BACKGROUND STORIES

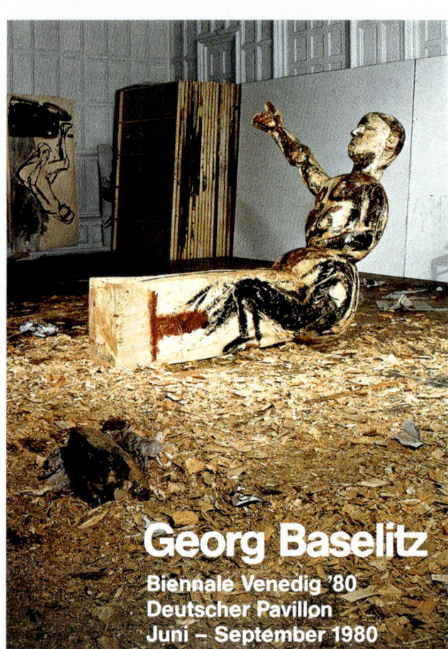

Exhibition poster, *Georg Baselitz*, German Pavilion, Venice Biennale, 1980

ogive shape, which gives the figures a clear-cut appearance. The appearance of individuals that art never really managed to age, as it should have. Baselitz has often reiterated the importance that he attributes to the archeological metaphor, as if it were a question of digging into the earth to find what was buried there. More generally, he believes that all discoveries are tied to impenetrable and subterranean connections that we absorb via contact with our feet, in communication with our head: "Feet are my earth wire … For me the reception via an earth wire is much better than through an antenna."[1] It is not coincidental that the choice of bronze gives us the impression that these two individuals, stylized as though showing up as for a formal event, are essentially in contact with the earthly aspects of their existence. The way in which their bodies are settled corresponds to the very definition of sculpture, which derives from the Latin verb *stare*, to stand upright. From this principle as old as time, the sculptor effectively calls up the biographic substance of an artistic trajectory that he had begun thirty-five years prior with *Modell für eine Skulptur* (*Model for a Sculpture*). In its own way, this piece aspired to become a sculpture according to principles that its era refused to share, and which have not fundamentally changed since then. As a result, there were a number of misunderstandings at the 1980 Venice Biennale. But since the beginning, Baselitz has had a precise idea of what he wants to accomplish. As a result of its simple and unpretentious nature, wood carved with a power-saw has consistently remained his favorite material. He has continued to exploit its density and naturalness, despite introducing bronze in 2003 in a different dimension. On the other hand, each sculpture is not always the beginning of a whole program; it simply allows the artist to enter into communication with what painting cannot express.

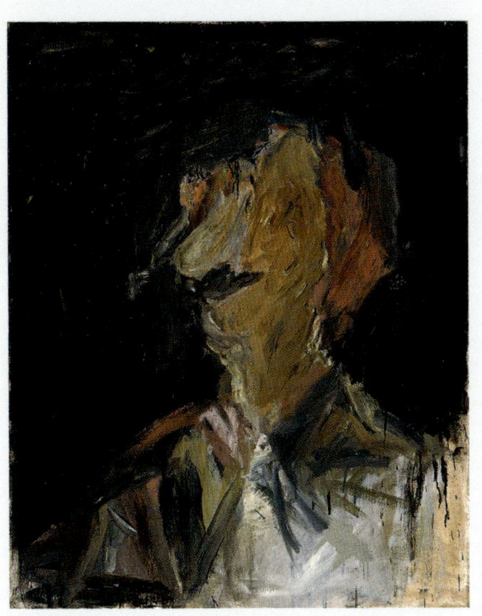

Georg Baselitz, *Portrait F. v. Rayski III*, 1960

The connection that the artist spoke of in 2011 authoritatively established the distance required between figures and their environment. Under the appearance of a social convention destined to brave history, it implies a form of alterity, which, in our eyes, is resistant—in the name of a principle that is not external, but on the contrary internal to the sculpture. This characteristic establishes a union between the two figures, and their ability to confront the world together.

How did we get here? This could be the beginning of a long narrative, of which this exhibition would be the newest version. Designed around the theme of the recent *Black Paintings* (realized in 2012 and 2013), this exhibition nevertheless also intends to examine the artist's earlier periods. From this perspective, his *Black Sculptures* certainly have a significant role, in order for us to both discover a source or origin, and to explain the on-going changes reflected in the artist's oeuvre. Baselitz has always been wary of interpretations: "I love to think, to say, to make the opposite."[2] The possibility of making something—his only goal—entails a kind of rupture that he first and foremost directs towards himself.[3] He speaks of errors or mistakes not as things to correct or improve, but as elements capable of producing something new. As Baselitz has often said, he wants to start over from the beginning. To start from zero, fully knowing that such a clean slate does not truly exist and that subterfuge must be used to get there. Baselitz already attempted this when he produced *Rayski-Kopf* (*Rayski Head*); he wanted it when he decided to invert the motif and today, in his sculptures, he wants it more than ever. "I believe that the sculptures that really matter have not yet been made,"[4] he declared in 1989 with regard to his ambitions. This conception behind Baselitz's art has not faltered over the years; in fact, it was

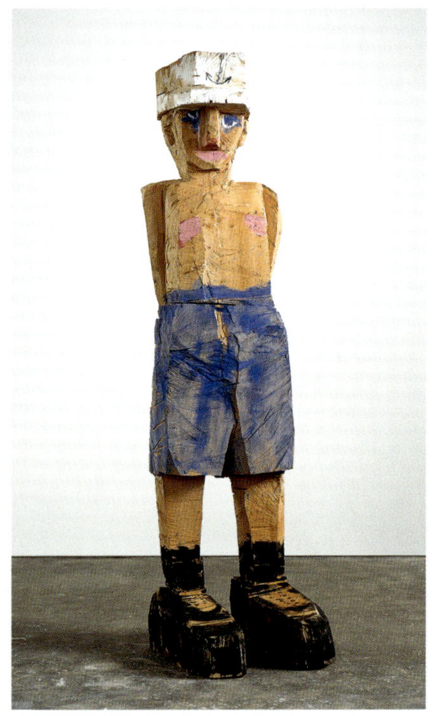

Georg Baselitz, *My New Hat*, 2003

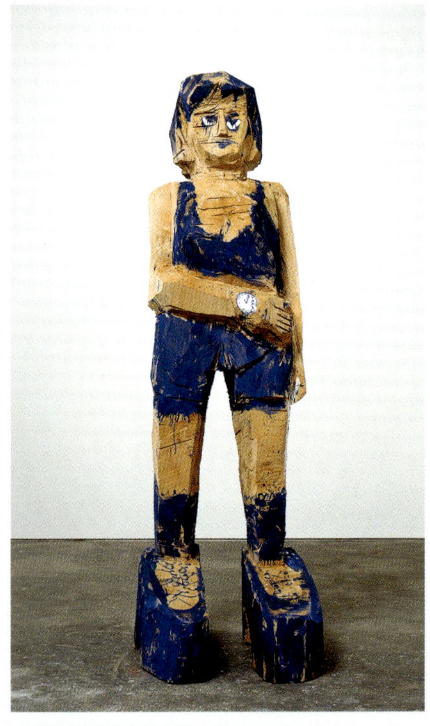

Georg Baselitz, *Mrs. Ultramarine*, 2004

even strengthened by the *Remix* group in 2005 and thus explains the extraordinary vitality of his work that is capable, at all times, of making decisions that play with the most exclusive of categories. Only the results matter in a (hi)story that is constantly amplified, depending on what remains concealed. The past being something that cannot remain what we believe it to be, the artist's decision becomes all the more unpredictable. If order must be imposed, it can only be the order of contradiction, which calls upon a grand unity. This unity is necessary so that the artist does not repeat himself: "The sculptures I make have never been made before, which is why I can make them."[5]

Sing Sang Zero confirms this by repeating identifying elements, its title letting us glimpse their persistence throughout Baselitz's oeuvre. The title seems less designed to explain its subject than to express what the sculptor might say to himself. It references both the present and the past tense of the verb "to sing" and is followed by "zero," where we might instead expect the past participle "sung" (a form which, following the past and present, would explicitly signify that an action has long since been completed). The appearance of the term "zero" in 2004 corresponds to an earlier self-portrait (*Der Veteran; The Veteran*, 2001) and is a repeated motif. Two opposing or complementary values are thus brought together: the biographical value and speculation regarding what counts as ordinary in life where, as Beaumarchais wrote, everything ends in song. A living zero that simultaneously cancels out and represents everything—an exclusive and untranslatable zero, existing solely to produce canvases. The result produces a title that we can only understand if we keep it as it stands, in the language that has been characteristic of the artist's work in recent years. A language that is

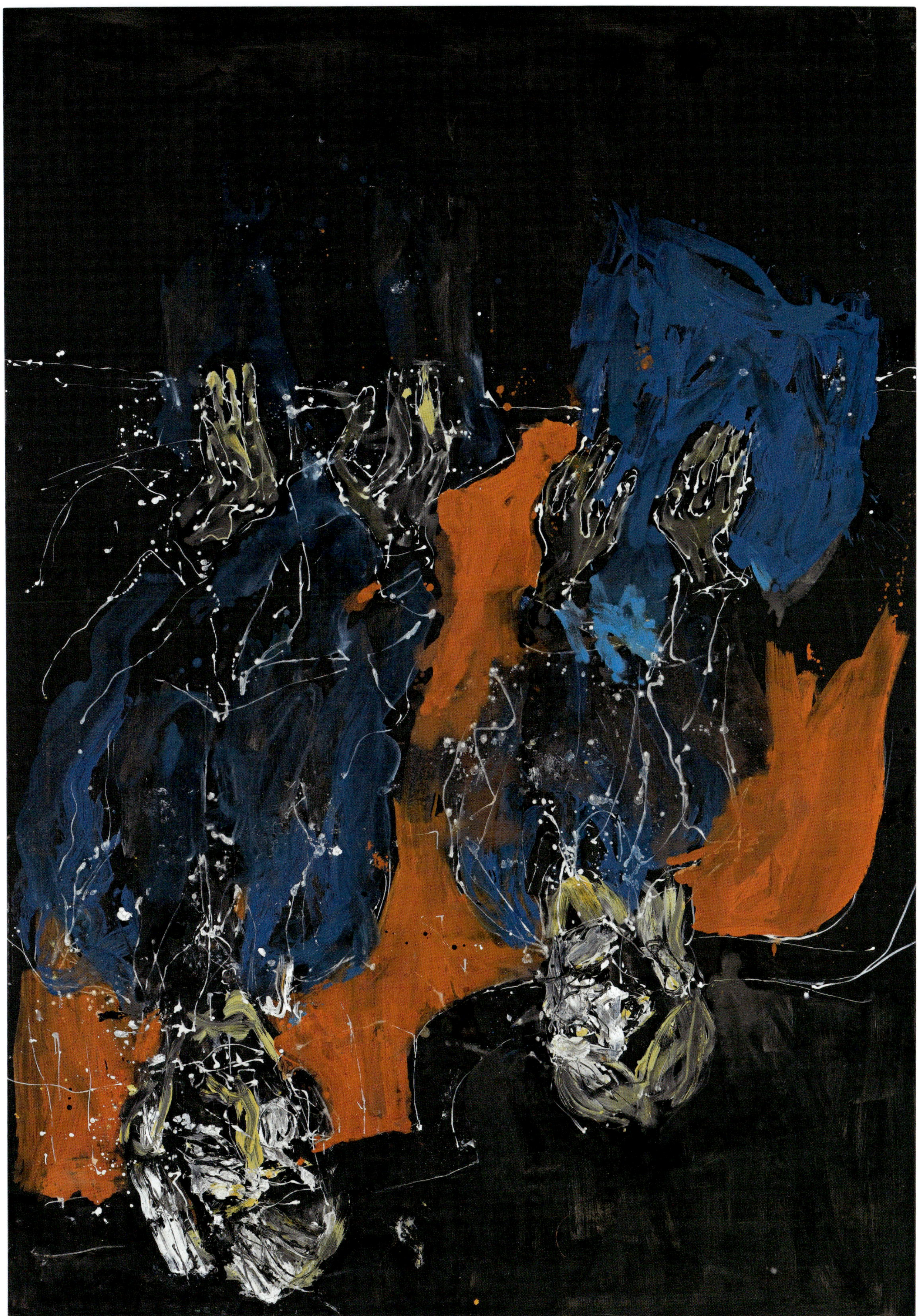

sometimes close to poetic flights of fancy, sometimes purely factual, but also at times capricious, playful, provocative and above all, endowed with a kind of freedom wrested from social judgment and interpretation. The paintings chosen to accompany the sculpture—*Zero* (2004, ill. p. 59), *Schlafzimmer* (*Bedroom*; 2009, ill. p. 105), *Negativ weiter links* (*Negative Further Left*; 2004, ill. p. 54)—allow us to envision how recent works have invented this memory of which sculpture represents the substance. The use of photographic negatives, or the remix of the 1975 painting transformed in the fashion of Otto Dix's *The Artist's Parents II* only represent some of the elements in play during this period that we can use to understand *Sing Sang Zero*. Even if the monumental cedar wood sculptures from 2003 and 2004 are not present, we can glimpse that a complex pictorial process allowed the author to discover, or rediscover, color and relief by contradictorily using black. *Meine neue Mütze* (*My New Hat*; 2003), like *Frau Ultramarin* (*Mrs. Ultramarine*; 2004), embodied a different kind of confrontation, first between the figures confronted with their pitiful image as Mediterranean bathers and then against the theme of "Death and the Maiden." The new cap depicted in 2003 possesses the child-like motif of the anchor, associated with the more violent skull emblem that is hidden in the back; this was not quite yet the same motif as would be incorporated into the 2009 sculpture, *Volk Ding Zero—Folk Thing Zero*. For this sculpture, which was cast in bronze and partially painted blue, the artist nailed onto the original wood structure a paper with the word "zero" written on it; this was borrowed from a promotional cap for a bankrupt paint company. Baselitz was first and foremost inspired here by a motif prevalent in Polish folk art: Christ, the

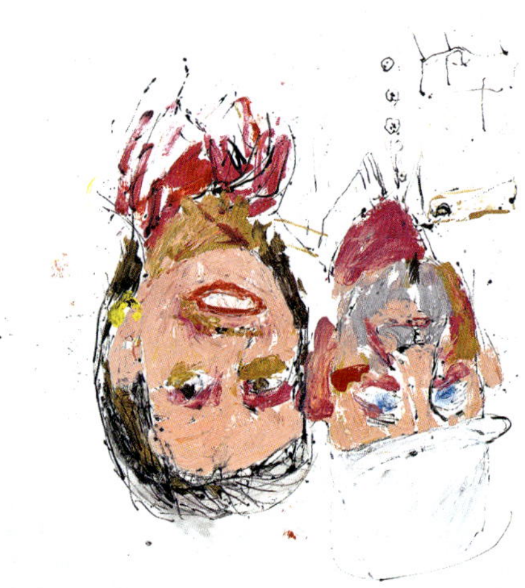

Georg Baselitz, The Veteran, 2001

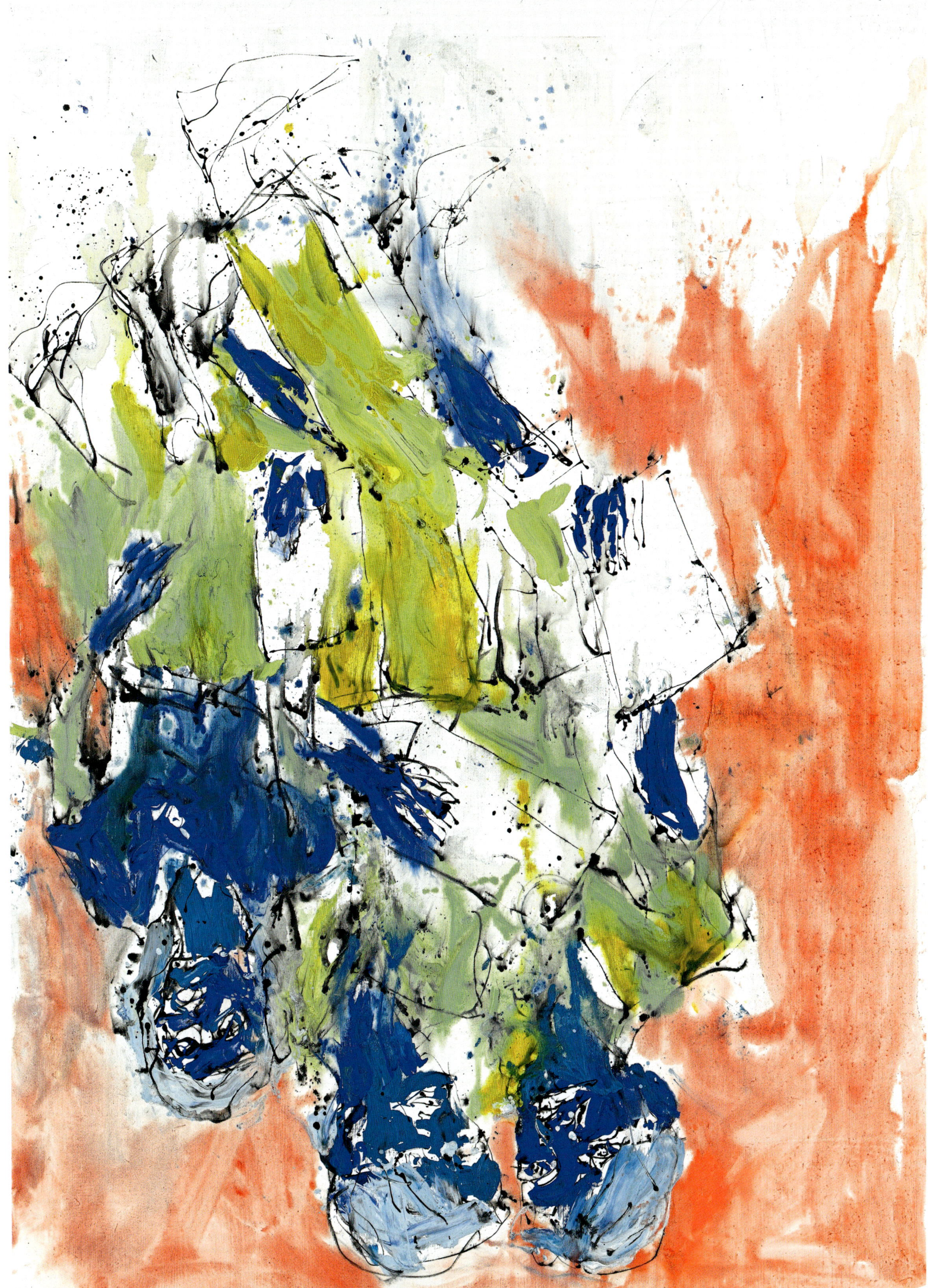

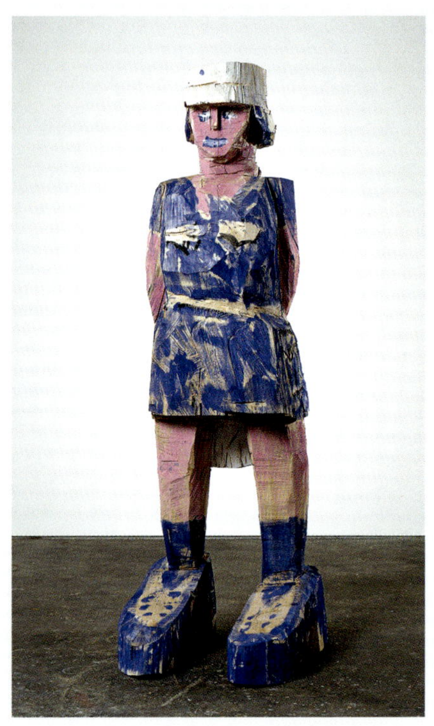

**Georg Baselitz, *Donna Via Venezia,*
2004**

Man of Sorrows, lost in grief on the side of the road. As a result, the promotional cap, which in its bronze versions was adorned with a metal plaque embossed with the artist's catch phrase, the emblem of his paradoxical solitude in today's Germany, no doubt evokes the derision of Christ, as well as the crucifixion's titulus "INRI," but is now distorted to transform its tragic Christian connotation. The black, high-heeled shoes leave no room for ambiguity, no more than the melancholic gesture where we see one of the most recent versions of the *Pathosformel* tradition. These continued and exaggerated transformations, also seen in *Dunklung Nachtung Amung Ding* (2009), confer to the 2011 sculpture a distant character, breaking with the more outrageous aspects that transmitted pathos and ridicule: the colors blue, white, and pink; the scorched and incised nature of the wood; the contemporary signs and symbols of vanity and desire; as well as the clownish, oversized shoes that simultaneously reveal its unpredictably comic and imperturbably serious presence. *Donna Via Venezia* (2004) belongs to this Felliniesque world that the bronze work of *Sing Sang Zero* no longer allows us to imagine, not even as a negative image. The entire element of exorcism, which had still been visible in the original wood version, seems now to have disappeared. But what has replaced it?

Louise Fuller (2013, frontispiece) is another large imposing sculpture, but this time endowed with huge feet, as though with such a title, everything could fly away in the blink of an eye. We cannot ignore the fact that the sculpture maintains a relationship with dance. Likewise, the figure itself gently parodies an actual dancer, whose history has been recently discovered after a long period of general neglect, due to a number of different reasons. The rings or hoops do not

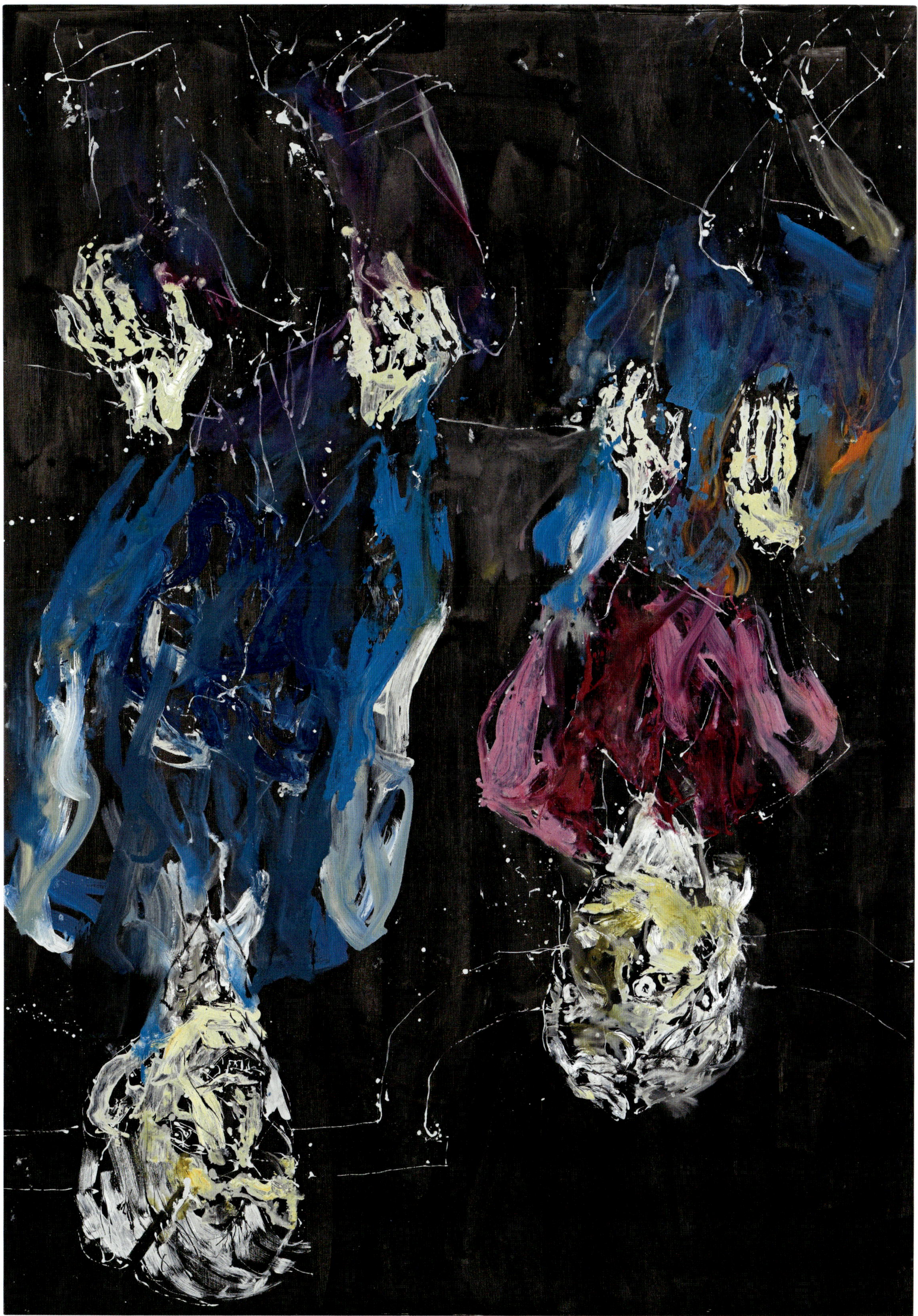

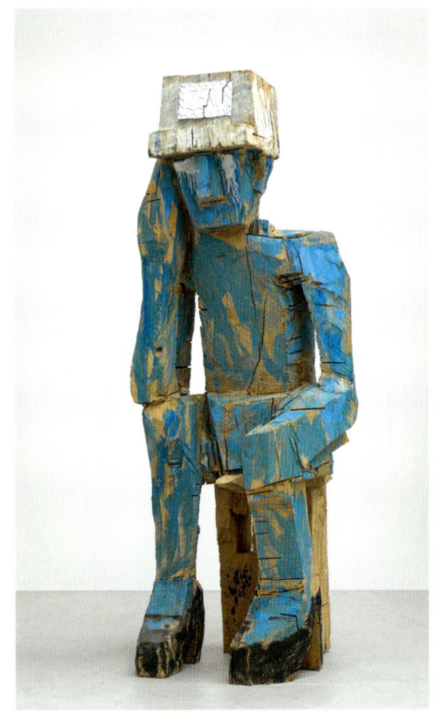

Georg Baselitz, *Volk Ding Zero—Folk Thing Zero*, 2009

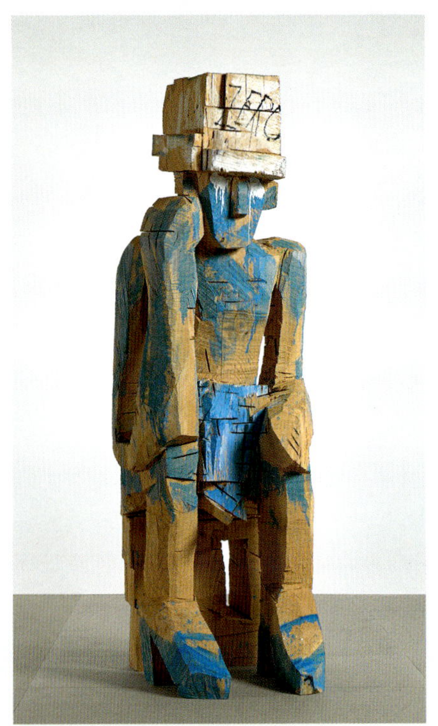

Georg Baselitz, *Dunklung Nachtung Amung Ding*, 2009

entirely obscure a torso that has been reduced to a vertical axis, from which two arms emerge, raised up in a gesture that recalls a pirouette triumphing over gravity. These four superimposed circles emphasize the contrast between the top and the bottom of the body. In the wooden model, the circles were kept in place by copper wires that rejected any attempt at illusion and whose function was intriguing. The bronze sculpture, on the other hand, faithfully reveals the waist with its irregular planes—a form of simplification that associates a rough and heavy aspect with the complexity of an unprecedented structure. The title of the work seems like an ironic epithet, contradicting everything we know about the light and airy dances of the real Loïe Fuller as depicted in the many photographs, films, and works that highlighted the fantastical efflorescence of her performances. It is worth noting that these performances, which revived the art of the dance at the beginning of the last century, used technical means that were very far removed from the rough-hewn tree trunks favored by Baselitz. There is nothing left of the butterfly or the orchid that enchanted music hall spectators when the dancer's body melted into a swirl of artificial lights and veils. The poet Stéphane Mallarmé wrote of the "vertigo of a soul as if aired through an artifice."[6] No trace either, among countless examples, of the "Flying Lady" that decorated the front of one particularly famous brand of English automobiles. Likewise, we can discern no allusions to other famous dancers, such as Gustave Courbet's *La signora Adela Guerrero, danseuse espagnole* (*Signora Adela Guerrero, Spanish Dancer*; 1851) or Édouard Manet's *Lola de Valence* (1862), which recall the "pink and black" prestige of nineteenth-century Spain and a whole lineage of ballerinas that would seem entirely out of place here. The gauzy ideal of *Jugendstil* ("modern style"),

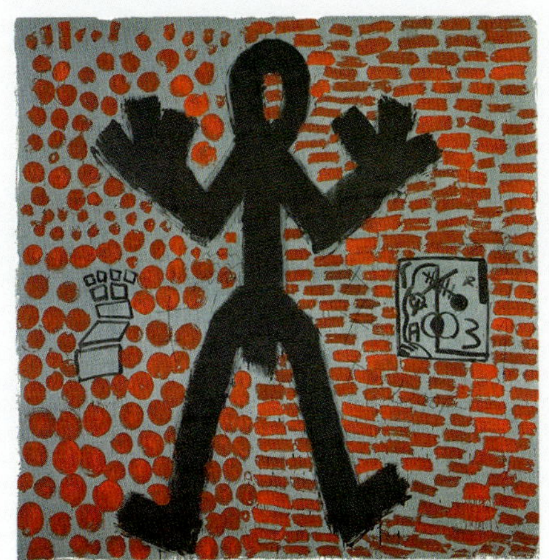

A. R. Penck, *Standart*, 1971

as embodied by René Lalique's figures, vases, and jewelry pieces evoke a time that has vanished as surely as the mammoths of our distant ancestors. Nevertheless, Baselitz's black sculpture cannot be reduced to something like the stick figure of A. R. Penck's *Standart*, despite a certain family resemblance conveyed via a relationship to the graphical sign or symbol. Rather than getting lost in a web of comparisons, we should perhaps return to the artist's oft-repeated definition of the ornament. Baselitz has always been highly interested in the use of rhythmical interlacing elements, as seen in gothic art and literature and most notably in cultures that prohibit the representation of bodily images, such as Islam. During the period when he produced the *Bildübereins* (*Picture Over One*) series (1991–95), and which was a time of important formal discoveries accompanied by theoretical texts, the painter expressed his interest for limitlessly expanding decorative forms: "I would like to develop an ornament, so to speak, that could be read with a figuration that would be embedded, integrated, incorporated inside."[7] In this regard, he speaks of abstract ornaments that more closely resemble arabesques, a shape that presents itself as a continuous ribbon, a form of writing that could give birth to a new image. Having taken the evanescence of the dancing body to its apex, *Louise Fuller* seems to introduce this higher form of abstraction. To use Mallarmé's terms once again, we might say that *Louise Fuller* "is not a dancing woman," "is not a woman," and "that she does not dance,"[8] because she is objectively a *thing*, a metaphor by which the sculpture enters into dialogue with a language that artists, from Edgar Degas to Robert Rauschenberg, have ceaselessly explored. Baselitz has given it the value of a sign: a hieratic sign whose relief asserts the primal expressiveness sought by Louise Fuller and others who were

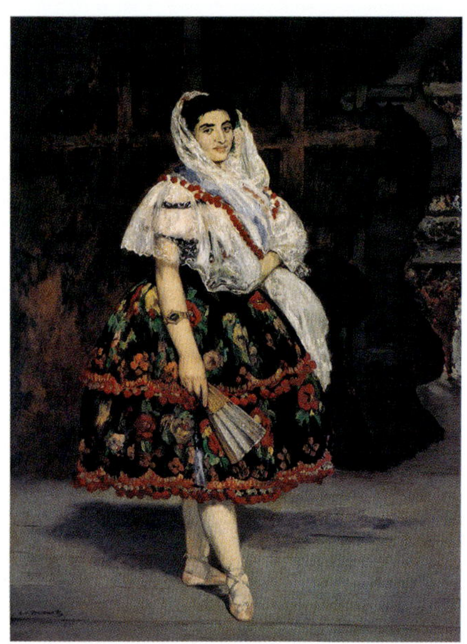

Édouard Manet, *Lola de Valence*, 1862

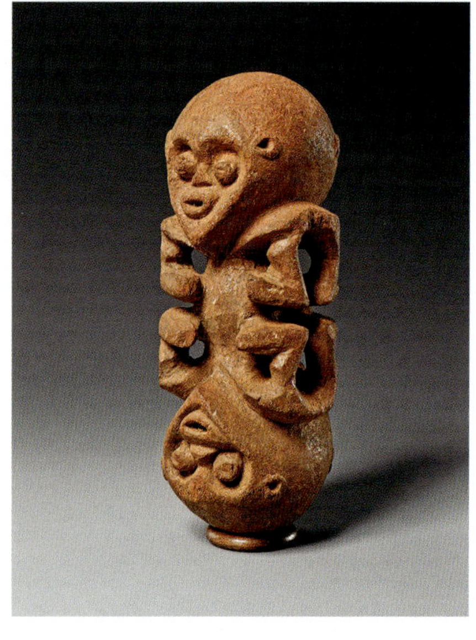

Two-headed Janus figure, *Mambila*, Nigeria–Cameroon border

inspired by her art—but with the aggressive character of a raw thing that recognizes no ancestors in its tradition. A sort of "sculpture" in his own style. Is a chainsaw not meant, after all, to cut out pieces?[9]

The sculpture was carved out of a single, one-hundred-year-old cedar trunk with a chainsaw. The rings that surround the sculpture's central body like a necklace also come from the original tree trunk, to whose circumference and measurements they allude. Photographs taken while the work was being created show the figure still ensconced in the wooden mass, where cross sections have begun to be cleared in order to produce the superimposed rings which would be, once separated from the "soul" of the tree trunk, artificially supported by copper wires. In the bronze version, we can see them lead all the way up to the dancer's arms, as if she had fingers to hold the wires and artificially play with them. Nevertheless, this work is not a variation on Olimpia, the automaton in *The Sandman*, the short story by E. T. A. Hoffmann, no more than she embodies another Coppélia or Salome. Beyond what the title suggests with relation to a particularly reference-laden story, especially for German art, Baselitz obviously conceived of his project by taking into account his materials. He created something whose physical source cannot be overlooked. Even more than with the circus horse of Éric Satie's ballet *Parade* and the tree of Charlie Chaplin's *Shoulder Arms*, the wood used here—from which the sculpture claims to free itself—acts in response to the improbable notion of an ornament that incorporates the human form. As published in the catalogue *Primitivism in 20th Century Art* by New York's Museum of Modern Art in 1987, after completing his work, Baselitz reached the conclusion that a Mambila sculpture from Cameroon seemed a more convincing analogy than any other.[10]

In this statuette, serrated discs are used to represent the body between the head and the base, shaped like a seat. The work was linked to certain sculptures by Constantin Brancusi; needless to say that the differences in design are great. Due to its autonomy with regard to design, *Louise Fuller* produces the maximum tension between a thing and an idea. She dances, so to speak, with a mental image and celebrates a body from which she frees herself with cutout segments that resemble the remains of another nature. The sculpture stands on a scene saturated with contradictory examples and, thanks to its difference, creates a void around itself.

For reasons that could be developed in an analysis of painting's "dark side," *Zero End* and *BDM Gruppe* (*BDM Group*; 2012, ill. p. 163) have been exhibited in the same room. Their soft black surfaces once again play an important role. Several versions of a recent series (2011–13) utilizing the eagle theme and modifying it until it practically disappears into the canvas's surface are linked to three paintings from 1992, two of which belong to the *Picture Over One* series. This series was conceived according to the principle of one painting being placed over another, thus reincarnating and varying an initial motif; in this case, the motif contained in 1965's *Die großen Freunde* (*The Great Friends*, ill. pp. 14–15), placed head to toe directly on the ground, a choice of method that fundamentally revived the concept of upside-down paintings. *Bilddreizehn* (*Picture Thirteen*; 1992, ill. pp. 50–51) and *Bildsechszehn* (*Picture Sixteen*; 1993, ill. p. 53) seem to extricate the

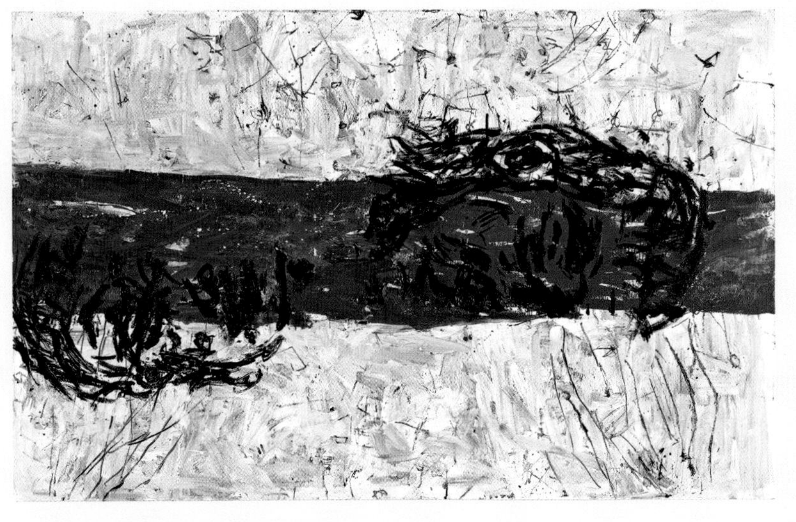

Georg Baselitz, *Picture Over One, 1991*

Sing Sang Zero, 2011

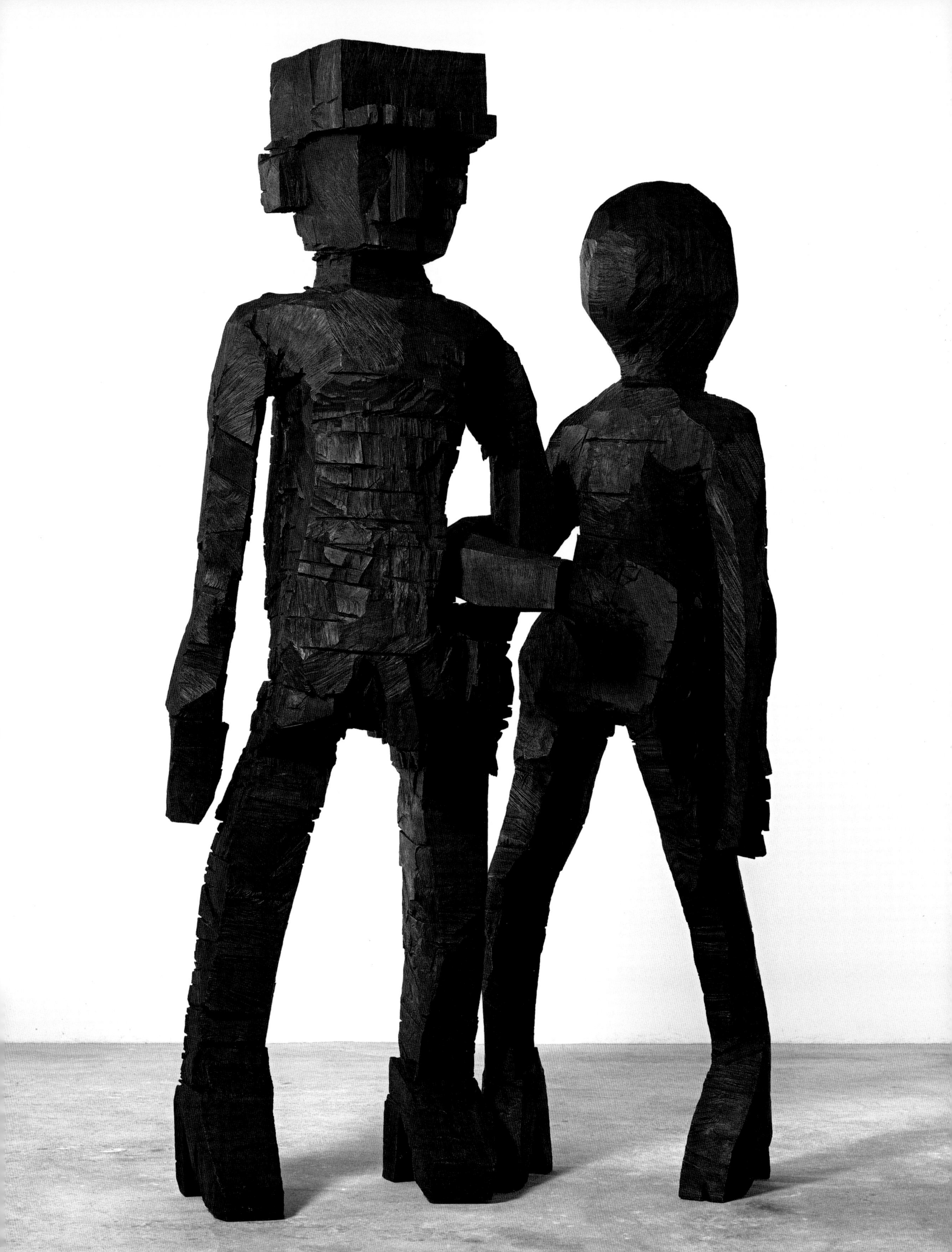

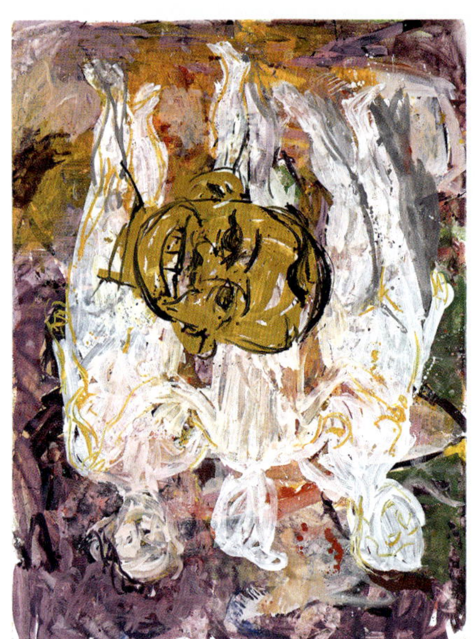

Georg Baselitz, *History as Background*, 1996

drawing from a dark background and multiply it. In order to obtain colored lines in the style of Matthias Grünewald—without really being able to see the whole motif—the artist pressed the paint tubes directly onto the canvas, to make the veins of his figures pop to the surface of the skin. On the contrary, *Dunkel age schwarzim* (*Dark Age Blackim*; 2012, ill. p. 184), *Da ben ar ufo* (*Op Ton*; 2013, ill. p. 193), *Zigfünfundreizehnneun* (*Tyfifethreteennine*; 2013, ill. p. 197), and a number of other canvases from the same series, whose more or less cryptic titles seem to trap viewers in a dense fog, combine form and content into one dark mass, riddled on its surface as in its depths with various impulsive strokes where the eye struggles to find what it constantly seeks: prosaically enough, something *to* see. The increasingly darker tones lead the viewer to the limits of the visible, a kind of visibility that is indefinitely saturated with indistinct presences, without nevertheless, managing to completely drown the motif in their obscurity.[11] It is possible to see here the beginnings of a connection with an inverted, two-headed sculpture such as *Zero End* boldly placed on the ground, as well as with a group that surged from the depths of the artist's memory: 1996's *Der Hintergrund Geschichte* (*History as Background*). In the latter work, the smiling face of a child—the artist when he was seven years old—reignites an irreducible disharmony.

BDM Group is not a title that was designed to leave viewers in the dark for too long, as it designates a group of three, clearly adolescent figures supposed to belong to the Bund Deutscher Mädel (BDM) during the Third Reich. The League of German Girls was the girls' wing of the Nazi Party's youth movement, the Hitler Youth. Since 1936, the League had welcomed girls between the ages of fourteen and eighteen to participate in a variety of activities, including

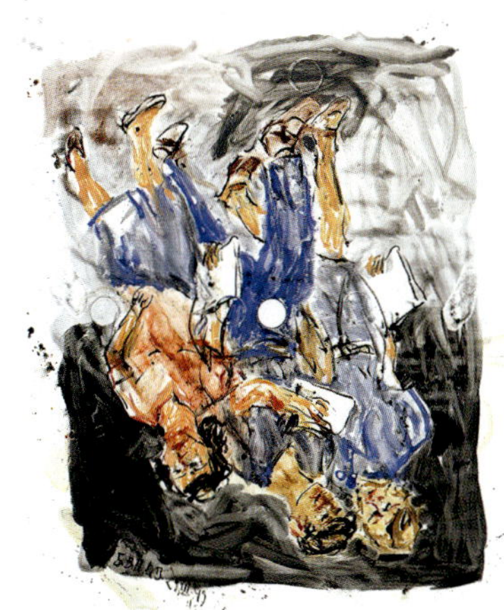

Georg Baselitz, *La Faculté ouvrière en marche (Boris Johanson, 1928)*, 1999

gymnastics, sports, hiking, folk dancing, and other pastimes that would exalt the cult of the *Führer* and encourage the principles of the Nazi Party. Propaganda pictures, films, and posters would invariably show the smiling face of a young blonde woman, healthy and happy, draped in a predominantly white uniform. "Be Faithful, Be Pure, Be German!" was the motto of this hierarchical organization, in which enrollment became mandatory on the eve of the war. Born in 1938 to a village schoolteacher, Hans Georg Kern was, likely despite his and his parents' desire, not old enough to participate in the Hitler Youth, the organization that brought together boys between ten and fourteen years old, commonly called "Pimpfe." In 1945, while Kern witnessed the collapse of his country over endless days, he recorded experiences that he would later use in his art. At different moments throughout his career, Baselitz gave shape to this living past, that he could only reach by thwarting the mechanisms of his conscience, its clichés, its taboos, and its shortcomings. Baselitz is in no way an illustrator of memories. At the price of radical decisions, his living memory enters into a relationship with ideas and information that transform it into a powerful means of formal invention. We have seen this in recent years, especially after the fall of the Berlin Wall, with *Dresdner Frauen* (*Women of Dresden*), *Familienbilder* (*Family Pictures*), and the series *Between Eagles and Pioneers*. If we were to take this question on its own merit, we would have to go back further in time, to the artist's adolescence and childhood even. The discovery of art and of the lived past, whose surprising dimension was revealed in a 2013 exhibition in Dresden titled *Hintergrundgeschichten* (*Background Stories*), here produces a new encounter where heterogeneous elements

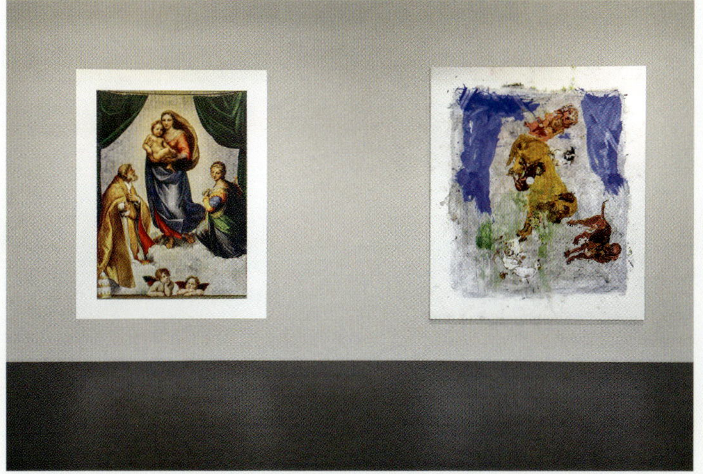

Installation view, *Georg Baselitz— Background Stories*, Staatliche Kunstsammlung Dresden, Royal Palace, 2013

BDM Group, 2012

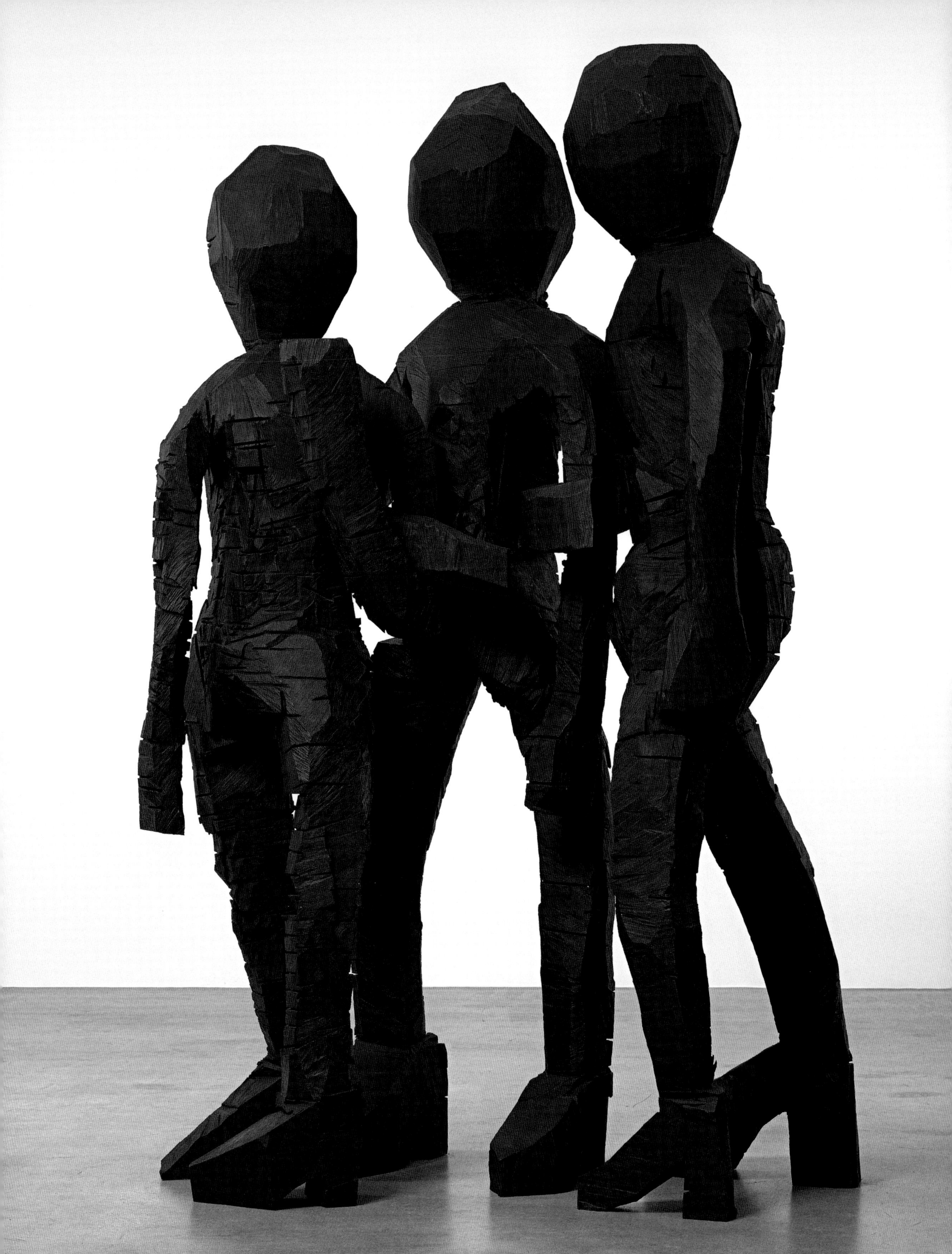

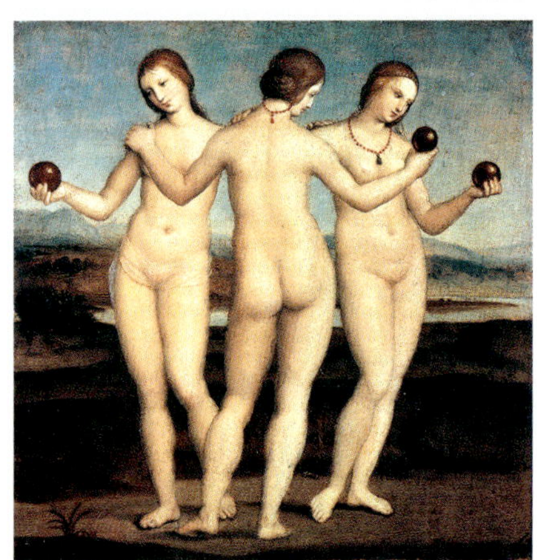

**Raphael, *The Three Graces*,
ca, 1503–05**

violently collide.[12] The theme of The Three Graces that spontaneously comes to mind, associated with its famous precedents in Raphael or Canova, is immediately contradicted by a conception of beauty that is very distant from the eroticism handed down to us by the Greeks. The harshness of the basic wood shapes, to which a bronze patina adds a sort of filter designed to endure for centuries, completely clashes with the marble ideal of the Neoclassical tradition which became, after 1933, the official style of Hitler's regime. Moreover, the black figures have little in common from with the white uniforms of the League of German Girls, as seen on films shot for special occasions. As far as we know, high-heeled shoes were also not part of their daily outfit. The sculpture nevertheless manages to convey a collective identity, with its blind, faceless heads, similar to wooden pins, while the bodies, legs, and arms do not entirely suppress what doubtless triggered this childhood memory: the prestige, the beauty, the radiance of order as embodied by the artist's family life in the village of Deutschbaselitz, when local boys and girls would parade on Sundays, arm in arm, as was common in the countryside.[13] The sculpture cannot be separated from its title and the memories that go with it, in so far as the bronze allows the woodwork to shine through, giving the lie to the totalitarian aesthetics of the Third Reich, whose favorite sculpture themes included heroic nudity, paganizing subjects like the Judgment of Paris, and the racist exaltation of physical "beauty," in particular that of the Aryan woman. Despite this, the black sculpture preserves the mark of the past by creating a rhythm of arms linked together, transforming the group of three young women into three charming comrades. If history must appear in this story, then "das Unheimliche,"

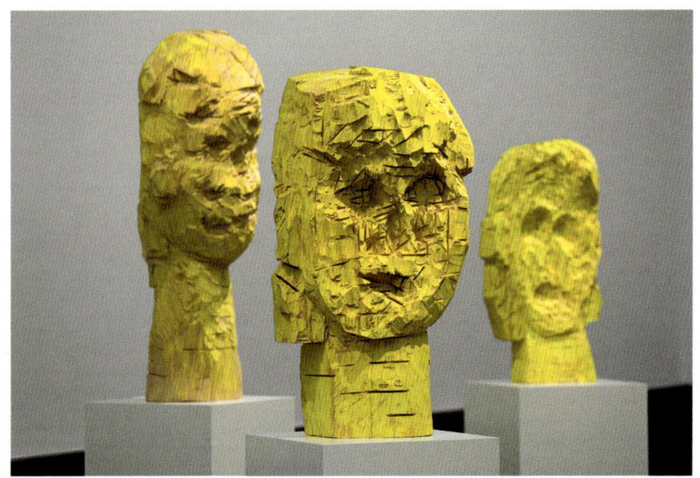

**Georg Baselitz, *Women of Dresden*,
1989–90**

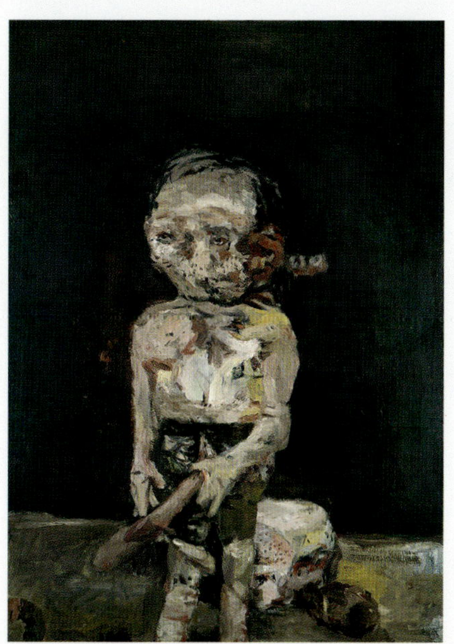

Georg Baselitz, *The Big Night Down the Drain*, 1962–63

the uncanny, imposes itself. This romantic notion par excellence was awkwardly translated into French by Jacques Lacan in 1959 with the neologism "extimité," the antonym of intimacy, as if the Fates in high heels had come to embody, on behalf of the Graces, a new, specifically German, role. The black surface does not hide a clear, bright side, which becomes even more dramatic and serious. It incorporates it completely to the point of making it disappear. At the most, the black coating allows us to glimpse what the trial of art represents so that the living past can impose itself, giving life before reason comes once again to order one's memories, sensations and emotions for outside interpretation. But this dimension of lucidity which fatally establishes itself should not lead us to ignore the presence of a dark source, whose troubling existence is revealed by these figures. They delve deep into the past to bring to light a reality that no analysis will be able to reduce. The black surface simply makes visible what is invisible to our eyes. It highlights a need for readability regarding these carefree figures, content freely existing before our eyes and fully conscious of the title that has been bestowed upon them. Their truth is not that of Herculaneum, but by a number of oblique paths they nevertheless grow closer to it.

The eagle is one of the most frequent motifs in Baselitz's paintings. In addition, it is probably the motif which, along with the early image of the upside-down tree, has most significantly expanded the scope of the artist's decision taken in 1969, following Marcel Broodthaers's establishment in 1968 in Brussels of his *Musée d'Art moderne (section XIXe siècle) Département des Aigles* (*Museum of Modern Art [19th Century Section] Department of Eagles*). In 1972, the author of *Die große Nacht im Eimer* (*The Big Night Down the Drain*) painted with his fingers

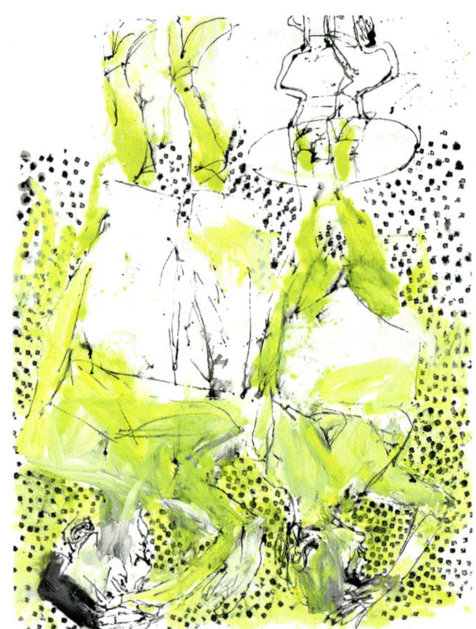

Georg Baselitz, *Prepared Late Time*, 2010

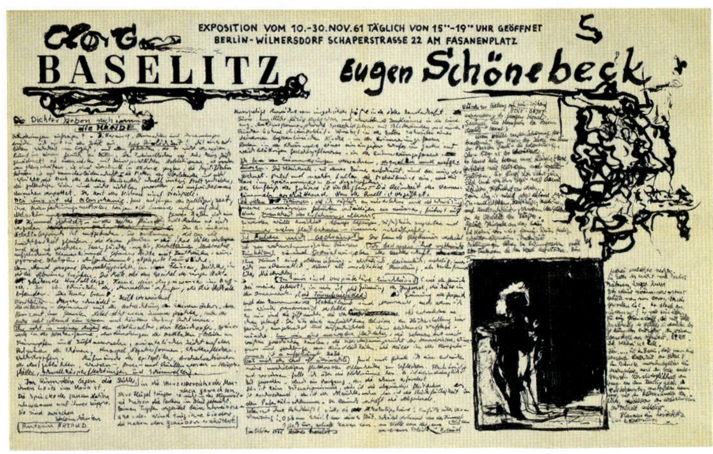

Poster, *Georg Baselitz and Eugen Schönebeck, First Pandemonic Manifesto* [1st version], 1961

a canvas that appeared to be free of the "majestic representation of art," whose persistent contemporary resurgences he avoided like the plague. The paintings from 2013, after those from 1979–80, bury forms in an ordeal that leads the eye to the edge of darkness, revealing the landscape of a world that is ignored by the full light of color. The painter is certainly a great admirer of the landscapes composed by Caspar David Friedrich, Johan Christian Dahl, Carl Blechen, Philipp Otto Runge, and Ludwig Richter, among others, but his intention was not to paint a nocturnal landscape. He wanted to re-envision the idea of the visible disappearing, replaced instead with a theme that has prompted numerous inventions in the history of art: anamorphosis, the grotesque, reconstructed heads, collages, the exquisite corpse, et cetera. By disconnecting words and letters, Baselitz instead used for his titles the graphical, phonetic and combinatory poetics of Kurt Schwitters, Hans Arp, Marcel Broodthaers, and the like to move towards a commentary that endlessly expands the scope of the question rather than answering it. We can try our best to decipher them—*Dunkel age schwarzim* / *Dunkel schwarz image* (*Dark Age Blackim*), *Da ben ar ufo* / oben darauf (*Op Ton*), *Zigfünfundreizehnneun* / *Neunzehndreiundfünfzig* (*Tyfifethreteennine*), *Heiteldunk* / *Dunkelheit* (*Nessdark*), *Flunkler Deck* / Dunkler Fleck (*Spark Dot*)—we will never get anywhere. An inflexible will evades anything that could resemble a definitive and stable state, established in a relationship of forms that is as constricting as that of common language. An irresistible spirit of rebellion reveals a range of possibilities that could be

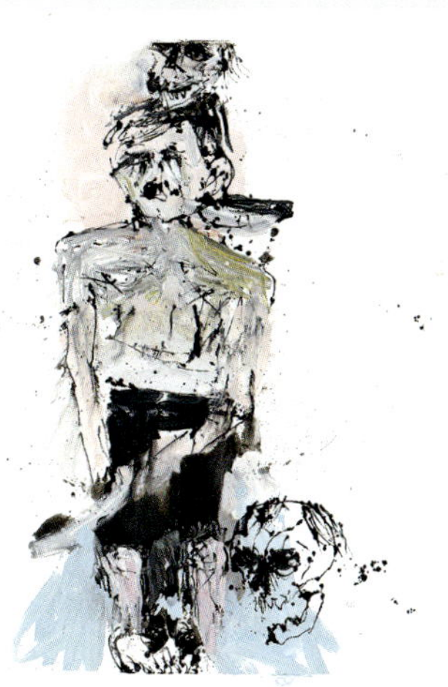

Georg Baselitz, *The Big Night from Back Then (Remix)*, 2008

compared to those available in music. But this passionate inebriation remains obstinately if dispassionately attached to its prey, painting, rejecting in a manner that is equally abrupt and ferocious the nighttime melody of the famous poem by Goethe, often set to music (in particular by Wolfgang Rihm): "Dämmrung senkte sich von oben" ("Twilight from Above Has Fallen"). The final words of this song become, for the needs of a canvas, *Ich esse stenk (Heast in Fall)* which is designed to discourage even the best of intentions. In the flux that seems to irreversibly carry away the cast-offs of old humanist interpretation, *Niemandsland* (*No Man's Land*; 2011–13, ill. pp. 188–89) arrives, against all expectations, to remind us of what the visible signifies, there where the consciousness of horror begins. Using a different format but also thanks to its intensity, through which miniscule traces of white pierce, the canvas alludes to the one Asger Jorn was still working on in 1972 on the eve of his death: *Stalingrad, le non-lieu ou le fou rire du courage* (*Stalingrad, The Non-Place, or the Mad Laugh of Courage*). Here again a savage conviction is fighting against the pathos of history, a conviction that is explained without being able to be represented. Unless it is forgotten under a layer of paint that takes a whole life to be reborn elsewhere, differently. The bronze sculpture *BDM Group* does not seek to represent the dimensions of a subject like *Stalingrad* or *Guernica*, but it also signifies, like *Women of Dresden*, the "no man's land" of memory—which we could also call the time regained of art.

Zero End comes after *Yellow Song* (2013, ill. p. 169) and *Marokkaner* (*Moroccan*; 2012). Even if the sculpture is not without similarities to some of the aforementioned works, for example because of the motif of the detached rings, it remains significantly different. The ornamental nature of the form relies

Yellow Song, 2013

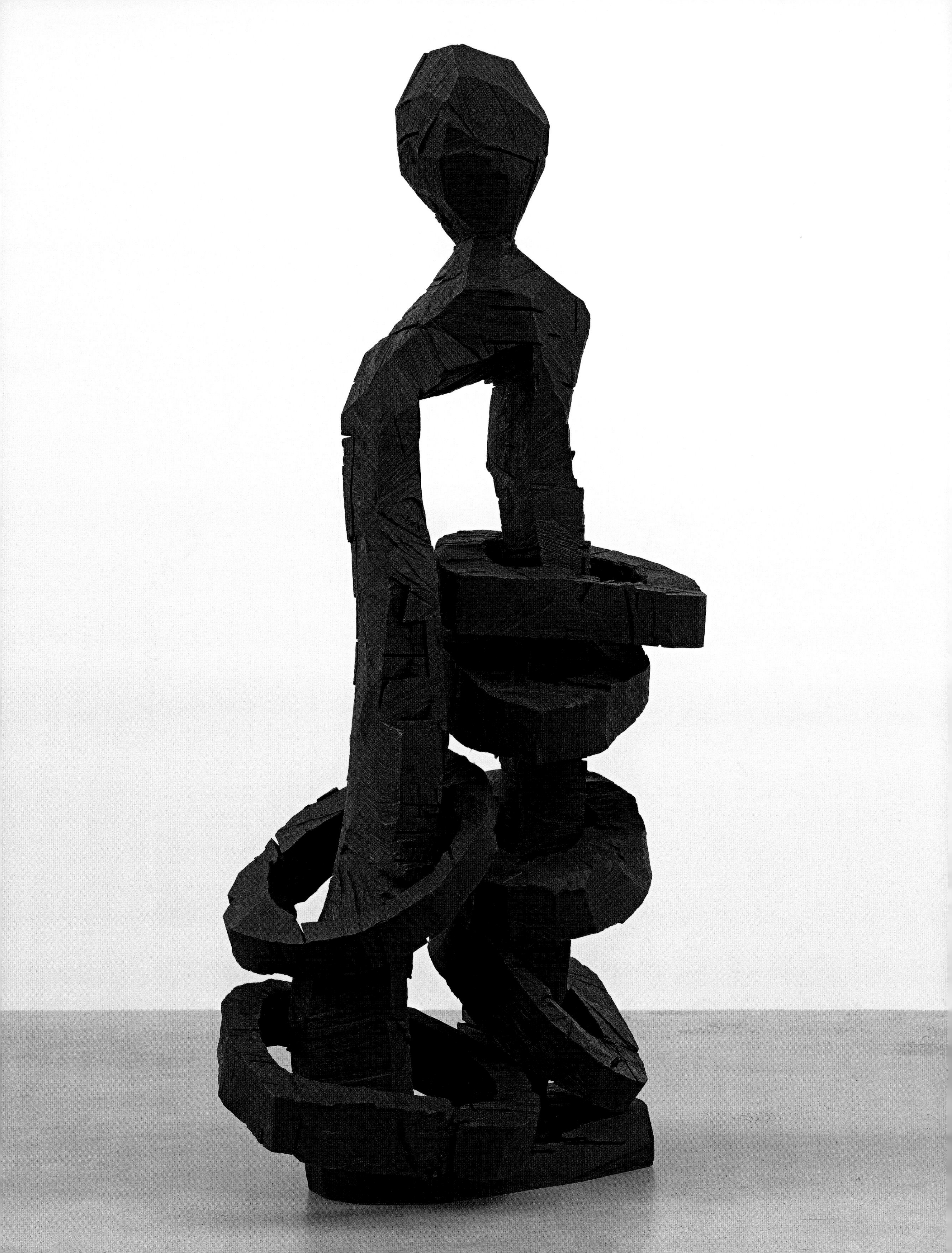

less on symmetry rather than on the reciprocal nature of two skulls, connected by a common trunk surrounded by an odd number of rings, which emphasize a voluntary asymmetry between the left and right sides of the sculpture. To take a particularly inappropriate example, Benvenuto Cellini's famous *Saliera* (*Salt Cellar*), which is conserved in Vienna, is a gold table sculpture that presents two complementary Roman deities, Cybele and Neptune, the earth and the sea. The female side and the male side of *Zero End* are more difficult to identify—or much more interchangeable—but perhaps they justify, without the help of any mythology, the idea of a division that is also complementary, analogues to the programmatic motif contained in the *Picture Over One*. The unity of the sculpture thus obtained, we are reminded of the tradition of recumbent statues, though we can of course immediately notice an obvious formal difference. In the 1965 painting *The Great Friends*, the two figures have an androgynous appearance that prevents us from embarking on a simplistic biographical interpretation. They

likewise recall the required duality that runs throughout the *Pandemonic Manifestos*. Baselitz's inventiveness is even more evident here, as the skull motif has, since antiquity, been one of the most common elements of funerary sculpture and still lifes. Today as yesterday its meaning is evident, even if we don't fully know what such evidence conceals. The painter used it moving towards greater readability in his 2008 *Remixes*, based on his 1963 paintings. But he also turned to it in a more cryptic manner in

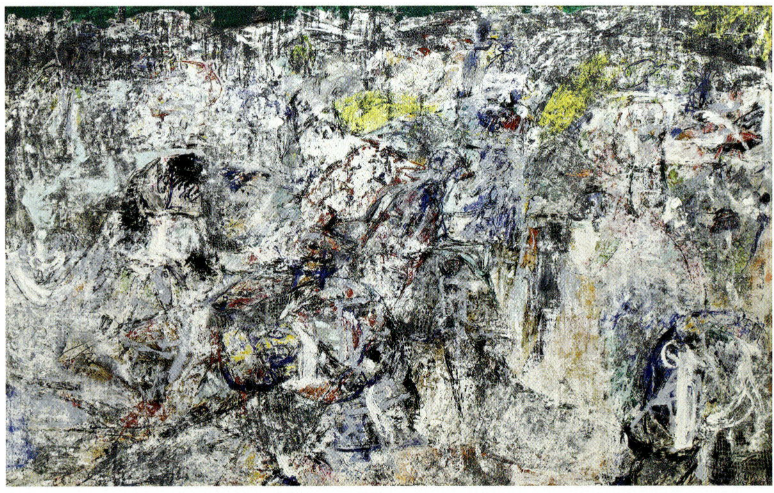

Asger Jorn, *Stalingrad, the Non-Place, or the Mad Laugh of Courage…*, 1957–60, 1967, 1972

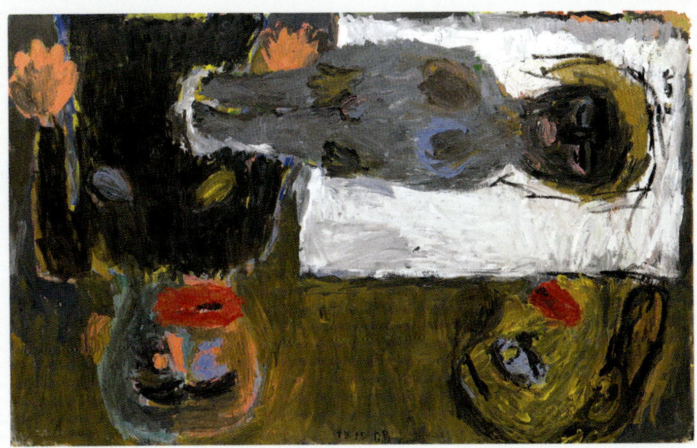

Georg Baselitz, *The Night*, 1985

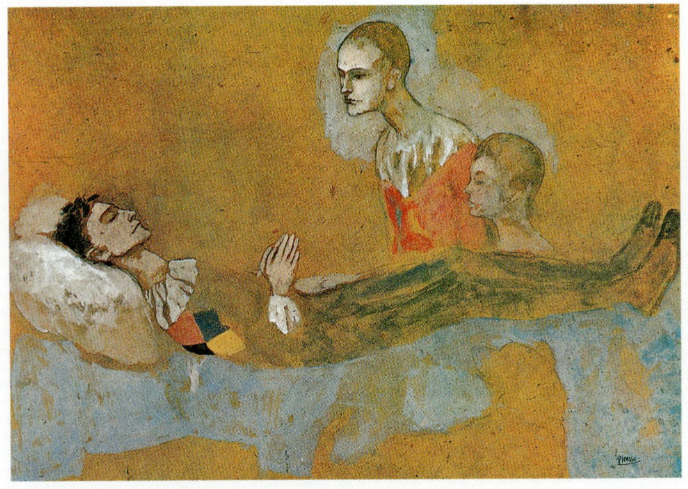

Pablo Picasso, *Death of Harlequin*, 1906

the extraordinary *Schwester* series (*Sister*; 1992–93), which combined black and white profiles with the Tachist signature of death. In 1989, we can also see in some drawings the same motif alternately flipped upside down and right side up like a playing card. Regardless, after having completed his piece, the sculptor was struck by the similarities with another stone Mambila statuette, this one from his personal collection, which had two antithetical faces positioned at its two extremities.[14] Of course, *Zero End* possesses neither the same dimensions nor the same history. If we wished to compare it with *Death of Harlequin* as depicted by Pablo Picasso, we would see that nothing remains of the Christian pietà. The sculpture rests on the floor with its main face turned towards us at ninety degrees. Obviously, we cannot reductively compare the sculpture to an amulet, nor can we consider it as a monument. Rather, should we not view it as a detached thing, which has left behind the symbolic order of vanity for a formal autonomy with no beginning nor end? The confrontation with the lived past only emerges stronger. What produced the fragmented intensity of *BDM Group* here pays witness to a more complete story that we do not know. A story that repeats itself and begins anew, which divides and unites because it remains unintelligible. More unintelligible perhaps than what Chronos and the skeleton holding

Louise Fuller, 2013

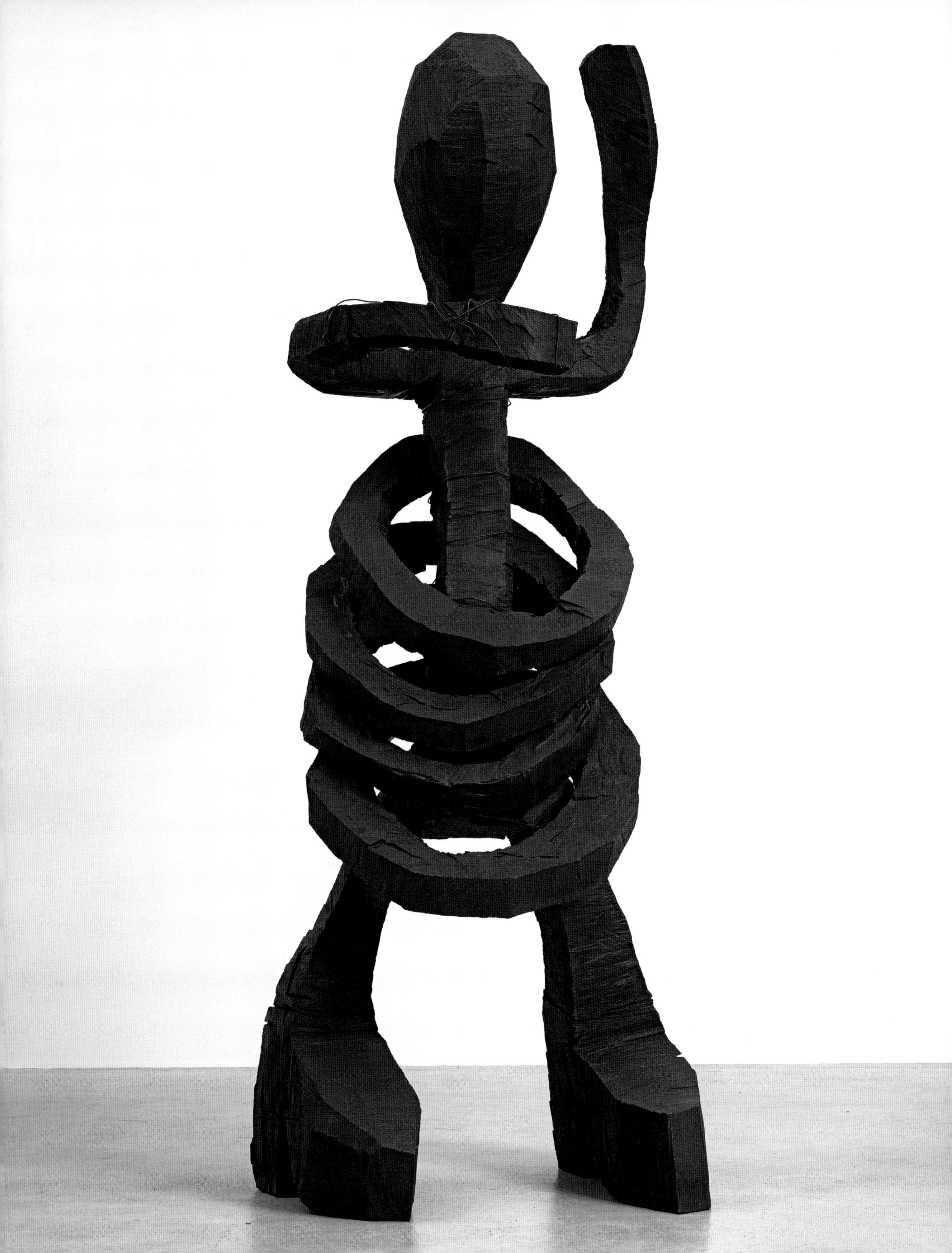

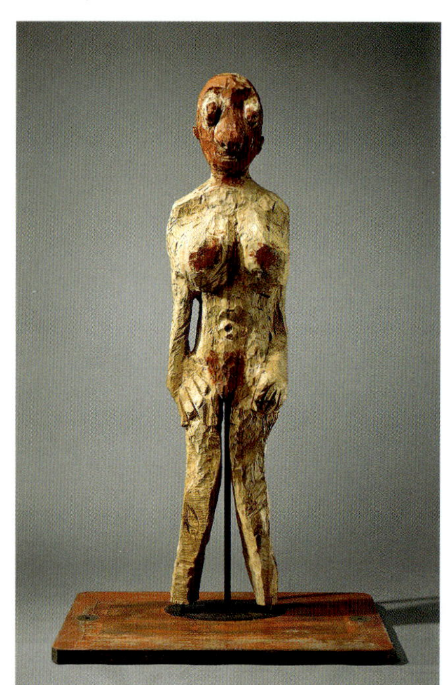

Georg Baselitz, *Greetings from Oslo*, 1986

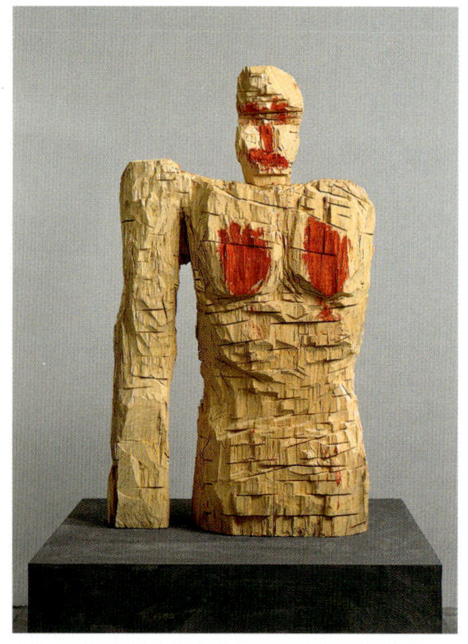

Georg Baselitz, *Mrs. Paganism*, 1984

the hourglass express, but also clearer thanks to what this story illustrates, what has been stripped bare and produced by the blind union of a life with art. No one would dream of saying that it is about the nothingness, although it is about what has tried to banish it since the dawn of time. It is not necessary to believe in spirits to understand it, but for a sculpture from another world, a spirit is needed. "Like an interlocutor for a connection," as the artist said in 1985.[15]

For Baselitz, sculpture has always been a more direct means of expression than painting. This was the case with *Gruss aus Oslo* (*Greetings from Oslo*; 1986) during the time of *Die Nacht* (*The Night*; 1985) or even with *Frau Paganismus* (*Mrs. Paganism*; 1994) during the time of the *Picture Over One*. This was again true for the *Black Sculptures* in relation to sets as contrasting as the *Black Paintings* from 2013 and the bold-colored canvases from 2011, elaborated based on drawings dating back to the period of the *Fracture Paintings* between 1966 and 1969.[16] Although the sculptor seeks to express something more directly, this does not mean that he wishes to simplify what he has to say. On the contrary, he believes that the artist should always follow multiple paths, produce several things, create the possibility of many connections, and change radical approaches with the same stubbornness, the same "obsession," in order to obtain something extreme that only sculpture will possibly be able to make simple, brutal, primitive. The black patina gives this energy a radiance that originates from the artist's past, rediscovered since 2005 and the *Remix* series. He discovers it thanks to an intelligence that he says he now wields more easily, without the mental blocks or scruples of youth. Not to envision aspects that would have been overlooked or concealed, but to obtain a new form of evidence. The evidence of an equivalence

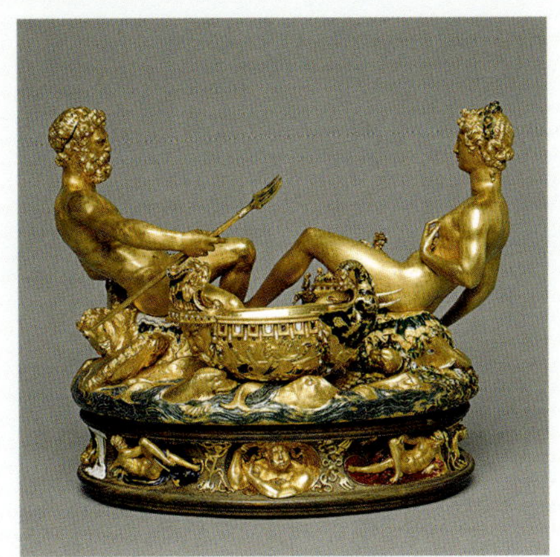

Benvenuto Cellini, *Salt Cellar (Saliera),* **1540–43**

with the work that he discovers archeologically. Doing so, he persists in a struggle begun in the East against everything that signifies the repression of art, everything that limits or destroys it. Even before he moved to sculpture, Baselitz had experienced the negation of art, from which he managed to extricate himself by performing a sort of backwards leap, finding in Ferdinand von Rayski a figure that was compatible with what he believed to be true. He has never been able to see himself as a modern painter, nor has he wished to. Even more so with sculpture, he has never felt comfortable with a tradition that stems from Michelangelo, passes through Auguste Rodin and culminates with Richard Serra. For Baselitz, African sculpture was an important alternative, not so he could imitate its methods like Pablo Picasso, Ernst Ludwig Kirchner or Karl Schmidt-Rottluff, but so he could have access to a high culture that did not consider form as the mere sum of its results. Today the situation is not at all the same, the painter possesses a vocabulary and does what he wants to do with an apparent ease that should not fool us. This facility translates a tireless reflection on what art is not, and on the contrary, what art is when we see it and we do not know what it is we are seeing. Baselitz's goal is to make things visible while painting on the ground, now on a white canvas, all the while knowing that it is impossible to reject visible forms. Such is the abstraction that allows him to obtain what he wants.

His recent *Black Sculptures* stem from an understanding that allowed the painter, after many years, to enter into dialogue with the celebrated painters of the pop art movement: Andy Warhol, Robert Rauschenberg, and then Willem de Kooning and Jackson Pollock who he discovered in Berlin in 1958, and now with Asger Jorn and the artists of the London School, Lucian Freud and Frank

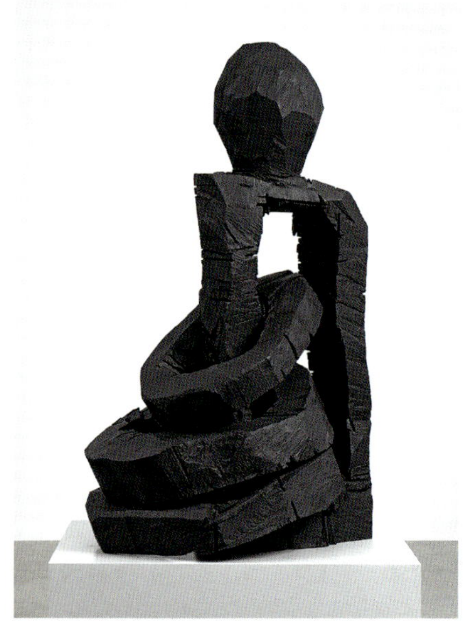

Hans Arp, *Cloud Shepherd* , 1953

Georg Baselitz, *Moroccan*, 2012

Auerbach. He began this dialogue by opening secret doors, by disturbing pre-conceived categories and ideas, but never by imitating or assimilating this group's ideas. "Intelligence" is the more or less ironic name that Baselitz gives to his absolute independence with regard to decision-making, denying the reign of objective reason in the art world. Most often, this takes the shape of a schematic form of classification or historical interpretation that he chooses to joyfully mock, refute, or demolish. This intelligence is not devoid of tricks and amusement, of complicity with its opponent and of the vital need for joyful, fraternal foolishness. It is the developed form of a dialogue began very early with individualities that helped to shape him, and that he has also sometimes helped us to rediscover. But with experience, it has become a fantastical means to invent another story. A story rediscovered in leaps and bounds, via its surprises and its depths. Hans Arp was the sculptor that opened the path for Baselitz towards an abstraction that was freed from geometry and its systems. Thanks to a title that evokes the final works of the *Cloud Shepherd, Yellow Song* can be seen as a kind of homage to an artist that knew how to attack from behind the doctrinaire mentality of his time:

"The man who wants to shoot a cloud down with an arrow will exhaust all his arrows in vain. Many sculptors are such strange hunters. What you have to do is fiddle something on a drum or drum something on a fiddle. Before long the cloud will descend, roll about on the ground in happiness, and at last complacently turn to stone. Thus with a wave of the hands the sculptor will realize the finest of statues."[17]

Less deliberately pedestrian than *Louise Fuller, Yellow Song* frees itself from opacity, of which only slices remain, falling down directly from the arms. The figure is but the instrument of an operation, which inherently produces an unveiling allowing a strange collar to uncoil towards the floor. The head that dominates this bizarre corkscrew embodies a principle of austerity that establishes itself as an internal rhythm. A song suffices to make us forget the crutch of naturalism; for once, everything seems to be supported by a secret union that requires neither shoes nor feet. "What I do," the artist declared in 1983, "is a kind of figuration, but I have no idea what it could be if there was no more figuration. And yet this figuration is independent of control or a connection with a real example or fact."[18] This still circles around the idea of the positive and the negative. The poorly squared-off rings are part of a minimalist figuration that does not result from an analytical process, but instead transforms the sculptor's aggressive act into a metaphor for what persists and resists a sensed, but unknown, idea. No more than the rings of smoke produced by a cigar can these circles shaped like messages tell us the nature of a thought. They speak another language that communicates with what must sing in a sculpture. "A great artist of the Stone Age knew how to conduct the thousands of voices that sang in him; he drew with his eyes turned inward." Thus spoke Hans Arp, the poet of *Opus Null* who said "Ich bin der Grosse Derdiedas."[19] A stone age as good as any other.

Recently, Baselitz has borrowed from the futurists their ardent rejection of the past and inverted it. From their hatred of "passatismo," he has forged the vengeful motto: "Avanti passato."[20] "Everything that is behind the painter is also ahead of him," Baselitz wrote in 1985 in his manifesto "Das Rüstzeug der Maler"

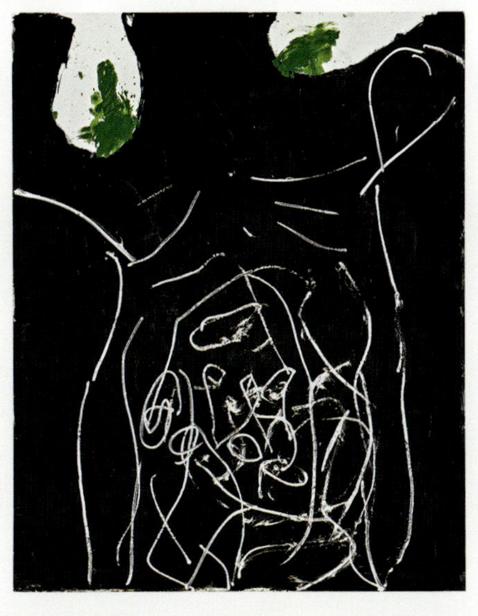

Georg Baselitz, *Sister Henri*, 1992–93

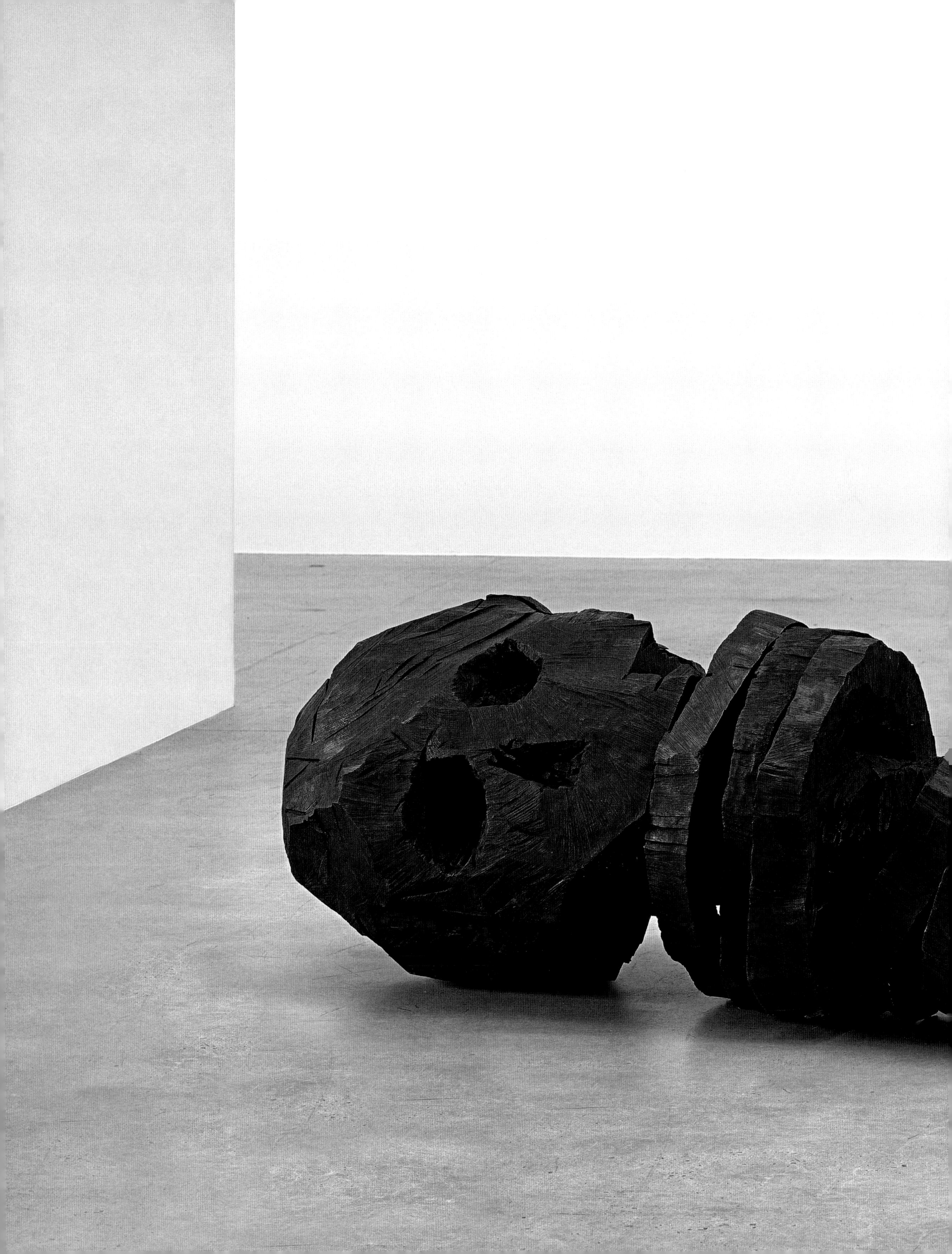

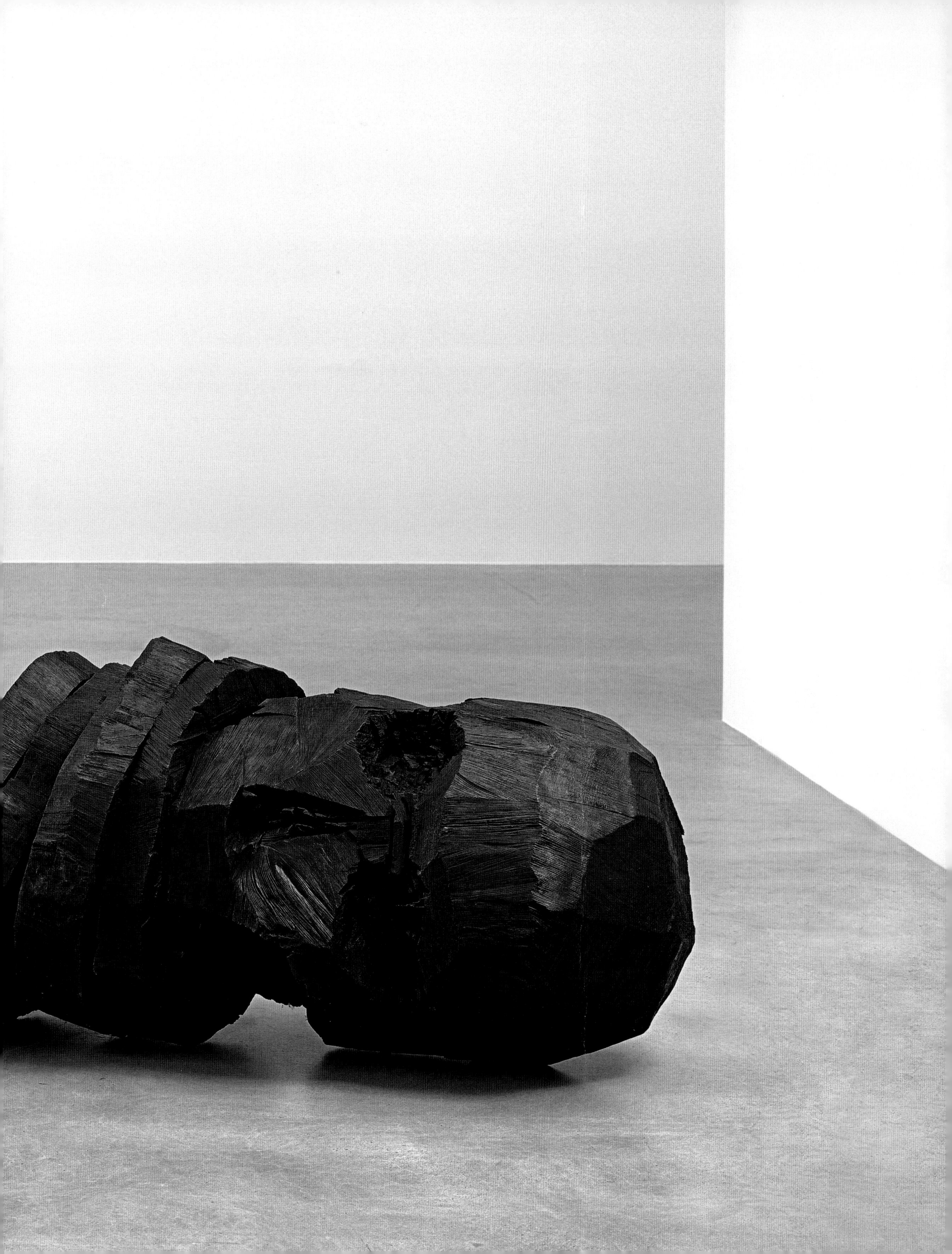

("The Painter's Equipment"). And if in 2006 he spoke of "looking forwards and backwards," he now adds that this is "not two steps forward and one step back, but three steps back and you are forward."[21] The past we are dealing with today is not the one that we believe it to be. It has been wrenched from its state as a compatible and presentable past to be brutally propelled forward. It has been pushed outside by a freshness in painting that is more provocative than ever. The figures of Marcel Duchamp and Piet Mondrian were its happy victims. In an iconoclastic fashion, the idea that any system of thought (and even the socialist realism of the *Russian Pictures* was a system of thought) could control history has been systematically undermined. Rrose Sélavy was taken at his word by painting, which treated him as an incorrigible rascal and the rotation of the Nazi swastika introduces itself into the abstraction of neoplasticism. From this resulted marvelously risky and audacious paintings, impatient to forge new paths by destroying the fetishes of a history that has been reduced to an explanation. The artist felt the need to say it: he is not a painter of history. He does not claim any consensus. He is nothing more than a German painter, and he has become this even more resolutely as his memory has become a force that relentlessly impels him. In these conditions, the past is something whose streaks, bumps, dark patches, relics, contradictions, and conflicts the *Black Sculptures* reveal. They evoke a presence as enigmatic as that produced by the *Braak Bog Figures,* an invention as different as African tribal art, a life beyond the grave that is as unpredictable as that of folk art. *Sing Sang Zero, Zero End*, and *BDM Group* are relevant to this biography of work that painting has for a number of years now struggled to develop in depth, so that the presence of a single work, an obstinately recaptured totality could unexpectedly

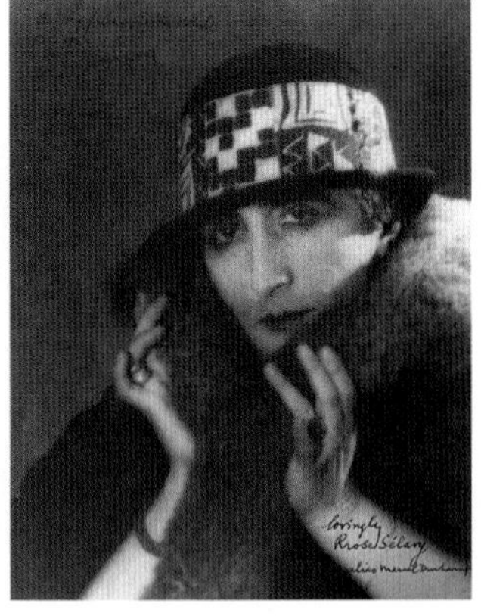

Marcel Duchamp,
Rrose Sélavy, 1921

emerge. Sometimes, as with *In London nicht, In Manchester Wadi Halfa* (*Not in London, in Manchester, Wadi Halfa*; 2011, ill. p. 137), or *Die Flügelhornistin Gracie Irlam* (*The Flugelhornist Gracie Irlam*; 2012, ill. p. 127), a direct allusion allows us to reflect on the full scope of the obsession engendered by a memory of destruction that imposes itself with the remix of the figures from *Neue Typ* (*The New Type*). In *The Emigrants*, in 1992, W. G. Sebald wrote about the fate of the painter Frank Auerbach in his graphite studio. Baselitz, as he had already done with Otto Dix, combines a world that has disappeared with another one, so as to establish the nostalgia and suffering that lives inside of him, the terrible *vivace* of his "avanti." The same goes for Asger Jorn compared with de Kooning, and for de Kooning compared to him. Separation and absence force the painter to find new avenues for reminiscence, which the silence of sculpture makes all the more visible. More visible thanks to an ornamental character, which transforms the rhythm of the figures that are disintegrating before our very eyes while sparing the essentials. Their size, their equilibrium, and their discordance between worlds that collide and contradict each other within them: folk art, African art, modern art, et cetera. The expression suggested by the artist in the sardonic English of connoisseurship, "German Tribal Art,"[22] is without a doubt the one that best embodies this challenging situation to tell a story, begun in Saxony, that is ceaselessly revisited and resumed. Georg Baselitz is certainly the artist who has moved the furthest away from the decorative motifs favored by Henri Matisse. His figures do not come from a universe of purity and innocence, like the master of the paper cutout dreamed of in Nice. In fact, his figures come from precisely the opposite realm. But all of a sudden he finds that black sculptures allow him to see the black and

Sacred figures from the Aukamper Bog near Braak, Ostholstein, ca. 500–400 B.C.

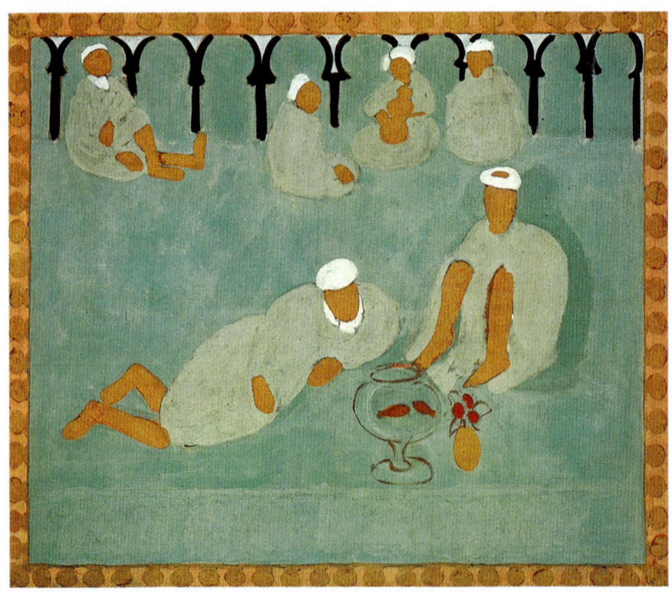

Henri Matisse, *Arab Coffeehouse*, 1911–13

white drawings of the Vence Chapel in a new manner, as if the ornament wielded a specific power over figuration, regardless of its nature. Everything seems to be carried further away by a single, powerful arabesque. By an Orient for which both artists felt a great attraction, due to a figuration tradition that was liberated from the weight of academicism. *Moroccan* is not a Moroccan who has traveled from Matisse's *Café arabe* (*Arab Coffeehouse*) in Tangier. It is a black sculpture like the others, and it once again calls upon a revelation that is nearby without ever becoming less foreign to itself. This sculpture is smaller than *Yellow Song* and appears to be placed on the ground like a Muslim might sit on his prayer rug. Finding exoticism in the work would probably be a mistake, but as always it requires very little to be transported. The wooden models for both of these sculptures were completed and painted yellow. Nothing was lost of a new image that a black patina invites us to sense below the impenetrable workings of form.

Special thanks to Julia Westner and Detlev Gretenkort for their invaluable help.

1 "Georg Baselitz in Conversation with Florian Illies" [2006], in *Georg Baselitz: Collected Writings and Interviews*, ed. Detlev Gretenkort (London: Ridinghouse, 2010), 282. Original citation: "Füsse sind meine Erdung, mir ist die Erdung wichtiger als die Sendung. Das Empfangen über Erdung funktioniert bei mir viel besser als über Antenne."
2 Georg Baselitz, letter to the author, May 5, 2014. "Ich liebe es das Gegenteil zu sagen, zu denken, zu machen."
3 "An Interview with Georg Baselitz by Jean-Louis Froment and Jean-Marc Poinsot" [1983] in *Georg*

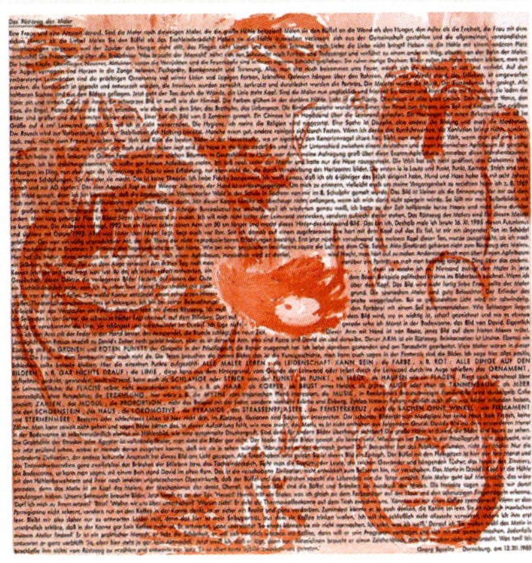

Georg Baselitz, *The Painter's Equipment*, 1985

Baselitz: Sculptures and Early Woodcuts (London: D'Offray, 1987), n. p. [15]. "Everything I do, and everything I think has just one purpose: to enable me to paint a picture. There is no other reason."

4 "Georg Baselitz in Conversation with Heinz-Peter Schwerfel" [1988], in *Georg Baselitz: Collected Writings and Interviews*, ed. Detlev Gretenkort (London: Ridinghouse, 2010), 196. Original citation: "Die wesentlichen Skulpturen sind, so glaube ich, noch nicht gemacht."

5 "Georg Baselitz in Conversation with Walter Grasskamp" [1984], in *Georg Baselitz: Collected Writings and Interviews,* ed. Detlev Gretenkort (London: Ridinghouse, 2010), 85 Original citation: "Die Skulpturen, die ich mache, sind bisher eben noch nicht gemacht worden, deshalb kann ich sie machen."

6 Stéphane Mallarmé, "Crayonné au théâtre," in *Oeuvres completes* (Paris: Bibliothèque de la Pléiade, 1945), 308. Original citation: "le vertige d'une âme comme mise à l'air par un artifice."

7 Georg Baselitz, *Charabia et basta: Entretiens avec Eric Darragon* (Paris: L'Arche, 1996), 76. Original citation: "Je voudrais développer pour ainsi dire un ornement que l'on puisse lire avec une figuration qui serait inscrite, intégrée, incorporée dedans."

8 Mallarmé, "*Crayonné au théâtre, Ballets,*" in *Oeuvres completes,*304.

9 See Georg Baselitz, "Painting Out of My Head, Upside Down, out of a Hat" [1993], in Diane Waldman, *Georg Baselitz* (New York: Guggenheim Museum, 1995), 247–49. Several times, the artist has mentioned the idea that the painter should find the means to supplement his "absence" in the creation of a painting.

10 Sidney Geist, "Brancusi," in *Primitivism in 20th Century Art: Affinity of the Tribal and the Modern*, ed. William Rubin, exh. cat. The Museum of Modern Art (New York, 1987), 2: 366. Referenced provided by the artist.

11 Michael Semff, "The Dark Side: Reflections on Georg Baselitz's New Paintings," in *Georg Baselitz: Le Côté sombre*, exh. cat. Galerie Thaddaeus Ropac (Paris, 2013), 60–63. See also the essay by Michael Semff in this catalogue, pp. 185–195.

12 *Georg Baselitz: Hintergrundgeschichten*, exh. cat. Staatliche Kunstsammlungen Dresden (2013).

13 John-Paul Stonard, "Baselitz Black or History as Background," in *Georg Baselitz: Le Côté sombre*, 27–30.

14 Georg Baselitz, e-mail message to author, May 6, 2014.

15 Georg Baselitz, "Sculpture," in *Georg Baselitz*, exh. cat. Musée d'art moderne de la ville de Paris (Paris, 1996), 171.

16 *Georg Baselitz: New Paintings and a Sculpture*, exh. cat. Gagosian Gallery, New York, 2012.

17 Jans Arp, *Arp on Arp: Poems, Essays, Memories*, in Documents of Twentieth-Century Art, ed. Marcel Jean, trans. Joachim Neugroschel (New York: Viking Press, 1972), 351.

18 "Georg Baselitz: Conversation between Jean-Louis Froment and Jean-Marc Poinsot," in *Georg Baselitz: Sculptures and Early Woodcuts* (London: D'Offray, 1987), 22.

19 "I am the great everything" (lit., "I am the great the/the/the").

20 Georg Baselitz, letter to the author, January 16, 2014. This expression parodies the vocabulary used by the Futurists. The polemical term "passatismo" was coined by Filippo Tommaso Marinetti in his *An Open Letter to the Futurist Mac Delmarle*: "L'Italia, più di qualunque altro paese, aveva un bisogno urgente di Futurismo, poiché moriva di passatismo," *Lacerba* (August 15, 1913). See Filippo Tommaso Marinetti, *Critical Writings: New Edition*, ed. Günter Berghaus, trans. Doug Thompson (New York: Farrar, Strauss and Giroux, 2006), 104. "Italy, more than any other country, was in urgent need of Futurism, for it was dying of an obsession with its own past." See also F. T. Marinetti, *Contro Venezia passasista;* Giovanni Papini, "Il passato non esiste," *Lacerba*, no. 2 [Florence], (January 15, 1914).

21 Georg Baselitz, letter to the author, January, 1 2014. "Blick zurück nach vorn" and "nicht zwei schritte zurück und einen vor, sondern drei zurück und man ist vorne."

22 "Anges et nains: German Tribal Art," [June 17, 1994] in *Georg Baselitz*, exh. cat. Musée d'art moderne de la ville de Paris, 217–19.

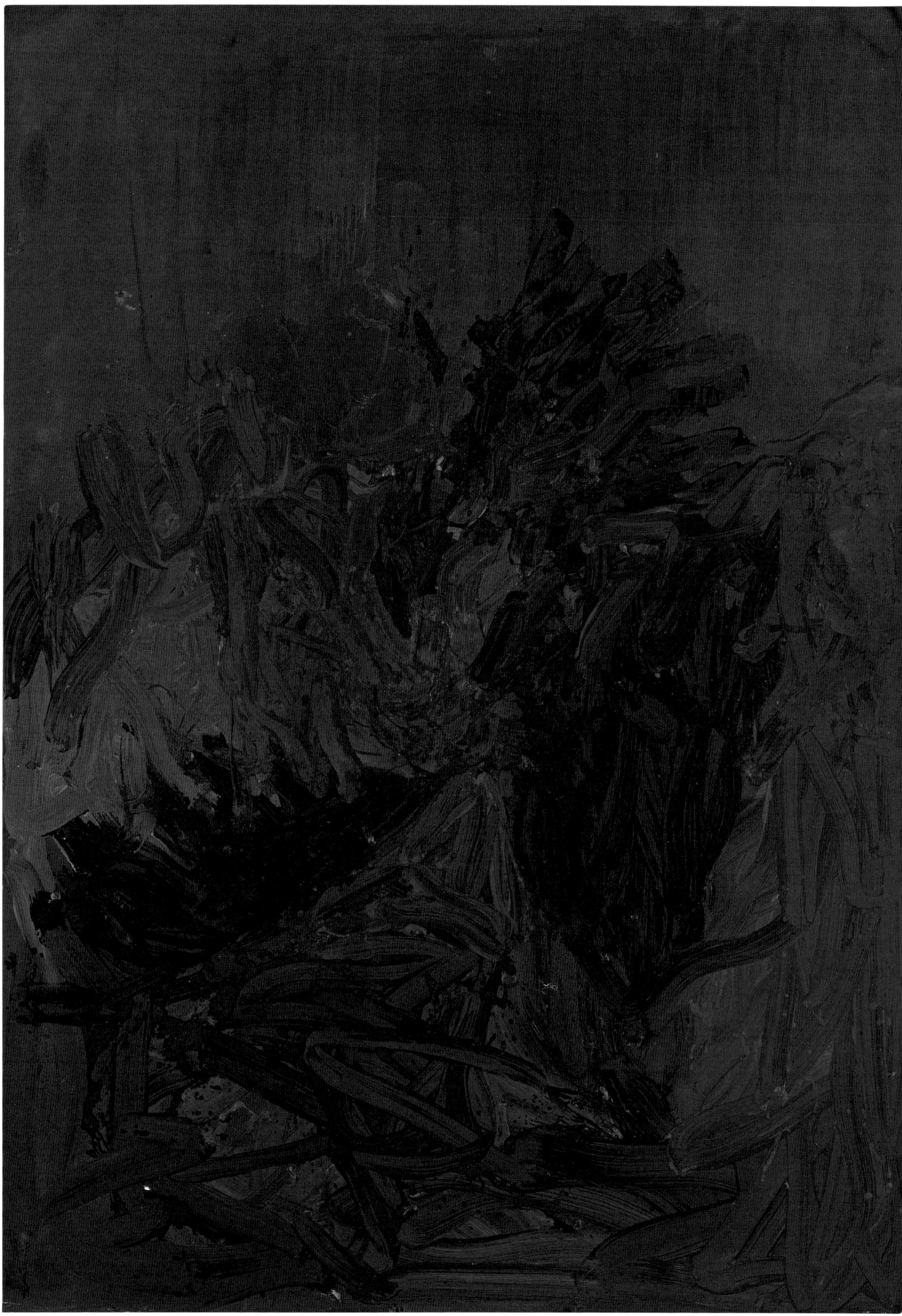

An almost uncanny silence fills these canvases. The monumental upright format is predominant, the paint spread over it, dark and densely opaque. At first, the viewer can hardly make out what is taking place on these surfaces. We are looking at apparently homogeneous anthracite or black fields of massive dimensions; then gradually—depending on the lighting—we recognize meandering brushstrokes which reveal subtly interwoven textures consisting of matte, muted shades of gray, brown, blue, and black. Emerging almost imperceptibly from these is the motif of the eagle with outspread wings—an early element of the artist's repertoire, present ever since in various forms in many of his drawings and paintings. The immediate starting point for his new pictures was *Finger-Painting—Eagle* (1972), the large painting from the collection of Franz, Duke of Bavaria, which is now a highlight of the Baselitz collection in the Pinakothek der Moderne in Munich. Like a tremendous chord, the bird's shimmering gray-black plumage stands in contrast to the bright, shiny blue background interspersed with gray and brown patches. Forty years later, the artist surprises us with a radically new pictorial concept that—in almost minimalist reduction—aims to eliminate all visible contrasts. Thus the painting process creates fields of overall dark shades in which all nuances are immersed to the brink of imperceptibility.

In these paintings, Baselitz reveals an almost somnambulic mastery of his material. His fluid, circling brushwork exerts a magnetism in whose force field the motif merges totally with the background. All the eruptive quality of his painting is still present, although it appears magically calmed, as if under a membrane. Vehemence turns into repose—but this is a repose that, far from superseding excitation, renders it all the more sublime. The flowing style makes

Michael Semff   For His Grace Duke Franz, on his 80th birthday

THE DARK SIDE:
REFLECTIONS ON GEORG BASELITZ'S NEW PAINTINGS

it appear as if the paint were being spread evenly, matching the flat, ornamental quality of the almost heraldic motif. Thus these pictures never show a tendency towards "composition," in the sense of placing different emphasis on specific areas. In his personal style—which, as ever, can be classed as expressive—the artist manages to strike a positively unexpressive note. Also in the color balance, without visible contrasts, any hint of external vehemence seems subdued. In the matte shimmer of slate and anthracite shades, which includes all the surrounding, predominantly dark tones, Baselitz achieves a greater unity of painting, in which ground, motif, and brushwork arrive at an equilibrium, canceling one another out. Oblique lighting shows the surface of the canvas vitalized, almost as in relief, by the process of painting in layers. Since as he paints, the artist cannot really see what is visible, he is almost feeling his way, leaving tactile traces, rather like embossed printing. He does not actually see what he is doing, rather feeling it in the gesture of his hand, through varying pressure on the canvas. Very rarely, there are minimal fragments of white, which—in contrast to the dark surroundings—have the effect of orientation guides on the vast surface of the painting.

For the invention of such an extreme pictorial model as that for these *Black Paintings*, the artist found this dynamic spread-eagle motif formally compelling. Every other motif in his figurative repertoire—which the *Remix* series presented, rejuvenated and as if reinvented, from 2004 onwards—would have emphasized the iconographic, narrative element all too superficially. This would not have served the process of abstraction involved in the unique series in his preceding oeuvre. What happened instead can unquestionably—if we look at the artist's strategies—be regarded as a magnificent intensification of his expressive potential to date. Retrospectively, from this standpoint it once more becomes clear just how much Baselitz's work has repeatedly managed to renew itself, without his methods of image-finding ever becoming redundant.

The artist's early decision to turn his representational motifs upside down—from now on to paint them inverted—proved momentous. For decades, this concept dominated Baselitz's creative process, the radical effect being his projected progressive purge of painting. From the beginning of the nineteen-sixties, in his engravings and figurative paintings, he had already vehemently resisted all current trends. Baselitz's rebellious spirit combined with his pronounced anachronistic aspiration to be a modern artist, as for instance in the most traditional graphic techniques such as soft-ground etching, aquatint, and chiaroscuro woodcut. From the start, in his insistence on this planned procedure, which included all manner of risks, it was the medium of engraving that had the urgency and the authenticity that set the standard to which he aspired for his entire later work.

By his own admission, Baselitz has frequently changed his method in the course of his over fifty-year career; his aim, however, has always remained the same. From 2005, in a tireless fury of creativity, he staged the complex pictorial world of his early paintings as a unique dialogue with himself; with the works in his *Remix* series, he achieved an unexpected advance in the field of pure painting—a territory he had never before approached in this way. It is hardly surprising that he was able, almost concurrently, to breathe new life into the other media of ink drawing and watercolor, engraving and woodcut, which

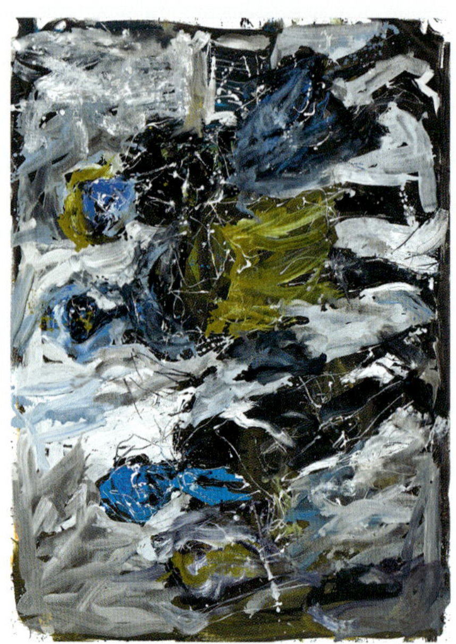

Georg Baselitz, *The New Flat*, 2012

he had brought to perfection over previous decades. The close artistic affinity of his works on paper with his painting oeuvre can be demonstrated particularly by the example of the *Remix* works, which reveal a kind of summary of his entire oeuvre. Baselitz's subject matter of recent years and up to the present day focuses on a specific system of references based on a subtle memory network, in which actual and imagined experience, the long past and the immediate present seem linked. Also with regard to genuinely artistic phenomena, this permeability may be observed in all the media he uses. There is hardly another artist of his generation whose work shows such a close and continuous cross-fertilization between the various genres. Thus the monumental watercolors painted between March and October 2002, exhibited shortly afterwards in the Albertina in Vienna, must indubitably be regarded as the precursor that inspired the *Remix* series. They seem to anticipate directly the luminosity, the new mobility, the glassy transparency, and the tendency to leave a white border like a passe-partout in works on paper.

In his oeuvre to date, Georg Baselitz has tested and explored, in a huge spectrum of variants, the essential driving forces as well as the antagonisms inherent in the process of painting. Everything in his work has evolved from the act of painting and from the reflection on this. As Eric Darragon remarks, the quest of the painter is directed exclusively at painting—at what it can discover through itself and against itself,[1] a kind of painting that seeks, renews, and expands itself according to what obstacles it encounters. Viewed retrospectively, the recent novel, image-generating function assumed by the photographic negative in Baselitz's work proves a necessary consequence of the inverted motif adopted over the preceding forty years. In 2012 he painted an exciting group of pictures based on a kind of inversion of color to its opposite. The starting point for this kind of artistic manipulation was the computer-aided conversion of images from the *Remix* series into photonegatives. This meant that the artist had no color copies from old catalogues to work from, as for his *Remix Paintings*, but instead the images processed into negatives, in which the original colors appeared reversed. This manipulated alteration of the color codes produces a stage towards abstraction, essentially undermining the construction of the images and their arrangement between ground and figure, by rendering interchangeable the dimensions of positive and negative, of fullness and emptiness between unfathomable black and blazing white.

Almost twenty years before these pictures were painted, Baselitz expressed something fundamental about his approach to painting, which still holds today: "I try to work without experience, without training, in a way I myself don't know. I don't want continuity … I set great store by waking sleep. I imagine handicaps. For instance, I lay the canvas on the floor, so as not to see what I'm doing…."[2] In 2010, he took up these ideas and continued them in a way directly linked with the secret of his latest pictures: "But then, thinking about extended brushes, or long arms, or painting behind the canvas or on the floor—what do you feel when you do that?"[3]

In this context, and looking at the group of *Black Paintings*, it is enlightening to remember five paintings from Baselitz's *Negative* series (2012): *Schon wieder eine schlechte Note* (*Yet Another Bad Grade*), *Die neue Wohnung* (*The New Flat*), *Stunde der Nachtigall* (*Hour of the Nightingale*), *Der Brief*

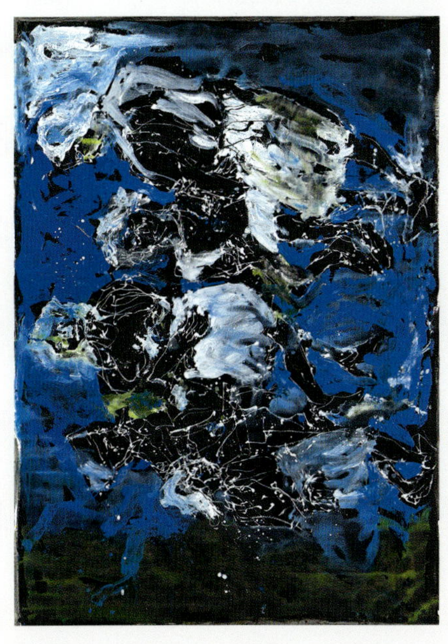

Georg Baselitz, *The Letter from the Front—The Negative*, 2012

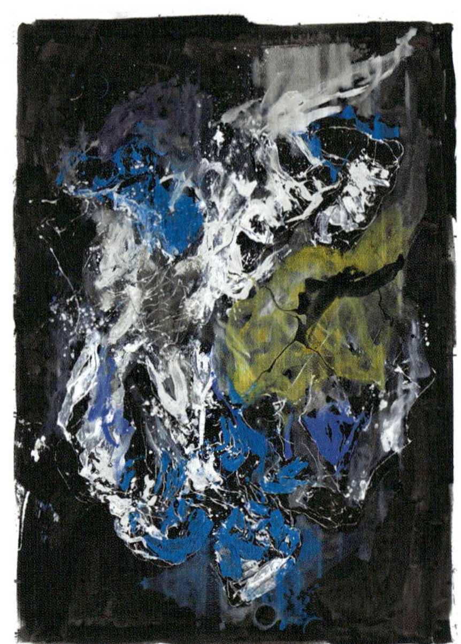

Georg Baselitz, *Hour of the Nightingale*, 2012

Pierre Soulages, *Peinture*, 1985

von der Front—Das Negativ (*The Letter from the Front—The Negative*), and *Schlechte Note* (*Bad Grade*). These are precisely the ones where the subject, largely dissolved, is sunk in the rectangular canvas, always trying to push out towards the edges. Nearly all of these paintings are characterized by an "all-over" texture in which the black background, showing through, is over-run in parts with a chalky, flickering white which sometimes appears to corrode it, and which allows room for only a few islands of blue or dirty yellow in varying density.

This description of the surface texture and the inner temperature of the paintings indicate the precise opposite of the abovementioned characterization of the *Black Paintings*. Thus it is obvious that the artist has once more accomplished a complete about-turn, a transformation of the inversion that marked the *Negative* series. This transformation is due to the emergence of the latest pictures, predicated quite unexpectedly on the aura of their sheer calm, which contains—apparently pent up subcutaneously—all the complex painterly experiences entailed in the gestural and coloristic transports of the immediately preceding canvases of the *Negative* series.

On his own admission, Baselitz thinks of the picture as a "skin"—the concept of "behind," that can also appear "in front." Here "the dark side"—as the artist has entitled his latest series—evidently alludes directly to the negative, blunt rear side of the photonegatives he used as a productive vehicle for his *Negative* series. It is this side, not its counterpart in the form of the shiny front, that appears to function compellingly as the foil for the *Black Paintings*. Only here, in miniature, is to be found that matte shimmer of anthracite and slate shades spread over the vast

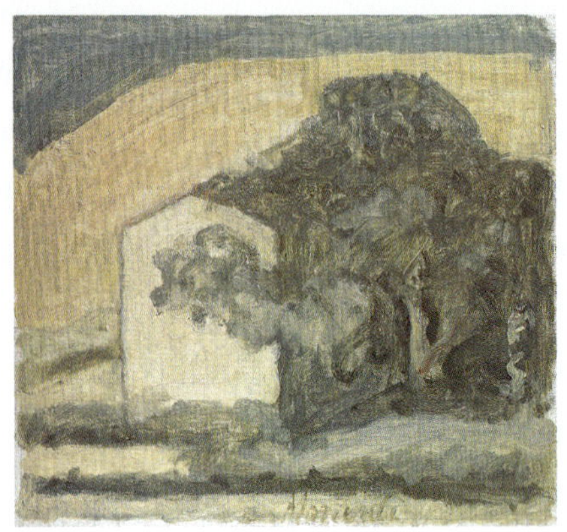

Giorgio Morandi, *Landscape*, 1963

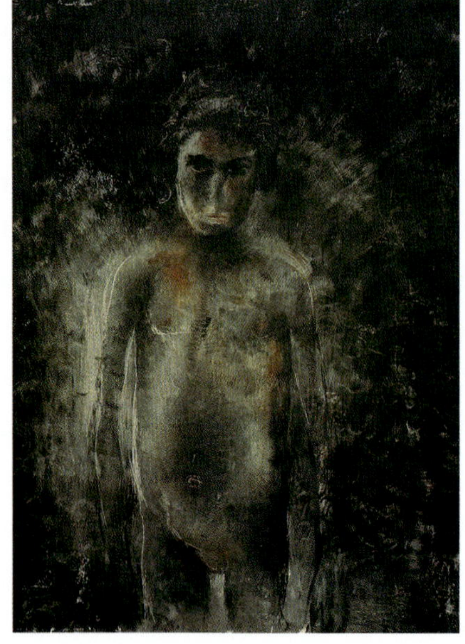

Jean Fautrier, *Grand nu noir*, 1926

surfaces where a subtle seething pulsation, like the far projection of an imaginary front, is still perceptible.

Apart from any tendency to virtuosity, it is in its very restraint that Baselitz's capacity as a painter demonstrates such perfection that one hardly even notices it. These paintings fascinate both eye and spirit through the art of subdued, smoldering passion. The brushwork has a resonant effect that intensively evokes the nuances of a *mezza voce* and sounds like an echo from another side. The artist has an apt metaphor for this: "… I think, for instance, you can play the piano better if you sit underneath the piano and play on it …"[4]

At work in the creation of these canvases was probably an unprecedented, extreme fusion of forces, which must first of all have most surprised the artist himself. With these paintings, he has achieved the culmination to date of his artistic potential, which attains unforeseeable areas of the unknown, far beyond the controllable intelligence of his pictorial thought. The content of his *Remix Paintings*—and thus also of their *Negative* variants—retreats in favor of virtual emptiness, in the sense of pure painting. The mentality of the color is reminiscent of early paintings by Jean Fautrier and, viewed from a distance, makes one think of the dark "calming effect" in the later paintings of Pierre Soulages. Wildness and calm become one—not unlike Giorgio Morandi's last landscapes.[5] Although the formats used by the two painters are quite incommensurable, in Baselitz's work the "subject" of the motif in the structure of the brushstrokes on the densely saturated ground of these canvases appears similarly neutralized in the extreme, almost dissolved. There dominates a movement, tamed in its wildness, of the painter's hand, that allows the form to emerge without

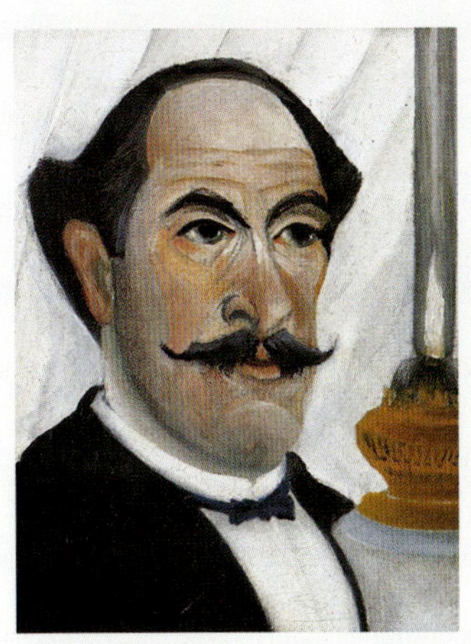

Henri Rousseau, *Self-Portrait of the Artist with a Lamp*, 1903

giving precedence to any detail. All the things on these canvases "are of equal importance and have their own place"—as Morandi found when he saw Henri Rousseau's *Self-Portrait of the Artist with a Lamp*. Prevailing here, without the slightest expressive urgency, is a restraint unusual for Baselitz, which, however, allows the subliminal presence of that positive, unrestrained force that is otherwise at his disposal. It may be described as a miracle of these "dark (verso) sides," to what extent they mitigate and balance out the contraventions of an imaginary "recto" in their strongest conceivable opposites. Time seems to have stopped here—not in the sense of standstill, but of exhaustion, calming "after the battle."

1 Eric Darragon, *Georg Baselitz: Das Negativ—Eine andere Umkehrung*, exh. cat (Salzburg: Galerie Thaddaeus Ropac, 2012), 17 and 19.
2 Georg Baselitz and Eric Darragon, *Darstellen, was ich selber bin: Georg Baselitz im Gespräch mit Eric Darragon* (Frankfurt am Main and Leipzig: Verso, 2001), 51.
3 Georg Baselitz, "Appropriation: Back Then, In Between, and Today" [2010], *Art Bulletin* 94, no. 2 (June 2012): 167.

4 Baselitz and Darragon, *Darstellen, was ich selber bin*, 103.
5 Giuseppe Raimondi, *Jahre mit Giorgio Morandi: Erinnerungen von Giuseppe Raimondi*, trans. Beate Taudte (Frankfurt am Main: Insel, 1992), 181.

Tyfifethreteennine, 2013

Heast in Fall, 2013

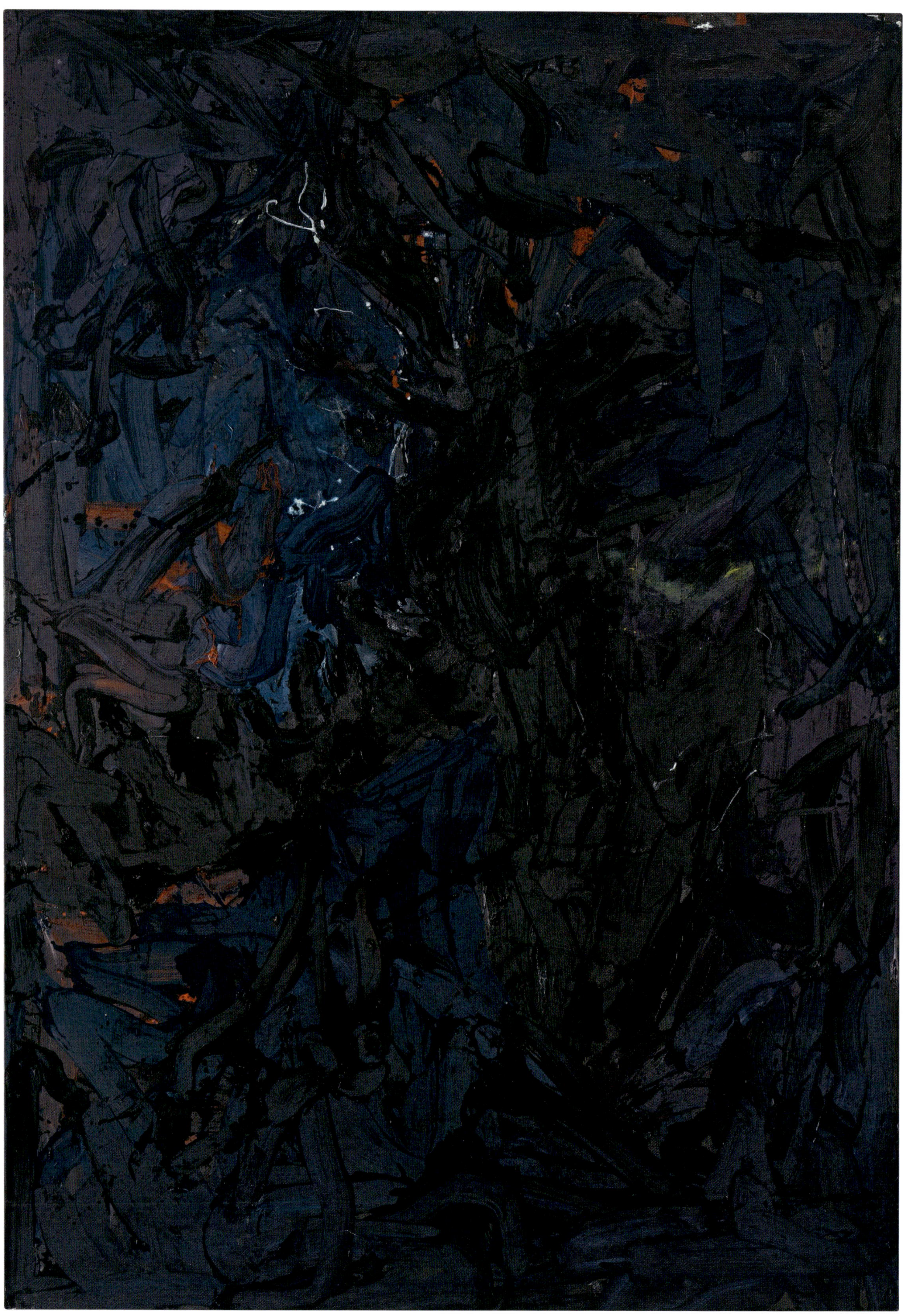

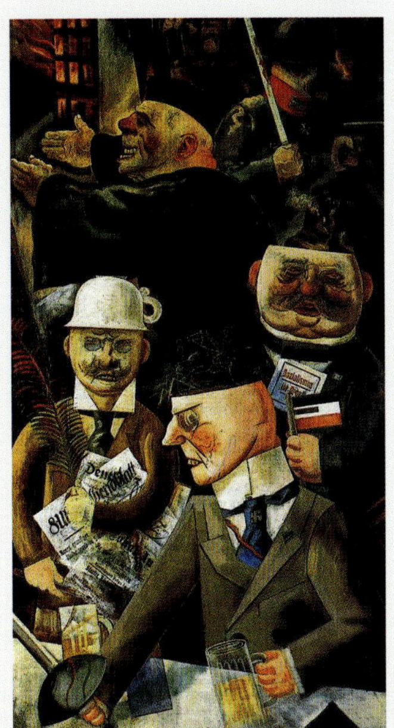

George Grosz, *The Pillars of Society*, 1926

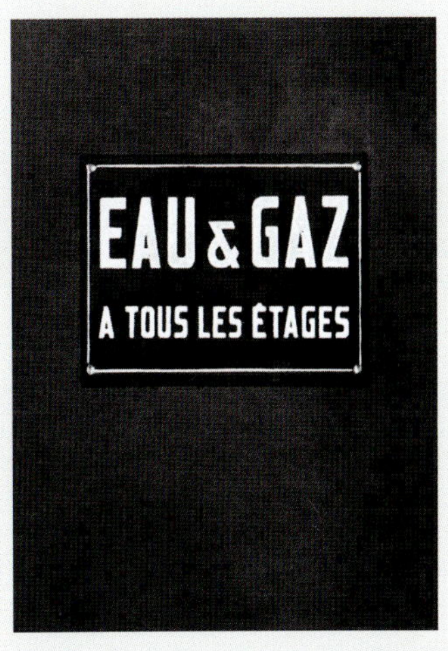

Marcel Duchamp, *Water & Gas on Every Floor*, 1958

discovered my talent and promoted it. But I knew, at most five years later, that this promotion comes to nothing and that I'd be better off letting it be. The hours diving in the South Seas are glorious, praise the Lord, because of everything one can see to the darkest depths of fish, monsters, corals, and colors. One is able to relax. Nothing more is required. At most, a game of solitaire on the beach. But then these stupid photographers and painters, these lusters after nature. When the airplane pushes up through the clouds, this expanse with stars or with blue skies, glorious, praise the Lord. Here, arias by Richard Strauss make a deep impression, but again, no pictures. The tin cans of shoe polish with the frog on the lid, two connected with a long piece of string and used as a telephone, back then, by us kids, glorious, praise the Lord. That gave pictures for the eye and ear. The breadth, the depth, the distance—first the frog was a prince, then a count, finally, a bastard.

The underground bunker in the woods, with walls covered with bed linen and my mother's green carpet on the dirt floor. When the soldiers were dead and the war ended, my friend and I moved in. A nice place for dreaming. We were well endowed with ammunition, too, from 8.8 caliber on down. The weapons were rusted. Before the secondary school painting advisor, Dr. Lachmann, set up his field easel in front of the old oak trees and began his little New Objectivity pictures, my high spirits to change the world in the future had no objective. I heard it rustling, but I lacked the form—no *Ahmung*, no *Lehnung*. Reading books was a great influence, and the paperback booklet with black and white illustrations of Italian Futurism, glorious, praise the Lord. Stuff of great pathos could also be found on stamps, Stalin for example, and in the romance novels of Jorge Amado. I was away more than I was here—more inside-outside than away-outside. That

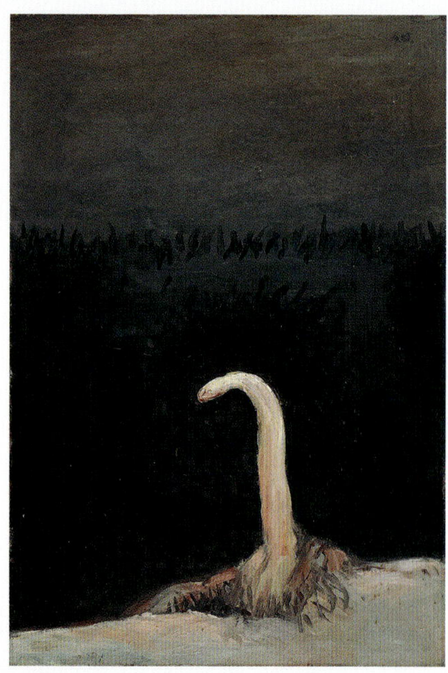

Georg Baselitz, *P. D. Stalk*, 1963

pictures meant freedom did not occur to me then. I thought to make paintings meant to draw attention to oneself. Oh well, it worked quite well in my bird's nest, or maybe better put, my rat's nest. The great prophets from the school desk next to me, the grand calculators and socialist creators of life forms, those I never saw again or heard of anymore. Presumably, they shriveled away. Also, the talented woman pianist gives only piano lessons. Even the great teachers shrink enormously after one leaves school. Why do memories tingle within us? Because one has rubbed against the wrong people? In this there is no difference in fact between the province and the metropole, at most, only in percentage.

There were many frogs in the sand pond. Before that it was slimy spawn, then the tadpole with the tiny tail, gradually it became amphibious, between land and water. With me, it was also slimy at first, and then crusted over. I, too, had my state between egg and hen. Sometimes it went like a bird, from tree to mountain and across the land. For example, the love fevers, the swank of bulging muscles, the trials of courage. Fantasy was only good for showing off (swanking). All records, everywhere, were broken. If it had existed at all, I have forgotten the envy, the comparison fails, also the incentives for faster or more efficient foraging in my milieu. The rich, whom I later met, were assholes, and the famous artists did not interest me at all at first because they existed too monumentally in another world. One just gets on easier with the starvelings, the so-called outsiders, and there were enough of them. One can hide if one does not want to be seen, but also if one does not want to see anyone.

This changed when the first paintings were made. Finally, I knew best what and how these were. The difference and the distance to what had come before

To dream oneself to the other end of the world was a childhood wish. I have dug, drilled, and trenched in the sand pit in order to come out again on the other side. Then later, years later, to find the past, the eon, the things from people who have been here before us, I have excavated at that same place for urns. Dr. Weissmantel, the history teacher, said that what I had brought to him were Slavic urns, 3,000 years old.

The game was not to lift oneself out of any old bad time into a better one. More than anything, curiosity propelled the discovery of what lay hidden in there, behind, and below. A good start for a painter's life, highly recommended.

Listening to the radio waves belongs to this curiosity. Putting one's ear onto the railway tracks (there weren't any nearby) or on the telegraph poles, or peering through the ice at the frozen lake, fired the imagination. Since 1942, in front of our house there stood giant electromagnetic listening dishes for the sky. Was something happening up there, airplanes with bombs, perhaps? One can hear various things with one's ear to the trunk of a tree, in any case, rushing water, like city dwellers hear the flushing system. *Eau et gaz à tous les étages.* The telephone wires sing far across the land. The red wood ants in their great piled-up castle sniff and rustle. Can you hear the sea in the conch? From where the wind comes was not so interesting, where it went was only further away. But the migrant birds passed through the sky in the formation of an arrow, or a wave, the starlings appeared as a cloud, the lapwings like whirled up leaves. Near Fort Worth I stuck my finger into the ground and oil came bubbling up. Over here, once in a while, a mountain crystal, or a fine ammonite in the creek.

Georg Baselitz

BACK THEN, IN BETWEEN, AND TODAY

**Francis Picabia, *"Carte à jouer"* or
The Cowardice of Subtle Barbarism,
1949**

Sometime later, I began with drawings and paintings, in a way like digging, drilling, evesdropping, ruminating, mining, as I thought about what lies behind or below. And so, transmuted into lines and forms, I have transported myself from my world into another one—not so far as to no longer recognize the relatives. Such good detergents did not exist back then. Somehow everything is still here, perhaps just in another place, upside down, or maybe not.

Worshipping heroes and listening to them, slipping into them and opening up the lid of their skulls like as George Grosz had done, it becomes inevitable—a leader leads by seduction.

But then, reflecting about elongated brushes, or long arms, or painting behind the canvas, painting on the floor, what do you feel below? Or letting something paint itself, pouring paint, letting it run, dropping, painting something stupid, painting everything over. Why did Picabia go that far, and then again he painted single dots onto it, like buttons on a vest.

The experience of firework music in Imperia—after all, we are living in the house of a relative of Lucio Berio, also a Berio, big iron "B" on the gate—the music began, the firecrackers blasted and up in the grandstand, we disappeared in the smoke. We couldn't see a thing and the music sounded only faintly, and dull. Groping in the dark? Falling into a trap? Anything can happen when it gets dark during the day. Now and again I slipped on a canvas wet with turpentine, like a wild boar in a wallow. If one can't hear music, maybe one can hear the worms in the wooden table, or the birds outside the window.

If sixty years ago Dr. Lachmann's mongoloid son had not looked out the window and grimaced when he saw me, I would perhaps have taken painting lessons, could not have been greater. The painting, *P. D. Stalk*, is more a ride on the "Moscow-Petushki" line, a trip to the end of the line, than a stroll in the supermarket of any pop artist.

For example, "Lenin and the Nightingale," Becher's idiotic Stalin poems, a roe deer … When Michael Jackson died, the obituary on the radio announced that the greatest musician of all time had died. He had received the most gold records. Damn bloody music is that, listened to by the damn bloody stupid. Becher is said to have been a snowbird on cocaine. More important, however, is that this crap poet was minister of culture. As for Lenin, please read "My Little Leniniana" by Erofeev. Lenin and Stalin with miniskirts and pumps. I, the painter, I'm getting into line, get into line, colleague. Hence the title, *The Forgotten Second Congress of the Third Communist International in Moscow 1920, on the right of the picture Ralf, next to him Jörg*. One may recall Breton, Aragon, and so on—the surrealists in the CP.

Now, Willem de Kooning is a leading figure, Tracey Emin, Cecily Brown, Richard Prince, and so on. I use method, stereotype, and particular shades of color because it feels good when these go through one's head. One should quote and see what the colleagues are doing. Sitting high in the incubator, there is a cozy, frictional heat. Still, few appear alongside Willem in my register.

When I had opened Trier's lid, it was nothing but *Ahmung* and *Lehnung* there, and also when I pushed Nay's color discs across the paper, there was a glorious feeling, praise the Lord. A fabulous, free, high-spirited mood, away over the neighbor's fence and into the distance, a condition similar to this: he who lies once is never believed again; or: when all dams are broken; or: when a reputation has been ruined, one can live without embarrassment. As long as

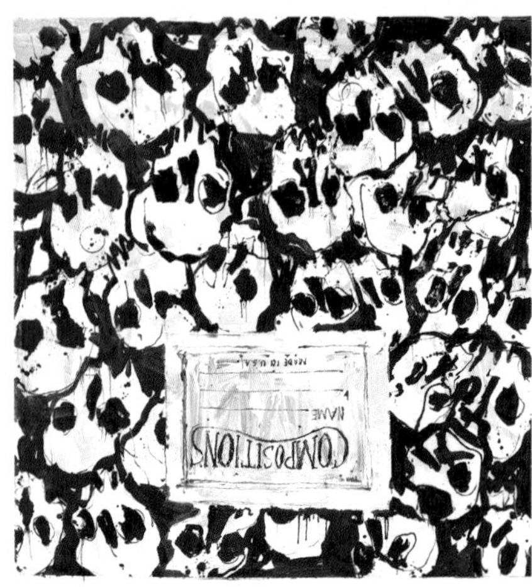

Georg Baselitz, *Folk Dance Made in U.S.A.*, 2009

the thread held, it all went well. But soon I was stuck again in the old muck. I didn't even want to learn French on account of the peculiar facial grimaces this required. Our teacher, Miss Härtel, said that we, as Oberlausitzers, were particularly suited for the French language. Miss Potzhuhn at the piano reeked of garlic, so playing the piano was also a lost cause.

I loved to look at pictures by Wols, back then, in 1957. But then the Americans came, this time not with chewing gum and chocolate but with Pollock, and the like. Glorious, this exhibition at our school, praise the Lord. In China, over thousands of years, over thousands of times, an alchemistic coffee cup from Meissen was already being broken. Is that a good aphorism for Europop from Saxony and Silesia? So far I have never cleaned toilet paper. We, Elke and I, are our own analysts. Our never-ending conversation about the past is reminiscent of two old apes picking the fleas from each other's fur, Elke says. Naturally, I have not only pondered. I have also dreamt in thought, putting together 1 and 1, planning and doing the next step, regardless of whomever was my helmsman in the little upper deck and whether he was choosing the right direction—this is not logical-biological but logical-visionary, and all of it before the discovery of the onboard computer. *Remix Paintings* are not like pickled cucumbers on the basement shelf. I have never ever greeted my own reflection.

That it occurs on a white surface, I have maintained into recent years. Something is there, not far removed from drawing, inside and on it, not just all over and about. Even my *Composition* after Lichtenstein is that way, quoted on it like fly dung, the music plays after it from the score sheet, and whether the thing can fly remains unclear. The lucky numbers for the next draw are: 1, 5, 19, 23, 38, 40.

Georg Baselitz, "Appropriation: Back Then, In Between, and Today,"
The Art Bulletin vol. 94, no. 2 (June 2012): 167–69.

LIST OF WORKS

Forgotten at Some Point—Sand Pond Dam, 2009
(page 103)
Irgendwann vergessen – Sandteichdamm
Oil on canvas
250×200 cm
Private collection, Vienna

Bedroom, 2009 *(page 105)*
Schlafzimmer
Oil on canvas
300×250 cm
Private collection

Unforgotten Then, 2009 *(page 107)*
Unvergessen damals
Oil on canvas
250×205 cm
Courtesy Galerie Thaddaeus Ropac, Paris / Salzburg

Willem Above, 2009 *(page 109)*
Oberhalb Willem
Oil on canvas
250×200 cm
Private collection

With Willem, 2009 *(page 111)*
Bei Willem, 2009
Oil on canvas
250×200 cm
Goetz Collection, Munich

Two Black Russians, 2010 *(page 113)*
Zwei schwarze Russen
Oil on canvas
250×200 cm
Private collection, France

Oh, a Shadow, Alas, 2010 *(page 115)*
Oh, ein Schatten, ach
Oil on canvas
250×200 cm
Goetz Collection, Munich

St. Anne United Field, 2010 *(page 116)*
St. Anna vereinigt Feld
Oil on canvas
300×250 cm
Private collection

Bird Deep, 2010 *(page 119)*
Oil on canvas
250×200 cm
Private collection

Portrait of Elke, 2010 *(page 121)*
Elkeporträt
Oil on canvas
250×200 cm
Private collection

The Flugelhornist Gracie Irlam, 2012 *(page 127)*
Die Flügelhornistin Gracie Irlam
Oil on canvas
400×300 cm
Private collection

Aarhus Is a Beautiful Country, 2011 *(page 129)*
Aarhus ist ein schönes Land
Oil on canvas
300×390 cm
Private collection

Wadi in the Evening, 2012 *(pages 124–25)*
Wadi am Abend
Oil on canvas
305×211 cm
Cantate LLP, Paris

Right or Left Turn?, 2011 *(pages 132–33)*
Rechts oder links herum?
Oil on canvas
300×400 cm
Private collection

Not in London, in Manchester, Wadi Halfa, 2011
(page 137)
In London nicht, in Manchester, Wadi Halfa
Oil on canvas
300×215 cm
Private collection

Once a Rod Like 1960, also a Stovepipe Like 60, 2011
(pages 138–39)
War mal Stock wie 1960, auch Ofenrohr wie 60
Oil on canvas
255×310 cm
Private collection

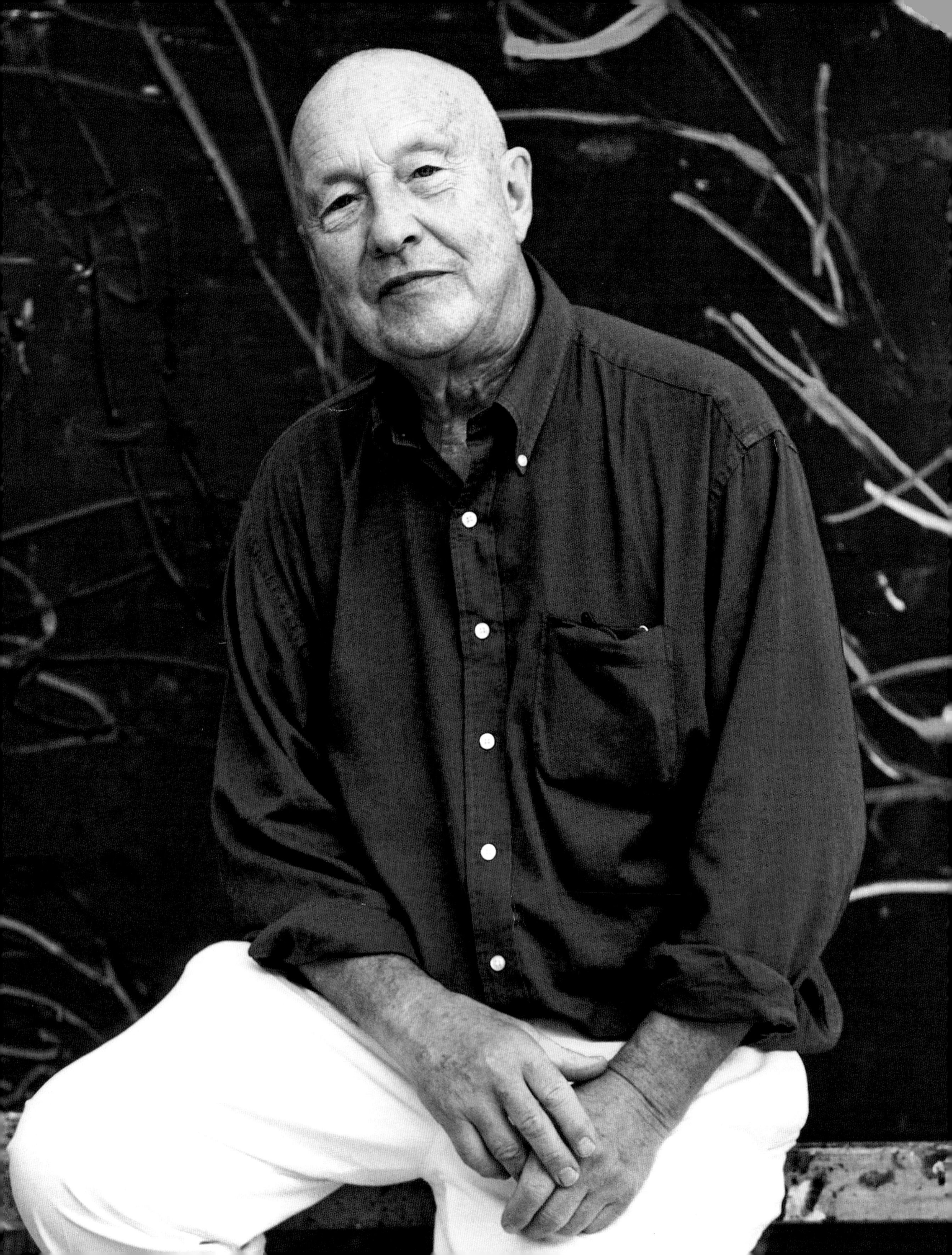

1938 Born on January 23, 1938 as Hans-Georg Bruno Kern in Deutschbaselitz, Saxony (Germany).

1956 Admitted to the Hochschule für bildende und angewandte Kunst in East Berlin; studies in painting with Walter Womacka and Herbert Behrens-Hangler.

1957 After two semesters, Baselitz is expelled from the academy for "sociopolitical immaturity." He continues his studies with Hann Trier at the Hochschule für bildende Künste in West Berlin, and graduates as a *Meisterschüler* in 1963.

1960 Produces his first valid works with the so-called *Rayski Portraits*.

1961 Takes the artist's name Georg Baselitz, borrowing the name of his birthplace. ■ *Pandemonium I* manifesto and exhibition with Eugen Schönebeck.

1962 Marries Elke Kretzschmar; birth of their son Daniel.

1963 First solo exhibition at the Galerie Werner & Katz in Berlin, which becomes an overnight scandal. Among the exhibited pictures, *Die große Nacht im Eimer* (*The Big Night Down the Drain*; 1962–63) and *Der nackte Mann* (*The Naked Man*; 1962) are seized by the public prosecutor's office. The ensuing court proceedings are concluded in 1965, when the paintings are returned to the artist.

1964 The first etchings are printed at the printing press of Wolfsburg Castle in Lower Saxony.

BIOGRAPHY

1965 Scholarship at the Villa Romana in Florence. ■ Exhibition at Galerie Friedrich & Dahlem in Munich. ■ Returns to Berlin; works on the *Heroes* series until 1966.

1966 *Why the Painting* The Great Friends *Is a Good Picture!* exhibition and manifesto at Galerie Rudolf Springer in Berlin. ■ Birth of son Anton; the family moves to Osthofen near Worms in Rhineland-Palatinate.

1968 Scholarship from the Kulturkreis im Bundesverband der Deutschen Industrie (Association of Arts and Culture of the German Economy at the Federation of German Industries).

1969 Begins to invert his motifs, one of the first such paintings being the *Der Wald auf dem Kopf* (*The Wood on Its Head*).

1970 First museum exhibition at the Kupferstichkabinett in the Kunstmuseum Basel. ■ Parallel to Art Cologne, Franz Dahlem presents the first Baselitz exhibition featuring paintings with inverted motifs at the Galeriehaus on Lindenstrasse.

1971 Moves to Forst an der Weinstrasse in Rhineland-Palatinate.

1972 Participates in documenta 5 in Kassel. ■ Studio in Musbach.

1975 Moves to Derneburg near Hildesheim in Lower Saxony. ■ Participates in the 13th São Paulo Art Biennial.

1976 Retrospectives at the Kunsthalle Bern, the Staatsgalerie moderner Kunst in Munich, and the Kunsthalle Köln. ■ Until 1981, maintains an additional studio in Florence.

1977 Appointment to the Staatliche Akademie der Bildenden Künste in Karlsruhe, where he holds a professorship from 1978 to 1983. ■ Withdraws his paintings from documenta 6 in Kassel in response to the participation of "official representatives of GDR painting." ■ First large-format linocuts.

1979 The exhibition *Schilderijen 1977–1978* is held at the Van Abbemuseum in Eindhoven. ■ "Vier Wände und Oberlicht oder besser kein Bild an die Wand" ("Four Walls and Skylight or Rather No Picture on the Wall at All"), lecture given at the Dortmunder Architekturtage on the theme of museum buildings.

1980 Completes the eighteen-part cycle *Straßenbild* (*Street Picture*). ■ In the German Pavilion at the Venice Biennale, Baselitz shows his first sculptural work, *Modell für eine Skulptur* (*Model for a Sculpture*), alongside works by Anselm Kiefer.

1981 Participates in the exhibitions *A New Spirit in Painting* at the Royal Academy of Arts in London, and *Westkunst* at the Cologne Messehallen. ■ Produces the series of *Orangenesser* (*Orange Eaters*) and *Trinker* (*Drinkers*) paintings. ■ Until 1987, maintains an additional studio in Castiglion Fiorentino near Arezzo. ■ First New York exhibition at Xavier Fourcade.

1982 Participates in documenta 7 in Kassel and the exhibition *Zeitgeist* at the Martin-Gropius-Bau, Berlin. ■ Intensified sculptural work.

1983 Produces the large compositions *Nachtessen in Dresden* (*Dinner in Dresden*) and *Der Brückechor* (*The Brücke Chorus*). ■ Participates in the exhibition *Expressions: New Art from Germany*, organized by the Saint Louis Art Museum, which tours the US. ■ Retrospective at the Whitechapel Art Gallery in London, later shown at the Stedelijk Museum in Amsterdam and the Kunsthalle in Basel. ■ Professorship at the Hochschule der Künste in Berlin until 1988, and from 1992 to 2003.

1984 Retrospective of the drawings at the Kunstmuseum Basel, which later tours. ■ Until 1992, member of the Akademie der Künste, Berlin.

1985 The Bibliothèque nationale in Paris mounts a retrospective of the graphic works, supplemented by an overview of the sculptural work to date. ■ Composes the manifesto "Das Rüstzeug der Maler" (The Painter's Equipment).

1986 Awarded the Kaiserring by the town of Goslar and the Art Prize of the Norddeutsche Landesbank, Hannover.

1987 Receives the French honor of a Chevalier de l'Ordre des Arts et des Lettres. ■ Maintains an additional studio in Imperia on the Italian Riviera.

1988 Completes the composition *Das Malerbild* (*The Painter's Picture*).

1989 Participates in the exhibition *Bilderstreit* in Cologne. ■ Completes the twenty-part painting *'45* and begins the monumental sculpture series *Dresdner Frauen* (*Women of Dresden*).

1990 The most comprehensive retrospective of the paintings to date takes place at the Kunsthaus Zürich, and then travels to the Kunsthalle Düsseldorf. ▪ Michael Werner publishes the artist's book *Malelade* with poems and forty-one etchings by Baselitz.

1991 Until 1995, works on the series *Bildübereins* (*Picture Over One*), which encompasses thirty-nine works.

1992 The 1989 Bordeaux, Château Mouton Rothschild, is presented with a label designed by Baselitz. ▪ Receives the French honor of a Officier de l'Ordre des Arts et des Lettres. ▪ Delivers the lecture "Purzelbäume sind auch Bewegung und noch dazu macht es Spaß" (Somersaults Are Also Movement, and They're Fun Too) at the Münchner Podium in the Kammerspiele as part of the series "Reden über Deutschland" (Talking about Germany).

1993 Designs the sets for a production of Harrison Birtwistle's opera *Punch and Judy* at the Dutch National Opera in Amsterdam.

1994 Writes the manifesto "Malen aus dem Kopf, auf dem Kopf oder aus dem Topf" (Painting Out of My Head, Upside Down, Out of the Hat). ▪ Completes the cloth-covered sculpture *Armalamor*, which is installed in 1996 in the entry hall of the new building of the Deutsche Bibliothek in Frankfurt am Main.

1995 First large retrospective at the Guggenheim Museum in New York, which then travels to the Los Angeles County Museum of Arts, the Hirshhorn Museum and Sculpture Garden in Washington, D.C., and the Nationalgalerie in Berlin. ▪ Begins a series of family portraits based on old photographs.

1996 Comprehensive retrospective at the Musée d'Art Moderne de la Ville de Paris. ■ Completes the sculptures *Sentimental Holland* and *Mutter der Girlande* (*Mother of the Garland*).

1997 Tour begins of an exhibition of the *Portraits of Elke* at the Modern Art Museum of Fort Worth, and thereafter at the North Carolina Museum of Art, Raleigh, the Carnegie Museum of Art, Pittsburgh, and the Museo de Arte Contemporáneo de Monterrey, Mexico. ■ The Deutsche Bank shows its Baselitz collection at the State Exhibition Hall New Manege in Moscow, and thereafter at the Städtische Kunstsammlungen Chemnitz and the Johannesburg Art Gallery. ■ Completes the sculpture *Mondrians Schwester* (*Mondrian's Sister*).

1998 The Museo Rufino Tamayo shows the first overview of Baselitz's works in Mexico City. ■ Completes the large-format paintings *Friedrichs Frau am Abgrund* (*Friedrich's Woman at the Abyss*) and *Friedrichs Melancholie* (*Friedrich's Melancholy*) for the Reichstag Building in Berlin.

1999 *Reise in die Niederlande 1972–1999*, exhibition at the Stedelijk Museum, Amsterdam. *Gravures Monumentales 1977–1999*, exhibition at the Musée Rath in Geneva. ■ Honorary membership of the Royal Academy of Arts in London. ■ First prizewinner of the Rhenus Kunstpreis.

2000 Honorary professorship at the Academy of Fine Arts in Kraków. ■ *Im Walde von Blainville/Malerei 1996–2000* (*In the Woods of Blainville/Painting 1996–2000*) exhibition at the Essl Museum of Contemporary Art in Klosterneuburg near Vienna.

2001 *Sculpture versus Painting*, exhibition at the IVAM, Centre Julio González in Valencia. ■ First prizewinner of the Julio González Prize in Valencia.

2002 Receives the French distinction of a Commandeur de l'Ordre des Arts et des Lettres. ■ Produces the series of monumental linocuts *Belle Haleine*.

2003 *Monumentale Aquarelle* (*Monumental Watercolors*), exhibition in the Albertina in Vienna, thereafter at the Frac de Picardie in Amiens. ■ Completes the self-portrait *Meine neue Mütze* (*My New Hat*) as an over-life-sized sculpture. ■ Prize for best work at the first Beijing International Art Biennale. ■ Receives the Staatspreis of Lower Saxony.

2004 Completes the over life-sized sculpture *Frau Ultramarin* (*Mrs. Ultramarine*), a portrait of his wife. ■ Retrospective at the Art and Exhibition Hall of the Federal Republic of Germany. ■ Prizewinner of the Praemium Imperiale, Tokyo. ■ Honorary professorship at the Accademia di Belle Arti, Florence. ■ Works on the series of *Negative* portraits, *Spaziergang ohne Stock* (*Stroll without a Stick*), and *Ekely*.

2005 *Attori a rovescio*, exhibition with Benjamin Katz in the Villa Faravelli in Imperia, Italy. ■ Begins the *Remix* series. ■ Receives the Austrian Order of Merit for Science and Art.

2006 Retrospectives at the Louisiana Museum near Copenhagen and the Fondation de l'Hermitage in Lausanne. The Lausanne retrospective is shown in a slightly modified form the following year at the Museo d'Arte Moderna in

Lugano. ■ *Remix* exhibition at the Pinakothek der Moderne, Munich; shown the subsequent year at the Albertina in Vienna. ■ Honorary citizen of the city of Imperia. ■ Relocates his studio and residence to Bavaria.

2007 *Russian Pictures*, exhibition at the Musée d'Art Moderne, St. Étienne, and subsequently at the National Museum of Contemporary, Seoul and the Deichtorhallen, Hamburg. ■ Baselitz exhibits at the Venetian Pavilion of the Venice Biennale in dialogue with Emilio Vedova. ■ Major retrospective at the Royal Academy of Arts in London.

2008 *23. Januar 1938*, exhibition and 70th birthday party (together with Jonathan Meese, born on the same day) at the gallery Contemporary Fine Arts in Berlin. ■ Retrospective at the Museum MADRE in Naples. ■ *Baselitz: Top*, exhibition at the Kunsthalle Würth, Schwäbisch Hall. ■ Completes the series *Mrs. Lenin and the Nightingale*.

2009 *Gemälde und Skulpturen, 1960–2008* (*Paintings and Sculptures, 1960–2008*), retrospective at the Museum der Moderne, Salzburg, and thereafter in modified form at the Rudolfinum in Prague. ■ Completes the monumental sculpture *Volk Ding Zero—Folk Thing Zero*. ■ *Dresdner Frauen* (*Women of Dresden*), exhibition at the Staatliche Kunstsammlungen Dresden, Gemäldegalerie Alte Meister. ■ *50 Jahre Malerei und 30 Jahre Skulptur* (*50 Years of Painting and 30 Years of Sculpture*), retrospective at the Museum Frieder Burda and at the Staatlichen Kunsthalle, Baden-Baden.

2010 *Remix*, exhibition at the Helsinki Art Museum, Tennis Palace, accompanied by photographic portraits by Benjamin Katz, as well as the exhibition *Pinturas recentes/Recent Paintings*, at the Pinacoteca do Estado de São Paulo. ■ Begins the series of *Elke* nudes, followed by the blue *Eagle* series and the double-portraits *Seid bereit, immer bereit* (*Be Prepared, Always Prepared*). ■ Honorary citizen of the city of Castiglion Fiorentino.

2011 Begins the *Herfreud Grüßgott* series and *In London gesucht und nichts gefunden* (*Sought in London, Nothing Found*). ■ The exhibitions *Re-Mixed* at the Kunstverein GL Strand in Copenhagen, *À la pointe du trait, gravures*, a retrospective of the print works at the Musée Cantini in Marseille, and *Lustspiel, Neues aus dem Atelier/New Works from the Studio*, an exhibition with Arnulf Rainer at the Arnulf Rainer Museum in Baden near Vienna. ■ *Baselitz Sculpteur*, comprehensive retrospective at the Musée d'Art Moderne de la Ville de Paris. ■ Completes the sculptural pair *Sing Sang Zero*.

2012 Produced early in the year are the large-format *Auf dem Weg nach Manchester* (*On the Way to Manchester*), and in spring, the paintings based on color negatives. ■ *Romantiker kaputt: Gemälde, Zeichnungen und Druckgrafik aus der Sammlung GAG*, an exhibition at the Kunstmuseum des Landes Sachsen-Anhalt, Stiftung Moritzburg, in Halle. ■ Completes the sculpture *BDM Gruppe* (*BDM Group*), consisting of three figures, which is displayed that following summer in the garden of the Victoria and Albert Museum in London. ■ Receives the French honor of a Chevalier de la Legion d'Honneur.

2013 *Werke von 1968 bis 2012* (*Works from 1968 to 2012*), 75th birthday exhibition at the Essl Museum, Klosterneuburg near Vienna. ■ Works on additional sculptures and on the *Black Eagle* series and *Willem raucht nicht mehr* (*Farewell Bill*). ■ *Hintergrundgeschichten* (*Background Stories*), exhibition at the Residenzschloss (Royal Palace) of the Staatliche Kunstsammlungen Dresden. ■ *Le récit et la condensation*, exhibition with Eugène Leroy at the Musée des Beaux-Arts Eugène Leroy in Tourcoing, France. ■ *Besuch bei Ernst Ludwig* (*A Visit with Ernst Ludwig*), an exhibition at the Kirchner Museum Davos.

2014 Produces the large-format self-portraits. ■ *Tierstücke. Nicht von dieser Welt* (*Animal Pieces: Not of This World*) exhibition at the Franz Marc Museum in Kochel am See. ■ *Georg Baselitz—Damals, dazwischen und heute* (*Georg Baselitz: Back Then, In Between, and Today*), exhibition at the Haus der Kunst in Munich.

Georg Baselitz lives and works at Ammersee (Bavaria) and Imperia (the Italian Riviera).

Compiled by the Archive Georg Baselitz

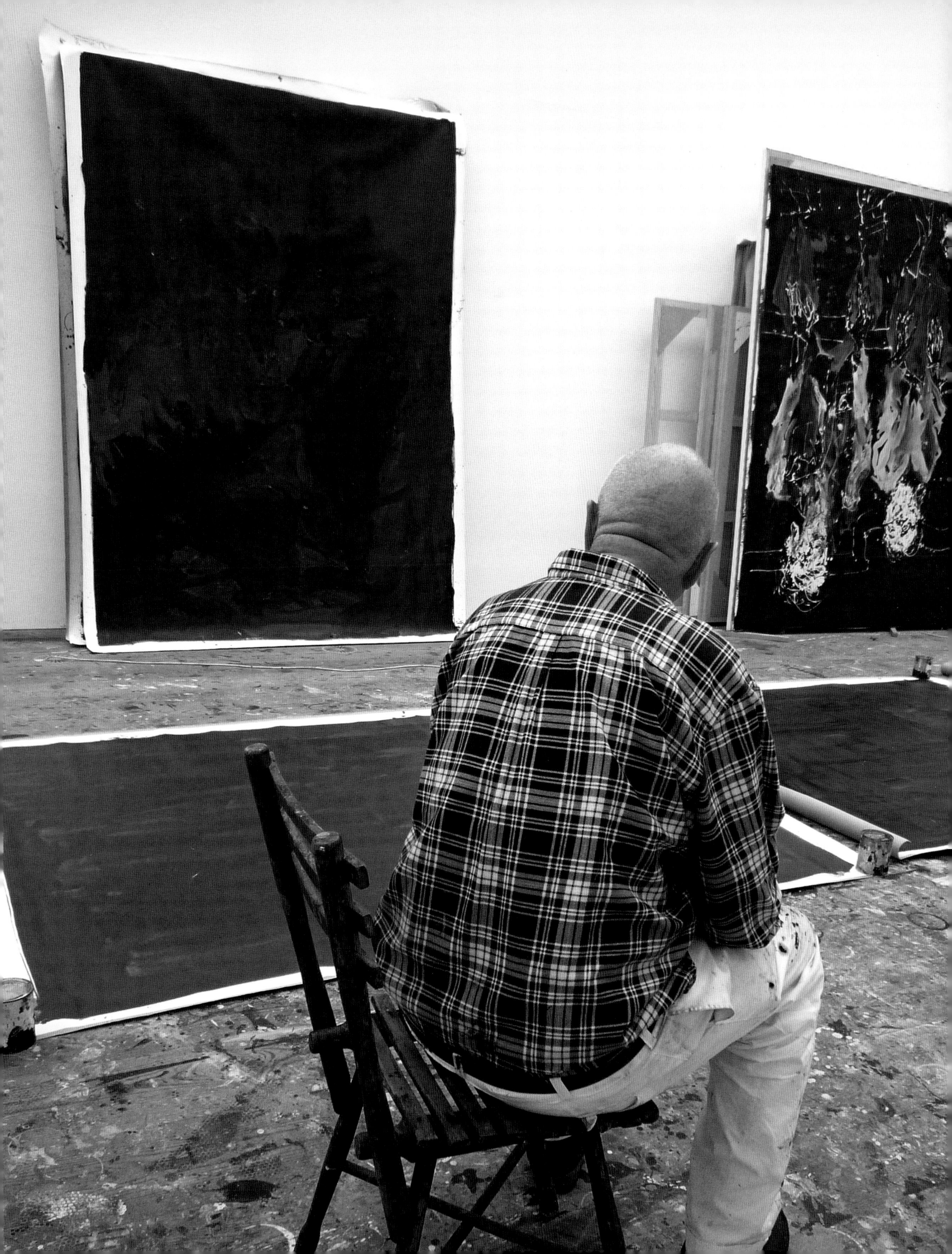

This catalogue is published on the occasion of the exhibition
Georg Baselitz: Back Then, In Between, and Today
held at Haus der Kunst in Munich, from September 19, 2014 to February 1, 2015,
and at the Powerstation of Art (PSA), Shanghai, from March 20 to June 21, 2015

We would like to thank our shareholders for their annual support of the program:
Freistaat Bayern, Josef Schörghuber Stiftung, Gesellschaft der Freunde Haus der
Kunst e.V.

The exhibition was supported by Galerie Thaddaeus Ropac, Paris / Salzburg,
Gagosian Gallery, New York / London, and White Cube, London

Stiftung Haus der Kunst München, gemeinnützige Betriebsgesellschaft mbH
Director: Okwui Enwezor

Team: Tina Anjou, Stephan N. Barthelmess, Sabine Brantl, Daniela Burkart, Sylvia
Clasen, Arnulf von Dall'Armi, Patrizia Dander, Martina Fischer, Elena Heitsch, Tina
Köhler, Anton Köttl, Isabella Kredler, Teresa Lengl, Anne Leopold, Julienne Lorz,
Iris Ludwig, Karin Mahr, Marco Graf von Matuschka, Miro Palavra, Glenn Rossiter,
Andrea Saul, Cassandre Schmid, Anna Schüller, Sonja Teine, Ulrich Wilmes

Prinzregentenstrasse 1 · 80538 München
Tel. +49 (0)89 21127 113 · www.hausderkunst.de

Curator of the exhibition and editor of the catalogue: Ulrich Wilmes
Authors: Georg Baselitz, Eric Darragon, Okwui Enwezor, Michael Semff,
Katy Siegel, and Ulrich Wilmes

Prestel Verlag, Munich
A member of Verlagsgruppe Random House GmbH

Prestel Verlag	Prestel Publishing Ltd.	Prestel Publishing
Neumarkter Strasse 28	14-17 Wells Street	900 Broadway, Suite 603
81673 Munich	London W1T 3PD	New York, NY 10003
Tel. +49 (0) 89 4136 - 0	Tel. +44 (0) 20 7323 - 5004	Tel. +1 (212) 995 - 2720
Fax +49 (0) 89 4136 - 2335	Fax +44 (0) 20 7323 - 0271	Fax +1 (212) 995 - 2733
www.prestel.de	www.prestel.com	www.prestel.com

Library of Congress Control Number is available; British Library Cataloguing-in-
Publication Data: a catalogue record for this book is available from the British
Library; Deutsche Nationalbibliothek holds a record of this publication in the
Deutsche Nationalbibliografie; detailed bibliographical data can be found under:
http://www.dnb.de

Editorial direction: Gabriele Ebbecke
Assistance: Katharina Kümmerle and Constanze Holler
Copyediting: Leina González
Translations: German–English: Ian Pepper; French–English: Sarah-Louise Raillard;
Christian Katti: "Georg Baselitz: Back Then, In Between, and Today"
Design and layout: SOFAROBOTNIK, Augsburg & München
Production: Cilly Klotz
Origination: farbanalyse, Cologne
Printing and binding: Kösel, Altusried–Krugzel
Typeface: Giorgio, Graphik
Paper: 150 g/m², Hello Fat Matt 1,1 f.

Printed in Germany

ISBN 978-3-7913-5402-6 (Trade edition English)
ISBN 978-3-7913-6566-4 (Museum edition English)
ISBN 978-3-7913-5401-9 (Trade edition German)
ISBN 978-3-7913-6565-7 (Museum edition German)

H A U S D E R K U N S T